MAD TO BE SAVED

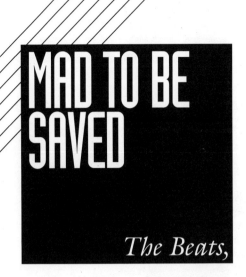

MAD TO BE SAVED

The Beats,

the '50s,

and Film

DAVID

STERRITT

Southern Illinois University Press
Carbondale and Edwardsville

01 00 99 98 4 3 2 1

Grateful acknowledgment is made to City Lights Books for
permission to reprint a portion of a letter by William Burroughs to
Allen Ginsberg published in *The Yage Letters* by William S. Burroughs
and Allen Ginsberg and a portion of "Pull My Daisy" by Allen
Ginsberg, Jack Kerouac, and Neal Cassady published in *Scattered
Poems* by Jack Kerouac.

Library of Congress Cataloging-in-Publication Data

Sterritt, David, 1944–
      Mad to be saved : the Beats, the '50s, and film / David Sterritt.
            p.   cm.
      Includes bibliographical references and index.
      1. Beat generation.   2. Motion pictures and literature—
United States—History—20th century.   3. Literature and society—
United States—History—20th century.   4. American literature—
20th century—History and criticism.   5. Experimental films—
United States—History and criticism.   6. Motion pictures—United
States—History and criticism.   7. Nineteen fifties.   I. Title.
PS228.B6S755   1998
810.9'0054—dc21   97-43376
ISBN 0-8093-2180-7 (cloth : alk. paper)   CIP

The paper used in this publication meets the minimum requirements
of American National Standard for Information Sciences—
Permanence of Paper for Printed Library Materials,
ANSI Z39.48–1984.⊗

For Jeremy and Craig

CONTENTS

■ CONTENTS

PREFACE

■ The purpose of this book is to explore the sensibility of the Beat Generation, its interactions with mainstream and experimental film during the years after World War II, and the interactions of all these with American society and culture of that era. The volume is not intended as a literary study, a historical overview, or a "film book" in the usual senses of those terms. It shifts among the fields of interest named in its title—Beat writing, the '50s, and film as a representative and influential mass medium—in order to illuminate the knotty relationships between establishment and antiestablishment thought during a complex and multifaceted period.

Interactions between the Beats and experimental art-making on one hand, and conventional society and media on the other, were marked by what might be called a logic of hostility, since both camps had ample reason to suspect and resent key aspects of the other's ideological stance. Hence, any attempt to understand the associations that linked them must travel down indirect, oblique, and ever-twisting pathways—seeking out connections as tenuous and tentative as the Beat enterprise itself, often detectable only through subtle impressions they left on the sociocultural fabric of '50s America as a whole.

To examine such tracings as thoroughly as possible, I have divided the study into two complementary parts. The first looks at Beat-related issues in terms of historical context and theoretical analysis, while the second focuses on specific works, artists, tendencies, and interactions. The devotion of more attention to some areas of concern (e.g., race) than to others (e.g., sexuality) is a result of the vast range of possibilities offered by the topic and does not indicate definitive conclusions as to the relative importance of these issues. In keeping with the Beat spirit, a certain amount of intuitive, associational, and (occasionally) spontaneous bop reasoning has been employed, meant to keep my arguments from becoming too solemn and to connect with the idiosyncratic pursuit of irresistible interests that so often characterizes Beat writing and experimental cinema themselves.

ACKNOWLEDGMENTS

■ Many people helped this project in many ways, some directly and frequently, others indirectly and perhaps unwittingly. My first thanks go to Robert Stam of New York University for the invaluable suggestions he made along the way. Similar thanks go to Robert Sklar, William Simon, and Richard Allen of New York University and to Charles Musser of Yale University, especially for their enlightening comments on the final draft. My colleague Lucille Rhodes of Long Island University provided both friendly and scholarly support. Annette Insdorf of Columbia University and Ray Carney of Boston University have provided much encouragement over the years, as has my old friend Vlada Petrić of Harvard University.

My former companions on the New York Film Festival selection committee—Richard Peña, Wendy Keys, Stuart Klawans, David Ansen, Carrie Rickey, and especially Phillip Lopate—deserve a zillion thanks for sharing with me the breadth of their knowledge, the sincerity of their enthusiasm, and more laughs than I'll ever be able to remember. My coworkers at *The Christian Science Monitor* have also been supportive for many years, as have many of my colleagues on the New York Film Critics Circle. In the filmmaking world, the words and movies of Stan Brakhage and Ken Jacobs have long been a source of inspiration, as have the great talents and valued friendship of Ernie Gehr and the late Warren Sonbert. Fred Camper shared his thoughts with his usual irreverence and humor, and especially heartfelt appreciation is due to Walter Hitesman for eye-opening ideas on all manner of topics, help in locating the most elusive books, and other contributions so thoughtful and insightful that nobody else could have provided them.

The timely completion of this project was aided by a major grant from the C. W. Post Research Committee of Long Island University, for which I am grateful.

Not everyone who helped can be mentioned here, but most of the others know who they are and how much I appreciate their input. My greatest debt is the closest to home. Ginnie Sterritt put up with even more absence and aggravation than usual as this book was being written and deserves the utmost gratitude for her forbearance and support. Ditto for our sons Jeremy and Craig, whose energy and humor have been a sustenance throughout.

MAD TO BE SAVED

INTRODUCTION

Beats, Visions, and Cinema

The Beat Generation was a generation of beatitude, and pleasure in life, and tenderness. But they called it in the papers Beat mutiny, Beat insurrection—words I never used. Being a Catholic, I believe in order, tenderness, and piety.

—Jack Kerouac to William F. Buckley Jr.,
Firing Line, 1968

Recent history is the record of a vast conspiracy to impose one level of mechanical consciousness on mankind.... The suppression of contemplative individuality is nearly complete. The only immediate historical data that we can know and act on are those fed to our senses through systems of mass communication.... America is having a nervous breakdown.

—Allen Ginsberg, "Poetry, Violence,
and the Trembling Lambs," 1959

Writers are potentially very powerful indeed. They write the script for the reality film.

—William S. Burroughs, "A Historic Memoir of
America's Greatest Existentialist," 1977

The Beats

■ The so-called Beat Generation flourished in the United States between the mid-'40s, when World War II drew to a close amid widespread uncertainty as to what the American future might hold, and the mid-'60s, when the so-called Hippie movement took over as the nation's most influential countercultural phenomenon. The term "Beat Generation" has been used in different ways by different historians, sociologists, critics, and commentators. For some it connotes the entire youth culture of the first postwar decades. For others it refers to a particular handful of authors, poets, dreamers, and dropouts whose activities reflected a conscious determination to rebel against what they perceived as a highly oppressive sociocultural atmosphere. While the label is regrettably imprecise, it suggestively evokes a youth-centered ethos that felt the weight of conventional social norms as a burden at once punishing and exhausting—inflicting on individuals a sense of being both "beaten," or assailed and tormented, and "beat," or worn down and defeated.

The early Beats have been likened to the Existentialists who emerged in Western Europe at approximately the same time. Both groups were driven by a commingling of alienation, anxiety, idealism, and intellectual energy, and both rejected the social given in favor of an aggressive insistence that humans must define themselves and their reality through their choices, decisions, and actions.[1] The actions of the Beats took the form of a negative dialectic that sought to oppose conventionality, materialism, repressiveness, regimentation, and corruption with the opposites of those qualities; this activity led the group to what critic Gregory Stephenson describes as a libertarian-egalitarian-populist-anarchist orientation that proposed not political rebellion but rather "a revolt of the soul, a revolution of the spirit" (6) that would gather strength as its adherents flung accepted notions of logic, sense, and sanity to the winds and, in Beat chronicler John Tytell's evocative phrase, "danced to the music of the absurdity they saw around them" (9). The importance of absurdity is a key notion for Beats and Existentialists alike, and has played a provocative role in postwar art (e.g., the Theater of the Absurd) and philosophy.

The negativity that prompted the Beat sensibility to its early stirrings never vanished from its social, spiritual, and aesthetic expressions, as later events in Beat history—from William S. Burroughs's radical rejection of linear prose to Jack Kerouac's ultimate embrace of a withdrawn and alcoholic life—have demonstrated in ways both metaphoric and literal. Yet the Beats during their ascendancy were by no means a recessive group. Indeed, they were strikingly productive, counterattacking the '50s idea of rationalized consensus with literary acts reflecting a Romantic insistence on the moral, ethical, and spiritual potency of creative selfhood. Their sense of energy and community were drawn partly from the fascination with language that such core Beats as Kerouac, Burroughs, and Allen Ginsberg displayed in the prose and poetry that made them famous. In addition, they were invigorated by the great outpouring of artistic experimentation that began in the '40s, including the bebop jazz of Miles Davis and Charlie Parker, the proscenium-free theater of Julian Beck and Judith

Malina, and the abstract-expressionist painting of Jackson Pollock and the New York School.

To their enthusiasm for various artistic forms the Beats added a sophisticated awareness of the bohemian tradition—with roots a century old on both sides of the Atlantic when the Beats began making their contributions to it—and a passion for street-level city life. This passion was sparked by the hustlers they met during their nighttime wanderings and above all by the hipsters who preceded the Beats as a paradigmatic American counterculture: quintessentially urban rebels who prowled "through our cities like [members] of some mysterious, nonviolent Underground" (1988b, 73), as Beat fellow traveler John Clellon Holmes phrased it. Hipsters took the risks of what Norman Mailer called, in a widely influential Beat-sympathetic essay of 1957,

> the decision . . . to encourage the psychopath in oneself, to explore that domain of experience where security is boredom and therefore sickness, and one exists in the present, in that enormous present which is without past or future, memory or planned intention, the life where a man must go until he is beat, where he must gamble with his energies through all those small or large crises of courage and unforeseen situations which beset his day, where he must be with it or doomed not to swing. (588)

Other influences on the Beats included the transcendentalism of Walt Whitman and the romanticism of William Blake; major figures in Dadaism and Surrealism, with whom the Beats shared a group identity, a preference for subversiveness that was sociocultural rather than directly political, and a leaning toward extremism in thought and expression; and the more radical of the post–World War I writers known as the Lost Generation, from Hart Crane to Henry Miller and Ezra Pound, all of whom anticipated the Beats in their determination to replace the most widely disseminated views and values of their age with new, more viable ideas. In the spirit of all these predecessors and progenitors, the Beats combined outrage at a status quo perceived as senseless (at best) and psychotic (at worst) with a determination to create what the early Beat figure Lucien Carr called a "New Vision" of art (Charters xviii);[2] this vision would be dynamized by "world-and-mind weariness, the continual moulting of consciousness, and the spirit's arduous venture toward its own reconciliations" (1988b, 89), which Holmes saw as the underrecognized and

undervalued foundation of the Beat sensibility. The forerunners who inspired them were less the official intellectuals of canonical wisdom than a
heterodox collection of real and apocryphal friends, family members, and
half-imagined heroes whom Kerouac called, in one of the most frequently
cited passages of Beat literature,

> the mad ones, the ones who are mad to live, mad to talk, mad to
> be saved, desirous of everything at the same time, the ones who
> never yawn or say a commonplace thing, but burn, burn, burn
> like fabulous yellow roman candles exploding like spiders across
> the stars and in the middle you see the blue centerlight pop and
> everybody goes "Awww!" (1991, 8)

Given the energy, inventiveness, and ethos-challenging carnivalism
that surge through so much Beat writing, turning even "world-and-mind
weariness" into a productive arena for exploration and adventure, the
phrase "positive negation" might be more appropriate than "negative
dialectic" to describe the group's thought and activity. The latter term
suggests somber opposition to a deadening society perceived in the near-
apocalyptic terms of, say, the Frankfort School's critique of the modern
sociopolitical era. By contrast, positive negation suggests a stance—in
keeping with the ideas of Mikhail Bakhtin, the innovative Russian theorist of carnivalism and dialogism—that is not merely antithetical, even
toward a scorned status quo. Rather, in the words of Bakhtin exegete
Michael Gardiner, it incorporates "the positive pole of popular-festive energy" (57), tapping into sensory and experiential knowledge so as to entail
not nihilism or despair but affirmation, renewal, and the inversion of that
which is rejected.[3]

Such a conception cannot be applied to the Beats in overly generalized
terms, since important aspects of their collective *oeuvre* do have despairing
and even nihilistic tendencies. One thinks of the electrifying hallucinations and corrosive metaphors that coexist with the manic humor and explosive satire of Burroughs's dyspeptic world, and of the profound sadness that courses through a good deal of Ginsberg's outwardly gregarious
work.

Perhaps most poignantly, one thinks of how the exuberance and
exhilaration of Kerouac's early *On the Road* (1957) and *The Dharma
Bums* (1958) were shadowed by the insinuating self-doubt and self-pity of
The Subterraneans (1958), which themselves gave way to the ineluctable

discontents of *Tristessa* (1960) and ultimately to the nightmares that erupt in *Book of Dreams* (1961), *Big Sur* (1962), and *Desolation Angels* (1965). Even in his early works, the presence of happiness is often accompanied by a tentative and worried undertone. "In fact I realized I had no guts. . . . But I have joy" (90), says the Kerouac surrogate in *The Dharma Bums* at a hard moment during a mountain-climbing expedition. This self-analytic statement sounds affirmative enough at first, but glossing it, critic Warren French notes that Kerouac's idea of joy was accompanied by the necessity for Lenten regret, reflecting his acceptance (ever since his Roman Catholic childhood) of the notion that unfettered happiness "is a release valve from the tensions of life that must be paid for with long periods of repentance [and] demands too much energy to sustain itself in the human condition" (126).[4] Kerouac seems instinctively to have viewed carnivalistic pleasure as affording only a temporary catharsis and a quickly dissipated sense of liberation. In this attitude, he reminds one of the medieval subjects described by Bakhtin as "too weak before the forces of nature and society" to resist the "seriousness of fear and suffering in their religious, social, political, and ideological forms. . . . Freedom granted by laughter often enough was mere festive luxury." The bright side of this situation is that when "distrust of the serious tone and confidence in the truth of laughter" did occur, they brought with them "a spontaneous, elemental character" (1984b, 94–95). Spontaneity and an elemental distrust of all seriousness—including his own—were among Kerouac's most appealing traits. Although he saw carnivalistic joy as ultimately a temporary and unsustainable phenomenon, it never entirely departs from his work, even at junctures where what he calls a "Beethoven gloominess"[5] threatens most boldly to take over; and his insistence on utterly intuitive writing with audaciously self-inventing structures ("spontaneous bop prosody") bears out his continual resistance to a closed-off or "official" vision of the world. In this openness and open-endedness, his *oeuvre* bears out Bakhtin's claim that "the carnival sense of the world . . . knows no period, and is, in fact, hostile to any sort of *conclusive conclusion*: all endings are merely new beginnings; carnival images are reborn again and again" (1984a, 165).

In sum, the Beats as a group generated a carnivalistic aura in many of the works that have lived most vividly in the popular imagination, such as Kerouac's peripatetic *On the Road*, Burroughs's uproarious *Naked Lunch* (1962), and Ginsberg's visionary "Wichita Vortex Sutra" (1966), which proclaims: "No more fear of tenderness, much delight in weeping, ecstasy /

in singing, laughter rises that confounds / staring Idiot mayors / and stony politicians . . . " (1984, 395). As urgent as their denial of the sociocultural status quo consistently was, and as deeply felt as their own sorrows persistently were, their rebellion was finally a positive phenomenon, producing art that aspired to be celebratory, transcendent, and transformative. This carnival sensibility had special importance in the '50s, a rigorously normative age when restrictive dogmas, doctrines, creeds, and screeds of official thought were striving mightily to exercise unchallenged hegemony over all within their reach. When the young Ginsberg equilibrated his "Howl" (1955–56) by juxtaposing anguished cries of "Moloch! Moloch! Nightmare of Moloch! Moloch the loveless! Mental Moloch! Moloch the heavy judger of men!" with ecstatic yowls of "The word is holy! The soul is holy! The skin is holy! The nose is holy! The tongue and cock and hand and asshole holy!" (1984, 131, 134), he was practicing a richly Bakhtinian aesthetic in which high and low are scrambled, the lower body is celebrated and sacramentalized, and the staring Idiot mayors of the established system find themselves turned on their richly deserving heads.

Unfortunately, similar things cannot be said of much other cultural production in the postwar era, including the Hollywood cinema, which generally tried to function as a guardian of traditional values and the sociopolitical status quo. Even in the largely monologic domain of American film, however, currents of carnivalistic subversion managed to make themselves felt with surprising frequency. These currents emerged in the work of studio renegades who turned the industrial apparatus to their own sly purposes, in "personal" works or excursions into comparatively flexible territory such as *film noir* melodrama, and also in the efforts of avant-garde experimentalists who functioned as artisans outside the industrial setting. Like the Beat writers, these filmmakers were a minority—often a beleaguered one—within their field. But the best of them believed deeply in the necessity of confronting the social given with new and daring ideas, and their activities helped enrich and expand the Beat challenge to an increasingly ossified society.

Beatness

> How frail, beat, final, is Tristessa as we load her into the quiet hostile bar. . . .
> —Jack Kerouac, Tristessa

A sense of the derivation and evolution of Beat attitudes can be gleaned from the history of "beat" as a descriptive term. The first to employ this adjective in something like its Beat Generation meaning appear to have been jazz musicians and street hustlers[6] for whom it meant "down and out" or "poor and exhausted" (Charters xvii). Burroughs learned it in 1944 from Herbert Huncke, a friend whose interest in drugs and street survivalism became an inspiration for all the Beat writers. Other core Beats picked up the word in turn, charging it with their own nuances and connotations. Ginsberg found its "original street usage" to suggest "exhausted, at the bottom of the world, looking up or out, sleepless, wide-eyed, perceptive, rejected by society, on your own, streetwise" (Charters xviii). Kerouac interpreted the term through the grain of Huncke's voice, recalling how his friend "appeared to us and said 'I'm beat' with radiant light shining out of his despairing eyes." Bringing his own associations to it, Kerouac noted possible echoes of "some midwest carnival or junk cafeteria" (1959b, 42) and connected it with a "melancholy sneer" worn by "characters of a special spirituality who didn't gang up but were solitary Bartlebies [*sic*] staring out the dead wall window of our civilization" (Charters xviii). These associations accorded with Kerouac's opinion that his generation shared

> a kind of furtiveness. . . . Like we were a generation of furtives . . .
> with an inner knowledge there's no use flaunting on . . . the level
> of the "public," a kind of beatness—I mean, being right down to
> it, to ourselves, because we all *really* know where we are—and a
> weariness with all the forms, all the conventions of the world. . . .
> So I guess you might say we're a *beat* generation.[7]

In his first and most conventional novel, *The Town and the City* (1950), Kerouac wrote of someone "wandering 'beat' around the city" on a search for money or support, and in his later novel *Desolation Angels*, he said the term "beat" originally implied "mind-your-own-business," as in "beat it" (Foster 7). Kerouac further reported, in his 1958 essay "The Philosophy of the Beat Generation," that the Beat Generation concept was first embodied by a handful of friends (including Burroughs, Ginsberg, Huncke, Holmes, and himself) who had long since moved from New York and gone their separate ways; yet the concept had sprung back to life after the Korean War when "postwar youth emerged cool and beat . . . bop visions became common property of the commercial, popular cultural world. . . . The ingestion of drugs became official . . . even the clothes style of the beat hipsters carried over to the new rock 'n' roll youth . . . and the Beat Generation, though dead, was resurrected and justified" (Charters xxi). The following year, in "The Origins of the Beat Generation," he wrote that "Beat" meant "poor, down and out, deadbeat, on the bum, sad, sleeping in subways" (1959b). In an appearance on Steve Allen's television show he observed, rather cryptically, that "Beat" meant "sympathetic."

Perhaps the most resonant of Kerouac's contributions to the word's developing usage is his punning association of "Beat" with the notion of beatification. In Kerouac's early novel *On the Road*, narrator Sal Paradise, a Kerouac surrogate, says of protagonist Dean Moriarty (a surrogate for Neil Cassady, who strongly influenced Kerouac's early evolution as a thinker and writer) that he "was BEAT—the root, the soul of Beatific" (161).[8] This marks another connection between Kerouac's writing and his longtime susceptibility to the Roman Catholic beliefs that he learned in childhood, particularly the notion of a "dark night of the soul" leading to a state of grace. Yet this usage did not wrench "Beat" away from its roots in down-and-outness, as Holmes—an author associated with the Beats, although not a member of the core Beat group—indicated when he wrote of it in 1952:

> More than mere weariness, it implies the feeling of having been used, of being raw. It involves a sort of nakedness of mind, and, ultimately, of soul; a feeling of being reduced to the bedrock of consciousness. In short, it means being undramatically pushed up against the wall of oneself. A man is beat whenever he goes for broke and wagers the sum of his resources on a single number; and the young generation has done that continually from early youth. (1952, 10)

The Beats and Visual Thinking

What Lee is looking for is contact or recognition, like a photon emerging from the haze of insubstantiality to leave an indelible recording. . . . Failing to find an adequate observer, he is threatened by painful dispersal, like an unobserved photon.

—William S. Burroughs, Queer

A pungent visuality often pervades Beat writing and thinking. Beats and their commentators have cited concepts drawn from contemporary music (especially jazz improvisation) more often than visual art when identifying key influences on Beat works; yet practices in fine-art production (especially action painting) and cinema also played an important role in shaping and crystallizing Beat notions of creativity. For instance, in the second half of an *Evergreen Review* piece called "Belief & Technique for Modern Prose"—a 1959 article that is really a fragmented "list of essentials" for generating spontaneous writing—Kerouac returns with striking regularity to visual metaphors that suggest his strong investment in pictorial, cinematic, and mind's-eye imagery:

16. The jewel center of interest is the eye within the eye
18. Work from pithy middle eye out, swimming in language sea
21. Struggle to sketch the flow that already exists intact in mind
22. Dont think of words when you stop but to see picture better
25. Write for the world to read and see yr exact pictures of it
26. Bookmovie is the movie in words, the visual American form
30. Writer-Director of Earthly movies Sponsored & Angeled in Heaven (57)

Kerouac's interest in verbal "sketching" has been traced to a friend's suggestion, early in his career, that he "just sketch in the streets like a painter but with words" (Tytell 143). Major consequences ensued when he followed this advice, and *On the Road* changed from what had promised to be a conventional story (in the Thomas Wolfe-like vein of *The Town and the City*, perhaps) to a complex and superenergized verbal tapestry modeled partly on the jazzlike flow of breath patterns but also on the ideal of transcribing streams of mental imagery with all their experiential ebbs, flows, and upheavals.[9]

Additionally, Kerouac had been fascinated by movies in his early years. He had a special fondness for French films; coming from a French-Canadian family,[10] he spoke English haltingly as late as age eighteen. He was particularly taken with the Walt Disney production *Fantasia*, which he saw fifteen times at Manhattan's well-known Thalia revival theater (Nicosia 32, 112). With the boldly colored forms and freewheeling movements of its most imaginative sequences, this film may have influenced the color symbolism and shifting visual perspectives found in his most adventurous books. He was not immune to dreams of success as a Hollywood screenwriter, moreover, or to avant-garde visions of producing a reflexive film about himself and his friends, capturing them in their real-life personae and perhaps filming both the performers and the crew unawares "so that the movie would also reveal the process by which it was made" (Nicosia 274, 470). The film *Pull My Daisy* (1959), in which Kerouac played an important off-screen part, is rather different in nature but has a hint of this ambience about it.

Kerouac was not alone among the Beats in cultivating an important visual component within his work. Ginsberg conceived his first enthusiasm for Zen Buddhism as a result of exploring what he described to Cassady as the "sublimity and sophistication . . . learning and experience" of Asian painting. In poetry he wished to use tensions between words much as Paul Cézanne used space between colors, and he found in Cézanne a use of juxtaposed planes and synaesthetic "*petite sensation*" that induced "eyeball kicks" similar to those Ginsberg had experienced in mystical visions of his own (Schumacher 153, 95, 197). He was interested in cinema as well, and harbored occasional ideas about film production. During a period of comparative financial security in the mid-'50s, for instance, he fantasized about making (among other projects) a kind of Buddhist science-fiction movie with "Burroughs on Earth" as its title (Nicosia 469–70).

As for Burroughs, the greater part of his work is grounded in a vast mythology of conflict between humanity and a parasitic enemy (known as the Nova Mob or the Board in most of its appearances) that has seized control of human consciousness through manipulation of images and words, turning the biosphere into a psychic battleground infested with "virus sheets constantly presented and represented before your mind screen to produce more virus word and image around and around . . . the invisible hail of bring down word and image" (1980, 68). Burroughs's major works constitute not only an account of this mythological struggle but also a line of defense against the Nova Mob's infiltration and control, insofar as the radical discontinuities of his montage-based prose (generated through deliberately disruptive cut-up and fold-in procedures) serve as antidotes to the enemy's lethal machinations, which are themselves as profoundly cinematic as they are ruthlessly monologic. "Remember i was the movies," says Mr. Bradly Mr. Martin, the arch villain of Burroughs's mythos, as one of his adventures reaches its final fadeout (1987b, 201).[11]

While it cannot be said that cinema played a specifically privileged role in the lives and works of most of the Beats, their inclinations toward nonliterary modes of expression (such as visuality and musicality) helped motivate an interest in film that asserted itself in many small ways and a few large ways (such as Burroughs's deployment of a recurrent "reality film" metaphor) at sundry points in their various careers. This interest represented, among other things, a creative response by the Beats to the relatively interesting state of American cinema during the period (the late '40s to the early '60s) that witnessed the major phase of their own activities as a "generation" with shared personal and aesthetic ideas. As already suggested, Hollywood studios during the long reign of the classical film-making style (which was largely unchallenged from the '20s to the early '60s) tended to think of themselves as sustainers of mainstream values and sociocultural consensus. Yet gaps and contradictions were always present in this enterprise—some were manifested in the flourishing of *film noir*, for instance, as cited above—and the '50s saw an increase in their number. On one hand, declining revenues and the new challenge of television led studios to relax their formula-bound production habits and loosen the constraints of self-censorship that had been enforced in one form or another throughout their history; these changes allowed a somewhat more fluid and at times even experimental atmosphere (in works by such innovative filmmakers as Samuel Fuller and Nicholas Ray, for example) to creep into commercial cinema. At the same time, a number of veteran filmmakers who had mastered Hollywood's most popular and productive idioms—and who in some cases had given those idioms distinctive inflections of their own, earning recognition as individualistic visual artists from a budding generation of *auteur*-oriented critics—were still actively at work within the studio system, taking advantage of its newfound (if still very limited) creative flexibility to shape some of their most personal and idiosyncratic work.

This is not to say that experienced directors like Alfred Hitchcock and John Ford or inventive newcomers like Fuller and Ray were giving postwar Hollywood as radical a jolt as the action painters were giving to postwar art, the beboppers to postwar music, or the Beats to postwar literature. As will be argued below, mainstream cinema remained a deeply monologic phenomenon in most respects. Nor can it be claimed that the Beats, either as moviegoers or as artists subject to influences from the cultural *Zeitgeist*, zeroed in on the most stimulating cinema that *was* being made. Kerouac, for example, was capable of recognizing a good movie when he saw one; in his novel *Vanity of Duluoz: An Adventurous Education, 1935–46*, he recalls "walking out of the Royal Theater all elated because I had just seen Orson Welles' *Citizen Kane* and by God, what a picture! I wanted to be a genius of poetry in film like Welles. I was rushing home to figure out a movie play" (104). Yet he repeatedly gave his affection to all sorts of films, ranging from critically respected works to movies designed for the most uncritical audiences. In the same novel, he describes the irresistible urge he felt as a Columbia University student to

> ride on down to Times Square and go see a French movie, go see Jean Gabin press his lips together sayin *"Ca me navre,"* or Louis Jouvet's baggy behind going up the stairs, or that bitter lemon smile of Michele Morgan in the seaside bedroom, or Harry Bauer kneel as Handel praying for his work, or Raimu screaming at the mayor's afternoon picnic, and then after that, an American doublefeature, maybe Joel McRae in *Union Pacific,* or see tearful clinging sweet Barbara Stanwyck grab him, or maybe go see Sherlock Holmes puffing on his pipe with long Cornish profile as Dr. Watson puffs at a medical tome by the fireplace and Missus Cavendish or whatever her name was comes upstairs with cold roast beef and ale so that Sherlock can solve the latest manifestation of the malefaction of himself Dr. Moriarty. . . . (76)

While this is an eclectic list, it smacks more of eager entertainment-hunting than of refined cinematic taste; that Georg Friedrich Händel biopic appears to have impressed Kerouac not with any musical or historical excellence it had to offer, for instance, but with a walloping dose of sentimental religiosity that made Kerouac literally cry (Nicosia 77).[12] Still, although such movies struck him for reasons having more to do with his personal moods and ephemeral emotions than with his fundamental aesthetic sensitivities, they were not merely a private quirk for him, like cheeseburgers or Twinkies for a renowned chef who respects simple pleasures and likes an occasional respite from elevated cuisine. They had a perceptible effect on his vision and on the writing that emerged from his highly heterogeneous inner life. It is hard not to think of a Walt Disney nature movie or cartoon from the '40s or '50s, for example, when reading a passage like this one in *Big Sur,* paradoxically one of Kerouac's most despairing works:

> I rose that following morning with more joy and health and purpose than ever, and there was me old Big Sur Valley all mine again, here came [the mule] good old Alf and I gave him food and

patted his big rough neck with its various cocotte's manes, there was the mountain of Mien Mo in the distance just a dismal old hill with funny bushes around the sides and a peaceful farm on top. . . . And there's the bluejay idiot with one foot on the bar of soap on the porch rail, pecking at the soap and eating it, leaving the cereal unattended, and when I laugh and yell at him he looks up cute with an expression that seems to say "What's the matter? wotti do wrong?"—"Wo wo, got the wrong place," said another bluejay landing nearby and suddenly leaving again—And everything of my life seems beautiful again. . . . (117–18)

Here such celebrated Kerouac personae as the peripatetic hipster, the transcendental mystic, and the jazz-inspired poet seem less in evidence than the fifteen-time viewer of *Fantasia* and the wide-eyed fan of Louis Jouvet's baggy behind. He shares his "bad taste" with other art-mavericks such as the Surrealists, of course, but they often seem more knowing and ironic in indulging their Kitschy proclivities.

Ginsberg appears to have developed somewhat more sophisticated tastes, yet without demonstrating a notably deep appreciation for cinematic excellence. Like his friend Kerouac, he loved movies from an early age, writing in his diary with precocious world-weariness at the age of eleven, "Movies afford me great pleasure and are about the only relief from boredom which seems to hang around me like a shadow." He received a jarring "nightmare vision of my own future" upon seeing Frederic March in Rouben Mamoulian's *Dr. Jekyll and Mr. Hyde* (1932) and wept sincerely at both the dying protagonist of James Whale's *The Invisible Man* (1933) and a lonely dog chasing after its prison-bound master in the finale of some lachrymose drama (Miles 1989, 26). In much later years, when he became a familiar face in avant-garde movies by a variety of filmmakers, he showed wide-ranging tastes in nonnarrative cinema, praising Andy Warhol's work and Barbara Rubin's audacious *Christmas on Earth* (1963), which he described as "a lot of porn, beauty, in which she made an art object out of her vagina. I thought that was in the right spirit" (Miles 1989, 334). This accolade may have been motivated in part by Ginsberg's personal affection for the filmmaker, however, since he was very close to her at the time of his exposure to her work.

Burroughs also showed an interest in film during much of his life, and cited screenplay writing as a major influence on his other literary work. "As soon as a writer starts writing a film script—that is, writing in terms of what appears on screen—he is no longer omniscient," he has said. The reason is that "information must be shown on the screen, unless the writer falls back on the dubious expedient of the off-stage voice. . . . You cannot get away with an indescribable monster. The audience wants to *see* the monster. . . . The ability to think in concrete visual terms is almost essential to a writer" (1993, 35–36). Yet for all his cogitation on visual thinking, his radicalism as an author, and his profound suspicion of mass media as manipulators of the mind and spirit, Burroughs's mature preferences in cinema appear to have followed mass taste—albeit the more adventurous aspects of mass taste—fairly closely. Discussing the motion pictures of 1969, he called Dennis Hopper's *Easy Rider* a "pretty good" film, praising the "great wide vistas that are really America. Kerouac would have loved that movie. . . . Or maybe he wouldn't have liked what it said the way he was talking those last years you could never be sure." (As will be shown later in this study, Kerouac's dislike for violence in films grew to almost paranoiac dimensions by the late '50s.) Haskell Wexler's ambitious *Medium Cool* was "[n]ot bad, a step in the right direction . . . with the *cinema verite* stuff, but not an exceptional movie . . . like [Sam Peckinpah's] *The Wild Bunch*." The film that really excited Burroughs was *The Damned*, which he called "a movie by a real master," a production that could only have been made by "a real European with roots that go way back" and who "knows how the European family works—and that is really what that movie is all about" (B. Cook 183–84). Luchino Visconti's melodrama about the Nazi era is indeed a worthwhile film, but Burroughs hardly seems to have hit upon particularly clever or original arguments for its merit.

Notwithstanding the inconsistencies in cinematic taste shown by the Beat writers, and the presence of much formula-bound cinema to bring out their worst instincts, it remains true that the Beats and the movies both experienced a very interesting phase in the postwar years—the former working to sustain vigorous literary careers, the latter finding new expressive possibilities as Hollywood nurtured (or tolerated) a minority of innovative filmmakers and television navigated its "golden age" of live production and media-specific experimentation. In addition, a new wave of avant-garde cinema emerged in the postwar era, conceived partly as a reaction to commercial film practice and partly as an outgrowth of aesthetic tendencies (poetic, nonlinear, expressionistic) that held little mainstream appeal but had well-established records in other art forms. This exercised a clear attraction for artists who wanted to adapt and extend Beat attitudes, ideas, methodologies, and practices in the field of cinema.

The interest of the Beats in visual expression, in high-energy communication, in multidimensional narrativity, in art sparked by spontaneous insight rather than canonical wisdom, in the possibility of a hip *Gesamt-kunstwerk* joining the pictorial, the musical, the verbal, and the physical into an orgasmic concatenation of aesthetic joy—all of this lured them at various times to the cinematic world, whether through direct participation, plans or hopes for such participation, an urge to write on cinematic subjects, or simply the desire to reflect a cinematically influenced *Weltanschauung* in works dealing with ostensibly different themes.

Beats and Cinema

The traces left in film history by interaction between Beat/avant-garde and mainstream/commercial discourses are often ephemeral. The reason is partly that the Beat writers deeply distrusted (at least when they gave the matter some deliberate thought) the sort of mass-produced culture that Hollywood represented, rightly or wrongly, for them and for most "establishment" intellectuals of the period. Hollywood took a complementary position of opposing Beat values (sexual license, anticonsumerism, utopianism, etc.) through strategies of mockery, co-optation, and containment. Under these conditions, it is not surprising to find the different camps occupying different portions of the sociocultural terrain.

Still, the crosswind of social questioning and cultural criticism that ran through Hollywood cinema during the '50s era—in the continuing output of *film noir*, the increasingly complex moral tapestries of a Douglas Sirk or a Vincente Minnelli, the escalating experimentalism of an Alfred Hitchcock, and so on—prevented Hollywood from congealing into the monolithic establishmentarianism to which its moguls generally aspired. This crosswind also provided Beat and Beat-influenced thinkers with provocative film-related material that they could readily identify and approve. Much the same happened with television, where the fluidity of still-emerging production modes offset commercial pressures enough to allow for occasional irruptions of Beat-reflective and even Beat-sympathetic expression. Also present on both sides of the Beat-Hollywood divide was a grudging fascination with the "other" that led Hollywood to occasional flirtations with the Beat spirit, and the Beats to occasional dreams of joining, purifying, and reforming the movie industry that held such decadent allure.

For these and other reasons there were numerous intersections between Beat and Hollywood activity; and even when they traveled down pathways that did not come close to converging, the very differences between their respective projects (in all the diversified forms that those projects took) can be read as symptomatic of the social, cultural, political, and economic environment that was shared by these two highly visible loci of artistic production. Like the Hollywood studios, the Beat writers wanted to communicate with a broad and diversified audience and were in fact widely known by the very stratum of American society—the middle class, the bourgeoisie, the squares—that was their most frequent and most avidly attacked target. They aspired to dissemination, respect, and influence just as actively as their studio-bred counterparts did, if with divergent motives and strategies. Their novels, poems, stories, and other works reflect actual, perceived, and fantasized realities of '50s culture as vividly as the period's movies and television programs do, if in different ways and with different goals; and their preoccupations and obsessions were received with interest by a wide range of Americans not limited to particular classes, communities, or degrees of aesthetic sophistication.

Movies and Beats, then, were equally integral aspects of the '50s scene. Fascination with the frontier and the rootless life gave impetus to Hollywood westerns as well as Kerouac's novels on the wilderness and the open road; interest in somatic expressivity spurred avant-garde ciné-poems as well as Ginsberg's breath-measured oral verses; and immersion in atomic-age terror and cold-war aggressivity spawned low-budget monster movies and experimental psychodramas as well as the zany deliriums of Burroughs's cut-up nightmares. The '50s provided fertile ground for all these artistic manifestations, which are as closely linked as they are dauntingly diverse. Much can be gained by considering each through the lens of the others.

Part

HISTORY, THEORY, CULTURE

One

The Beat
Generation
Meets the Lonely
Crowd

Historical Contexts

Once people hated to concede that their behavior was determined by anything except their own free will. Not so with the new suburbanites; they are fully aware of the all-pervading power of the environment over them. As a matter of fact, there are few subjects they like so much to talk about; and with the increasing lay curiosity about psychology, psychiatry, and sociology, they discuss their social life in surprisingly clinical terms. But they have no sense of plight; this, they seem to say, is the way things are, and the trick is not to fight it but to understand it.

—William H. Whyte Jr., "The Transients," 1953

I suppose I'll get married like everybody else. Have a big family, and can peaches, and make my own curtains. Probably get fat, too. It runs in my family.... Some girl'll take you in hand. She'll get you to dry dishes and pay life insurance, just like everybody else.... One of these days you'll be takin' the kids to the dentist and mowin' the lawn—don't you think you won't.

—Libby in Home From the Hill,
directed by Vincente Minnelli, 1960

You kill yourself to get to the grave. Especially you kill yourself to get to the grave before you even die, and the name of that grave is "success," the name of that grave is hullaballoo boomboom horseshit.

—Jack Kerouac, Vanity of Duluoz

American Society and Culture in the '50s

■ To understand the relationship between the Beats and American culture of the '50s, cinematic and otherwise, one needs to look at the social fabric of the United States as a whole. The postwar years are often cited as a paradigmatic time of conservatism, conformity, and consensus. Much evidence supports this reputation, although the situation is naturally more complex and contradictory than any brief characterization can indicate.[1]

A long-lasting economic boom started at the end of World War II and continued with varying degrees of strength throughout the '50s, '60s, and early '70s. This reinforced a superficial sense of power and even invincibility among Americans that was also fueled by other factors. One was the recent military victory by Allied forces and the American move into spaces formerly dominated by European imperialism. Another was a spate of new developments in science and technology, in the form of present realities and also of easily fantasized (and continually promoted) sources of increased ease and comfort in the imminent future. Still another was the fact that relative improvements in middle-class living conditions allowed many people to overlook ongoing inequities in the distribution of wealth.

Yet fear and distress were carving out privileged positions of their own. The growth of a credit-card economy facilitated the acquisition of debt and obligation as well as goods and services; mushrooming road and highway systems fostered rootlessness as well as mobility; suburban homes were comfortable but undistinguished and indistinguishable; an explosion of marriage, childbearing, and "togetherness" led to more household-oriented living and thence to new worries about education, juvenile delinquency, health care, and other family-related issues; and purchases of alcohol and tranquilizers boomed, indicating unease and insecurity despite the many signs of abundance that surrounded people in material fact and media representation.[2] Beyond the middle class, life remained bleak for African-Americans subjected to daily rituals of oppression, whether *de jure* in the South or *de facto* in the North, and circumstances were little better for members of other racial and ethnic minorities outside certain circumscribed domains where limited degrees of autonomy and power were tolerated by the xenophobic majority.

Many such problems were powerful enough to make their way into occasional major films from the Hollywood studios, from Martin Ritt's 1957 *No Down Payment*, with its sensationalized portrait of suburban discontents, to Vincente Minnelli's 1958 *Some Came Running*, with its nuanced suggestion that the Midwestern bourgeoisie maintained its emotional equilibrium through a skittish combination of good-life ideology and brain-dulling social drinking. A striking example of a '50s film that looks directly at social dysfunction is Douglas Sirk's 1959 production of *Imitation of Life*,[3] which shows how relentless racial norms relegate one African-American character to servant status and drive another to "pass" as white. Yet such a purposeful and potentially unsettling work might never have reached the screen if its criticisms had not been surrounded with melodramatic "entertainment value" that allowed racially insensitive audiences the luxury of focusing their attention on psychology, romance, and attractive furnishings rather than the movie's elements of forthright social commentary.

Meanwhile, the sexual prudery that prevented the *I Love Lucy* program from using the word "pregnant" on television (Albert and Albert 2) served the forces of sexism and homophobia by foreclosing any likelihood that the long tradition of compulsory sex roles and gender stereotypes might be openly and meaningfully discussed, much less ameliorated and rectified. Aggressive legal action against such Beat Generation works as Allen Ginsberg's poem "Howl" and William S. Burroughs's novel *Naked Lunch* stirred up paranoia over "different" and "daring" artistic activity, even when the writers were ultimately vindicated in court. In other fields, the manufacturing practice of "planned obsolescence" diminished the worth of consumer goods even when they seemed satisfactory in the short run. Freedom from labor became not an accomplishment to be valued but a problem to be solved—probably "the most characteristic of all our dilemmas," in Paul Goodman's view—as it was increasingly feared "that with the maturation of automatic and computer technology, either people won't *have* to work and will degenerate; or there won't be anything for them to work *at*, and they will be unhappy spending their time in trivial leisure activities" (1968, 165).[4]

In this atmosphere, employing potentially idle hands in the manufacture of superfluous, unnecessary, or downright useless items could easily be seen as essential to the public welfare; sure enough, the chair of the President's Council of Economic Advisors declared that the "ultimate purpose" of the American economy was "to produce more consumer goods" (Howard 46). And all the while the cold war (with its adjuncts of HUAC witch-hunting, McCarthyism, and the like) hung heavily over everything in American society, weighing down priorities in the political system, the economy, the scientific and technological sectors, the educational arena, and beyond, and incidentally producing what Goodman called "a tribe of brainy and university-trained people who are good for nothing else" (1968, 251).[5] Communism was seen as a disease to be combated or contained, and only a select few—such as former progressives whose exposure to leftism in the '30s had immunized them against further infection—could effectively defend the ideal of democracy.

Culture as Battleground

If the cold war between the United States and the Soviet Union was indeed a struggle of "universal faiths" (Pells 127), as the *New Republic* claimed in a 1949 article, it is not surprising that culture became an important battleground.[6] Novels by such authors as William Faulkner and John Steinbeck were chastised for bringing negative impressions of American life to a hostile world, and the very idea of cultural creativity as a profession could be regarded as inherently suspect—as in Nicholas Ray's film *In a Lonely Place* (1950), where the explosive and possibly dangerous personality of the Hollywood screenwriter played by Humphrey Bogart is connected by other characters with the creative energies that make him a "special" person. (By contrast, a police-officer character is praised by his wife for having what she proudly calls "average" qualities.) When it appeared that neither Soviet armies nor State Department commies were likely to overthrow the republic anytime soon, many American intellectuals turned to acclaiming the national fortitude that provided such invulnerability, explaining how free enterprise, economic growth, military strength, and political bargaining would ensure national security, the end of domestic conflict, and a fair share of opportunity for all.

Yet a current of anxiety continued to muddy this discourse. On one hand, the "consensus intellectuals" practiced what C. Wright Mills called the sociology of the "great celebration," earning much respect in professional and journalistic circles with their view that clear-headed management had superseded social and ideological wrangling in the face of contemporary problems. On the other, the most widely read and broadly influential social critics were those who warned, in sociologist Todd Gitlin's words, "that the heroic individual was paying a steep price—in autonomy and meaning—for the security and comfort he was reaping from the managed, bureaucratically organized society." The concerns of these authors (whose ideas reflect varying Marxist, liberal, and anticonformist backgrounds) are suggested by the titles of their most famous books, from *The Power Elite* by Mills and *The Organization Man* by William H.

Whyte to *The Hidden Persuaders* by Vance Packard and *The Lonely Crowd* by David Riesman and others. Offsetting enthusiasm over "the American way of life" as a solution to the ills of modernity was a worry that mass-produced social and cultural values were making "conformity" into a new kind of enemy (18–19).[7]

This fear is precisely what drew the core members of the Beat Generation into a common artistic community. Intellectually, psychologically, and spiritually, they were a heterogeneous group; as Burroughs has remarked, they "were not doing at all the same thing, either in writing or in outlook," and one "couldn't really find four writers more different, more distinctive" in many respects (Odder 52).[8] What made them "close personal friends of many years standing" and facilitated their group identity in the literary world was their shared horror of conformity, social engineering, and the death of spontaneous living.

Similar feelings were a key motivation for many avant-garde filmmakers of the time. Jonas Mekas, both a practitioner and a chronicler of the period's experimental cinema, reflected such sentiments when he stated in 1960 that the new generation of film artists was "by a dialectical necessity a generation of irresponsibility, disobedience . . . and these 'negative' characteristics should be encouraged." A similar message emerged when he commended new filmmakers (along with Harlem street gangs) for their "disrespect for officialdom, parenthood. Society without thieves, robbers, hooligans, is a dying worthless society in which all theft and murder is legalized, done from above" (D. James 1992, 40). Mekas's call for increased spontaneity and technical "impoverishment" was echoed by numerous other film experimentalists in word and deed—from Stan Brakhage, who sometimes called his radically individualistic works "home movies," to Taylor Mead, who in 1963 championed a specifically American cinema that would be not only "beat" but also "mongrel, wild, uncouth, naive, heartless, heartful, pornographic, licentious, insane, bold, bald, fat, monstrous, square enough for America—strong enough to release the monolithic freeze which periodically grips this land and is settling in again . . . " (48).

The Dangers of Adjustment

Thinkers closer to the intellectual establishment were more cautious and methodical in approaching the postwar trends toward sameness, other-directed thought, and uncritical group behavior. Still, many were forthright about their concern. Goodman, respected in many establishment circles even though his ideas often took highly individualistic turns, wrote as early as 1945 of what he called "sociolatry," defined as

> the concern felt by masses alienated from their deep natures for the smooth functioning of the industrial machine from which they believe they can get a high standard of living and enjoy it in security. . . . [I]t is a sociological standard energized by emulation and advertising, and cementing a sense of unanimity among the alienated. All men have—not the same human nature—but the same commodities. (1962, 33)[9]

A decade and a half later Riesman observed that the conforming or "other-directed" person is "too hard on himself in certain ways" and that "his anxieties, as child consumer-trainee, as parent, as worker and player, are very great. He is often torn between the illusion that life should be easy, if he could only find the ways of proper adjustment to the group, and the half-buried feeling that it is not . . . " (160). In the years between these statements, no less populist a journal than the *Reader's Digest* published an article on "The Danger of Being Too Well-Adjusted,"[10] and a 1955 book by psychoanalyst Robert Lindner entitled *Must You Conform?* described the contemporary world in decidedly unflattering terms: Society is "a stranger to men, and a hostile stranger at that"; young people are "helpless and hopeless, imprisoned by the blunders and delusions of their predecessors"; and modern leaders are "the prototype of mediocrity [and] the incarnation of the average," molded by the "commonplace, the vulgar and the unexceptional." As for the aggregated "Mass Man" who follows those leaders, he is "the psychopath *in excelsis*," a "mechanized, robotized caricature of humanity" and a "slave in mind and body, whose life signifies no more than an instrument of his masters' power, a lost creature without separate identity in the herding collectivity, a mindless integer of the pack . . . " (151, 28, 160–61, 23).

Such views have much in common with fears voiced by the Frankfort School writers. The sacrifice of individuality, Theodor W. Adorno asserted in 1938, "follows from the basic fact that in broad areas the same thing is offered to everybody by the standardized production of consumption goods. But the commercial necessity of concealing this identity leads to the manipulation of taste and the official culture's pretense of individualism, which necessarily increases in proportion to the liquidation of the individual" (Arato and Gebhardt 280). Mass-oriented culture certainly lies within the domain of the "consumption goods" at issue here, as when Hollywood movies lock into dependable formulas dictated by commercial pressures. Many an American thinker of the '50s—core Beats and film avant-gardists included—was troubled by such tendencies.

But even as conformity was being castigated by '50s intellectuals of a Frankfortian bent, others were pioneering a different view of consumption. None other than Riesman, the influential authority on other-directed behavior, observed as early as 1952 that cultural consumers "are not so manipulated as is often supposed; they fight back, by refusing to 'understand,' by selective interpretation, by apathy" and thereby "*interpret* the commodities and endow them with meanings" (Ross 53). Pointing toward the distinction between (dehumanizing) mass culture and (creative) popular consumption that would underlie much work by the so-called Birmingham and "cultural studies" writers in the '70s and '80s,[11] this notion suggests an inherent rebelliousness within the consuming population (related to what Bakhtin calls the carnival spirit) that stands ever-ready for spontaneous reaction against the leveling forces of commercial production.

Still, what gained ascendancy during the '50s was a less liberating perspective on the situation. If sociologists increasingly saw popular culture as benign, from Hollywood movies to top-forty radio shows, this was less because it provided an impetus toward creativity than because it helped teach contented and cooperative living in a consumption-oriented society. These authorities viewed shared culture as a tool for inducing people to join the great "natural" consensus which held, among other things, that modern managerialism in its many forms is equal to the challenge of modern dysfunction in *its* many forms.

*H*egemony, Common Sense, Discipline

Culture historian Andrew Ross has persuasively suggested that the liberal concern for social adaptation and cultural maturity concealed an antiradical agenda—to conserve cultural pluralism as a bulwark against collectivist ideas in politics and mass media. This defensive stance can be understood through Antonio Gramsci's concept of hegemony, whereby integrated social and political blocs articulate the interests of subordinated groups, forming an apparently spontaneous and self-sustaining consensus (Ross 55).

Such a consensus typically attempts to justify its dominance by appealing to self-evident or "common sense" truths. This is another concept important to Gramsci, who describes common sense as a "crudely conservative" grab bag in which one can find evidence of "anything that one likes" (345–46). Also relevant here is Michel Foucault's concept of the "episteme," a sort of epistemological grid that underlies the knowledge of a broad historical period, establishing what will be assumed as self-evident reality. It was not to foster individuality and egalitarianism that many '50s intellectuals promoted cultural diversity. Rather, it was to shore up the period's epistemological biases by conscripting movies, television shows, and other pop-culture products in support of the common-sense notion that change, manipulation, and self-improvement should be, in Riesman's words of 1961, "no longer oriented toward some social achievement but . . . used in a solipsistic way to adjust one to one's fate and social state" (150). This view encouraged a conservative avoidance of collective change and obscured the question of whether, in agreeing to change oneself, one is simply adapting without complaint to the social given.

This formula for self-absorption and self-discipline recalls Foucault's argument that modern Western societies have developed a new economy of power based on social and cultural "networks" that envelop "the body, sexuality, the family, kinship, knowledge, technology" (1980, 122), and just about everything else. It is small wonder that such a social order struck the Beats, the cinematic avant-garde, and other individualistic thinkers as worthy of vigorous attack, avoidance, or both. This explains Burroughs's urgent wish not only to unmask the forces of social, political, and spiritual control but also to manipulate fiction itself in such a way that sense-making loses its conventional functions and hence its usefulness as what Foucault would call a "disciplinary" agent.[12] Other members of the Beat group pursued similar goals, as did many avant-garde filmmakers, who rejected commercial-film restrictions and proprieties, and in some cases accepted a radically nonsubservient attitude toward sexuality and the body, staking out a clear division between themselves and their consensus-bound counterparts in the Hollywood studios. One audacious example is found in Brakhage's 1956 film *Flesh of Morning*, which depicts masturbation in a way that seems elliptical and stylized by standards of the '70s or later but is graphic enough to have put the filmmaker in danger of arrest and incarceration for exhibiting it.

Subjectivity and Subjection

Burroughs is closer than Brakhage to Foucault's perspective on social discipline and control. Foucault, a major theorist of the "death of the author," would find much to dispute in Brakhage's romanticized notions of the artist's ability to reenvision and reinvent the world. By contrast, Burroughs's fondness for melding and welding his own prose with that of others, literally carved out of context with blade or scissors, has a strong Foucauldian ring. Still, it is likely that the antiauthoritarian concerns of both Brakhage (preoccupied with freedom of perception) and Burroughs (obsessed with subjection and addiction) would lead them to agree with Foucault that in modern society the term "subject" has two meanings: "subject to someone else by control and dependence, and tied to [one's] own identity by a conscience or self-knowledge" (1984, 21).

It is exactly this double sort of power, yoked at once to externalized norms and internalized self-regulation, that many '50s intellectuals supported when they promoted popular culture as a route to harmonious social dynamics. Riesman's optimistic idea that audiences "fight back" and idiosyncratically "interpret" commodified culture accords with Foucault's view that ordinary people often have a clear awareness of social realities; but this argument was opposed by self-adjustment advocates who bore out Foucault's more pessimistic description of popular knowledge being blocked, prohibited, and invalidated by a power network that includes established intellectuals[13] (1972, 207). Embracing rather than interrogating dominant social, cultural, and political values, the group-adjustment gang did not seek to detach the perception of truth from the clutch of hegemony. Rather, this group turned to midcentury social science as an ideological tool for uniting bourgeois Americans within a system of shared beliefs. Worries about lonely crowds, power elites, hidden persuaders, and organization men would surely fade, it was assumed, as the American consensus became stronger and more sweeping in its grasp. Intellectuals who championed alternative views or subordinated groups were considered wrong not only for the opinions and constituents they chose to represent but also for their audacity in daring to challenge the unified popular will that made capitalism and democracy the bastions of security they surely were. "Unlike the majority of their predecessors for a century and a half," reported Goodman in 1960,

> most of our contemporary social scientists are not interested in fundamental social change. To them, we have apparently reached the summit of institutional progress, and it only remains for the sociologists and applied-anthropologists to mop up the corners and iron out the kinks. . . . Our social scientists have become so accustomed to the highly organized and by-and-large smoothly running society that they have begun to think that "social animal" means "harmoniously belonging." They do not like to think that fighting and dissenting are proper social functions, nor that rebelling or initiating fundamental change is a social function. Rather, if something does not run smoothly, they say it has been improperly socialized; there has been a failure in communication. (1960, 10–11)

But what if the message rather than the communication is the problem, Goodman goes on to ask? And what if this message—carried not only in "socially significant" discourses but also in those considered merely entertaining, diverting, and distracting from the cares of the day—is being heard *and* rejected by a significant portion of the population at which it is aimed?

The message of group-adjustment via self-manipulation was communicated clearly and forcefully in the years preceding the '50s period. Riesman notes a revealing progression in popular reading material, for instance. This progression begins with "success biographies" of the Horatio Alger type, lauding social and economic advancement via thrift, hard work, and similar virtues. It then shifts to inspirational literature of the Dale Carnegie or Norman Vincent Peale variety, including periodicals with such titles as *Journal of Living* and *Your Personality*, which recommend "self-manipulative exercises for the sake not only of business success but of such vaguer, non-work goals as popularity" (149–50). A similar trajectory is traced by historian Warren I. Susman, who notes the shift from "character" to "personality" as a popular preoccupation. The concept of character, established as early as the seventeenth century, is associated with such words as "citizenship," "duty," "democracy," "work," "conquest," "honor," "reputation," "morals," "manners," "integrity," and (especially) "manhood." The concept of personality did not replace the concept of character but became a rival in the first half of the twenti-eth century, eliciting such companion-words as "fascinating," "stun-ning," "attractive," "magnetic," "glowing," "masterful," "creative," and "dominant" (273–77). Interest in the bedrock qualities of character (epitomized by Alger and his breed) is partially displaced by the more ephemeral qualities of personality (elucidated by Carnegie and his ilk) and the manifold ways in which personality can (and should!) be molded and remolded until it suits the needs of the group, the organization, the sys-tem, the society, and the episteme so well that anyone and everyone will "get along" in the smoothest possible way.[14]

Even as they reinforce the social status quo, such developments sup-port an ideology of "individualism" that may oppose collective identity on a political level and foster self-absorption on an interpersonal level. One of the few filmmakers to show a keen interest in this area is Alfred Hitchcock, who explored personality-power as a force that can be either effective (e.g., *Shadow of a Doubt*, 1943, with Joseph Cotten as a dangerously personable monster) or ineffective (e.g., *Suspicion*, 1941, with Cary Grant as an in-sufficiently magnetic husband) within home and family situations. He also examined the social implications of individualism, most notably in *The Wrong Man*, his most specifically '50s-related work. Released in 1956, this film uses a documentarylike deliberateness (punctuated with occasional bursts of expressionistic camera work) to convey the sense of everyday life in a New York City suburb. Within this framework, it calls upon various strategies—from a screenplay based on real events to a visual style empha-sizing mundane detail—to mark the day-to-day experiences of its hero as joyless, repetitive, stifling, and entrapping. These qualities are not the re-sult of fate or destiny singling out the protagonist for unhappiness, not-withstanding the religious imagery of the story's climax. Rather, they are signs of his failure to question the authenticity of his socially molded "in-dividuality" and to realize that it is identical to that of countless others in his society, all of whom remain equally blind to the possibility of actions that might mitigate the bleakness of their surroundings and brighten their prospects for a better future.[15]

As aggressively as the self-adjustment message was disseminated in the '50s, then, the existence of a mainstream film such as *The Wrong Man*— and numerous others, including multilayered dramas by Ray and Sirk and the continuing output of the *film noir* cycle—indicates that this message did not triumph as thoroughly as social-science engineers wished. The authorities themselves were partly responsible for this circumstance. On one hand, consensus intellectuals promoted the notion of unified values as a defense against unruly forces of uncooperative, unindoctrinated, or downright un-American thought. Yet on the other, consensus within their own fields (sociology, psychology, criticism, etc.) was not strong enough to drown out dissenting voices—whether from unreconstructed Frankfortians fearing the deadening effects of top-down cultural production or more optimistic writers arguing that the effects of popular culture are not nearly as unifying as alleged. In short, consensus often proved ironically elusive for the consensus-mongers themselves. This situation did not strengthen their cause among thinkers inclined to skepticism.

Discovering the Rat Race

A more important spur to disinterest, noncooperation, and rebellion, especially among younger Americans and mavericks like the Beats and experimental filmmakers, was the declining reputation of the social system that the great consensus had (allegedly) produced and was (supposedly) uniquely equipped to defend. Unsolved social, political, and economic problems had not been totally eliminated from public discourse. Underclass miseries nagged at the American consciousness, however subtly, and managed to invade at least the periphery of public expression. Some intellectuals persisted in venting anger about American ills and criticizing other intellectuals for accepting the widespread presumption "that America consists exclusively of the middle class" (242–44), as Irving Howe put it in a 1955 article.

Still, if the term "rat race" was encountered more and more often during the postwar years—along with "the treadmill," its metaphorical cousin—the primary reason was not a radical alertness to the woes of minority groups and the inadequacies of intellectual critique. Rather, it was the fact that within the vaunted middle class itself, even successful group-adjusters and self-manipulators were becoming weary of the responsibilities and disillusioned with the rewards that their efforts brought. On a deeper historical level, moreover, self-doubt was fostered by such massive events as World War II, the Holocaust, wars supported by the United States in Korea and elsewhere, and growing decolonization. All these played a role in the emergence of such groups as the Beats in the United States, the Angry Young Men in Britain, and the Existentialists in France, as well as in the appearance of popular cultural products as diverse as the

American novel *What Makes Sammy Run?* and the English film *The Lone-liness of the Long Distance Runner*, for just two examples among many.

"*An apparently closed room in which there is a large rat race as the dominant center of attention*" was Goodman's 1960 model of the Organized Society, which he spelled with uppercase initials and populated with an all-male cast. The race is engaged in by "bright fellows who do not believe in it" but run "desperately . . . because they are afraid to stop" (1960, 159–60).

Also present in this room, however, are many who choose not to participate. Some are Corner Boys, endowed with more sense of community, more resourcefulness, and less repressive training than College Boys, but doomed by parental example and lack of alternatives to a late entry into the race, not a lifetime abstention. Nearby stand the Delinquents, who share many qualities with the Organized Society—conformism, snobbery, cynicism—but do not get the rewards of the rat race despite their ill-hidden esteem for it. Hollywood and Madison Avenue provide their heroes.

Present too are Bums who have broken down and flunked out of the race, acquiring superficial freedom but remaining trapped in their own corner of the closed room. Nationalities from abroad are represented by Britain's frustrated Angry Young Men, waspish and bitter toward the social shortcomings they see, and self-disdainful French Existentialist youths, who comment witheringly on the closed room without leaving it. Hipsters jump all over the place, widening the room's boundaries through their active subculture, but hobbled by their conviction that nothing exists other than rat races of various kinds, including their own insatiable craving for experience and love.

And amid this clamor one finds the Beats, who have either found good reason to question the race or have lacked the heart to begin it in the first place. On the plus side of their ledger, says Goodman, they are generally clever at deriving personal and cultural satisfactions from the relative poverty they embrace. On the minus side, their rejection of cultural tradition makes their art immature and parochial, and their weaknesses for notoriety and cynicism undermine their richest personal attributes. Like their companions in the apparently closed room, they are caught in a situation that is distant not only from the outdated social model of Progress but also from the model of Class Struggle, which has traditionally been conceived as taking place "in an open field of history, in which new values were continually emerging and the locus of 'human value' changing." In the apparently closed room, the only value system is the rat race itself. It is both shared and held in contempt by everyone present—a status quo that offers little motivation for basic change, "since there are no unambiguous motives to fight for and no uncontaminated means." No wonder it is "hard to grow up" in this environment (1960, 159–69).

Gray Flannel Men

In a feminist analysis of what she calls "the gray flannel dissidents," social historian Barbara Ehrenreich identifies two strands of protest among disaffected middle-class men during the '50s: one directed against the white-collar work world, the other against the suburbanized family life that such work was frequently meant to support. Conformity signified a sort of emasculation to such dissenting males, but there was little they could do about their plight, since the security of a steady job and the comforts of a bourgeois home were too seductive to allow for decisive movements toward fundamental change. Hence, the gray-flannel rebellion found itself stalled at the ineffectual level of a plaintive lament and a diffuse critique, rising at best to a "higher conformity" of deliberate acquiescence with the social given and perhaps (in Riesman's word) an "autonomy" manifested by a dim faith in the redemptive powers of, say, psychoanalysis or modern art.[16] Even the conservative Norman Podhoretz, no enemy of status-quo accommodation, found the latter mind-set too wishy-washy to tolerate and ridiculed the attitude that there is "great beauty, profound significance, in a man's struggle to achieve freedom *through* submission to conditions . . . " (Ehrenreich 52, 32, 40–41).

While it is hard to argue with Podhoretz on this particular stand, it is true that the gray-flannel rebels did not get very far with their insurrection. The uninterrupted continuation of unadulterated middle-class life-styles throughout and beyond the postwar period (even in the tumultuous '60s, when more drastic challenges were brought to bear) supports this contention in itself. So does much cultural evidence from the '50s, of which *The Man in the Gray Flannel Suit*, as both a Sloan Wilson novel and a Darryl F. Zanuck movie, is a representative example.

The popular film version, written and directed by Nunnally Johnson for Twentieth Century Fox in 1956, stars Gregory Peck as the eponymous white-collar worker who leaves a "safe" job with a vaguely identified "foundation" for a higher-paying slot at a Madison Avenue media and public-relations firm. The story takes many pains to protect the status of the hero, Tom, as a person of good intentions and clean conscience. These qualities shine through Peck's relentlessly dignified performance, and the screenplay uses a carefully calculated subplot about Tom's past indiscretions as a soldier overseas—he fathered an illegitimate child during a wartime love affair—to strengthen rather than diminish his virtuous image, since he and his wife Betsy (Jennifer Jones) agree to provide financial support for the (safely distant) child when they learn of his poverty-stricken life. On top of that, Tom's new job is a surprisingly altruistic one by Madison Avenue standards. The company's chief executive wants to launch a national campaign for better mental-health care, and Tom's task is to draft a speech that will enlist the medical community in this worthy cause. His biggest challenge is figuring out how to get his honest, constructive criticisms past the "yes-men" who have the boss's ear. In one scene, he convinces himself (although not Betsy, who wonders what happened to the "guts" he once had) that becoming a yes-man might be his own best course of action, on the ground that his opinions are not necessarily more valid than those of his boss or his colleagues. Ultimately he sets aside the temptation to curry favor, however, and speaks from his heart, earning more respect than ever from his hard-pressed but unfailingly gentle and introspective employer.

In some respects, the film wants to be seen as a critical exploration of Madison Avenue-type conformity, craftiness, and obsession with success. One of the yes-men is portrayed as ineffectual, the other as craven. Certain corporate practices, such as using irrelevant criteria as a basis for job placement, are called into question. Most important, the chief executive is depicted as a decent, caring man whose possibilities for happiness and contentment have been sadly brushed aside by the pressures of an all-consuming career. His heart is ailing; his marriage ended years ago; and now his misguided daughter is marrying a disreputable playwright instead of going to college like a nice girl. (The daughter is rich and pampered but vaguely Beat in her ostensible disdain for work, money, and "reasonable" behavior.) Tom resembles his son who was killed in the war, so the old man treats him with special warmth and consideration, earning affection from the film's audience as well as from Tom himself—especially when he tells Tom that he would do things differently if he had a second chance at life, investing less energy in his work and paying more attention to his home and family. (The obvious advantages that his family has reaped from his success—their material comfort, for instance, and the fact that his dead son could have avoided active service and therefore not been killed if he had taken advantage of the father's connections—are not discussed, presumably because they would complicate this aspect of the movie's message.)

In this manner, the film aggressively reinforces at least three important (and related) conventions of the '50s sociocultural paradigm. One is that both family and work are natural and necessary but are compatible with each other only if approached with modest and moderate goals. The second is that when a choice between business and home arises, the home must come first, or short-term happiness will be followed by long-term grief. The third is that nonconformity brings danger not only when it is manifested in the form of eccentric behaviors like those of the Beat Generation but also when it leads to intemperate pursuit of socially approved goals, such as top-level success in the business jungle. To be a "stand-out" is to be in peril, the story suggests, holding up Tom's boss—in despair over his private life, always moping about things at the office—as Exhibit A in its plainly rigged argument.

Thus, the way is paved for the film's ultimate statement, embodied in Tom's final decision about how to order his life. He has learned from his boss the price of too much hustle on the corporate ladder. And he has learned from Betsy the value of "guts" and honesty—which encourages him to foil the yes-men at work and then to confess his wartime romance and unacknowledged offspring at home. When this confession sparks a domestic crisis and threatens to destabilize his marriage, he remembers his boss's admonition that the business world needs two sorts of men: unflagging tycoons, who sacrifice everything to build mighty corporations, and nine-to-five soldiers, who do the daily drudgery needed for those corporations to stay afloat. Pondering his proper path, Tom realizes that he will be most content as one of the nine-to-fivers and that to evade this destiny—by accepting elevation to a new place at the boss's right hand, replacing the most craven of his yes-man colleagues—would be a tragic and needless mistake, leading to the certain ruin of his household and the sort of empty life that has given so many regrets to his aging employer. Proof of Tom's good sense in refusing advancement arrives quickly, as the boss reacts with understanding rather than anger, acquiring even more respect for Tom than he had before and acknowledging that he would make the same choice if he could. The moral is clear: Achieving too little may be Beat, but achieving too much wreaks just as much disruption on the American ideal, which is to fill one's appointed place in the status-quo system as contentedly and unobtrusively as possible.

A coda shows Tom and Betsy arranging with a kindly judge to send money regularly to Tom's faraway offspring—an act of such selfless compassion (especially on Betsy's part) that the overwhelmed judge declares it a privilege to know the couple and shakes his head in wonder at their virtuousness. No wonder Tom and Betsy smile warmly (if wanly) as they settle into their sedan, steer into the streets of suburban Connecticut, and take up their newly rigidified roles as average, normal, untemptable members of the bedroom-community bourgeoisie. Here, in DeLuxe color on the CinemaScope screen, is precisely what even a '50s conservative like Podhoretz could not bring himself to abide: the seductive assertion that beauty and significance may indeed reside in the struggle to achieve freedom via willed and willing submission to the social given.

Gray Flannel Women

Women occupied a complicated position in the male-defined and male-oriented discursive structure reflected in *The Man in the Gray Flannel Suit* and many other '50s cultural products. This position developed as the ideologies of consensus and "togetherness" promoted a gender-based division of roles and behaviors that led to differing yet complementary notions about females and the feminine.

To begin with, a sweeping avoidance of productive discussion about women was frequently grounded in contentions that their role in life was inherently "higher" than that of men—a rhetorical tactic that had been a commonplace of Victorian morality. Thus, in the course of an earnestly compassionate study of postwar "youth troubles," even such a well-intentioned critic as Goodman was capable of writing that a "girl does not *have* to, she is not expected to, 'make something' of herself. Her career does not have to be self-justifying, for she will have children, which is absolutely self-justifying, like any other natural or creative act" (1960, 13). So much for the fact that by 1960, forty percent of women over sixteen years old had jobs (Pells 214). And so much for all the personal, sociological, and political implications of such a statistic for women, their families, and a society that jealously guarded assumptions of "natural" family contentment, or at least "natural" family resignation.

Coexistent with this line of attack was a rhetoric of paranoia that surged through popular literature and journalism. Philip Wylie attacked women in general in his 1956 article "The Abdicating Male . . . And How the Gray Flannel Mind Exploits Him Through His Women," published in *Playboy*, and attacked mothers ("momism") in particular in *Generation of Vipers*, significantly his best-known book. In a 1958 series on American men, articles in *Look* magazine noted statistics that contrast vividly with Goodman's homely portrait of women—millions of females owned securities, their stock holdings were enormous, they made a majority of consumer purchases and helped with money management in most homes— while also suggesting that women tended to push men into ever-rising consumerism (part of a "keep up with the neighbors" conformity) and that "female dominance" could be "one of the several causes of the 'organization man' who is so deplored today. What he is doing is just building his own masculine world. His office is *his* castle" (Ehrenreich 37–39).[17]

Although the motivations of Betsy and Tom in *The Man in the Gray Flannel Suit* are slightly different, Betsy is built on a similar model during much of the film. She plays a virtual Lady Macbeth to her overcautious husband when he fails to be aggressive enough at the office; chiding him for a lack of "guts" at one point, she hesitates just long enough to hint that she might have said "balls" if the Hollywood censorship code had not constrained her. Only near the end of the story does she turn away from advocating tough-guy ambition for her spouse, instead accepting his choice of an equally "normal" ideology based on averageness (one recalls the happily normalized police officer of *In a Lonely Place*, cited above) and "fitting in."

By the terms of this interlocking set of postwar discourses, men obviously faced the duty of supporting women in their "higher" child-rearing and family-tending functions while defending themselves (and the best interests of their society) against the pressures and temptations to which women subjected them. Where would such a sociocultural situation lead? To the snazzy-jazzy pages of *Playboy* magazine, among other places. Here was a publication that confronted family-centered aspects of the postwar consensus with a proud rejection of family-magazine status (announced in its first editorial) and a clear-cut advocacy of masculine privilege. At last the male rebellion promised to leave its vagueness and diffuseness behind, spurred by Hugh Hefner's journalistic savvy and also by his wordy "philosophy," which soon started appearing in the periodical.[18]

If the innovations of *Playboy* represented not the beginning of the sexual revolution (a '60s phenomenon that commenced long after the magazine's 1953 debut) but rather a turning point in the previously half-hearted male revolt of the '50s, it was because they championed freedom from much more than sexual repression and decorum. A male, the Hefner message asserted again and again, did not have to encumber himself with any of the responsibilities connected with home and family in order to think of himself, or be thought of by his society and his peers, as a man. As potentially reorienting as this notion was, however, the *Playboy* mind-set remained generally conservative vis-à-vis the status quo, retaining a shameless fascination with money and a whole-scale acceptance of commodity culture. It also remained profoundly imbricated with the asserted privileges of male power, manifested in discursive structures that were scarcely more complex or enlightened than those that Hefnerism claimed to repudiate as puritanical, benighted, and outmoded.

Playboy is not mentioned in Vincente Minnelli's drama *Home From the Hill*, released by MGM in 1960, but the attitude held by some of this film's characters toward male privilege and domestic responsibility makes an interesting study in terms of the *Playboy* mind-set. A patriarch (Robert Mitchum) has struck an agreement with his wife (Eleanor Parker) that allows him to philander to his heart's content, indulging a predatory sexuality that he explicitly likens to the hunting that has filled his study with animal trophies; in return, the wife is allowed to raise their son (George Hamilton) with no interference or even participation by her husband. Thus does a powerful and influential man sustain the appearance of a socially proper household while divesting himself of moral and emotional responsibility for parenting and other substantive aspects of his role as a husband and father. But years after this arrangement has been made, he is dismayed to realize that his teenage son prefers collecting rocks, birds, and butterflies to the stalking, spitting, and shooting that "real men" enjoy. He promptly takes the lad in hand, giving him a gun and enlisting a more suitably socialized young man (the patriarch's illegitimate offspring, we later learn) to initiate him in the ways of the Texas wilderness.

Minnelli's vision in this film is fairly sophisticated. It ultimately depicts the "sissified" boy as fully capable of "real man" behavior—as when he matches his father's legendary feat of single-handed boar killing—and shows him rejecting the excesses of *machismo* while maintaining a level of humane sensitivity (e.g., standing up for his half-brother's rights at his own expense) that reflects the benign influence of his "feminine" upbringing. The film tellingly dissects *Playboy*-type values with its portrayal of a prominent man whose conception of power equates sexuality and masculinity with promiscuity and predation—all seen by the movie as arbitrary notions growing less from an inborn "human nature" than from unthinking capitulation to socially constructed norms. Such values reigned with tenacious power in a wide variety of shapes and guises throughout the postwar period and beyond.

Rationality, Irrationality, Pararationality

A naked lunch is natural to us,
  we eat reality sandwiches.
But allegories are so much
    lettuce.
      Don't hide the madness.
                    —Allen Ginsberg, "On Burroughs' Work," 1954

. . . I realized either I was crazy or the world was crazy: and I picked on the world. . . . And of course I was right.
                    —Jack Kerouac, Vanity of Duluoz

Shameful common-sense—I hope, I
    swear—
Will never come to me.

                    —Vladimir Mayakovsky

The contrast between two modes of thought, loosely defined as the rational and the irrational, provides a useful tool for exploring the relationship between mainstream (e.g., Hollywood, popular novels) and oppositional (e.g., Beat writers, avant-garde film) cultural production during the '50s era. On one side, associated with much mainstream culture, one finds the aspiration toward a Rational Society, rooted in logical social-scientific principles expected to justify or even eradicate social ills. On the other side, associated with many oppositional thinkers, one finds strong resistance to such aggressive rationalism. Indeed, one finds the embrace of an *irrationalism* that is at once utopian in spirit, vague in definition, and wistful in tone. This mode might better be called "pararationalism," since it is not entirely irrational but represents an alternative way of conceptualizing and employing reason and retains enough intellectual and psychological coherence to have (according to its proponents) significant value as an aid in reaching personal and/or social change.

To suggest this approach is not to set up an arbitrary dualism between reason, logic, and sanity in one camp and unreason, nonsense, and madness in the other. Nor is it to suggest rationality as a causal or explanatory framework vis-à-vis '50s society, or irrationality as a magical key to understanding Beat or avant-garde phenomena. There are plenty of areas in which the mainstream embraced irrational things, such as ridiculous fads (hula hoops, Davy Crockett merchandise) and carnivalistic entertainments (professional wrestling, Three Stooges movies), not to mention such geopolitical grotesqueries as the cold war, the nuclear-arms race, and the doctrine of mutually assured destruction. Conversely, the central Beat figures (Ginsberg, Burroughs, Kerouac) and many experimental filmmakers (Brakhage, Deren, Markopoulos) never relinquished their respect for aspects of classically rational culture.

But all this notwithstanding, postwar tensions between majority and oppositional thought rest partly on differing attitudes toward reason and its place in the social structure. One such attitude, exemplified by "official" ideas in journalism, education, and mass culture, sees rationality as indispensable for maintaining order (e.g., bureaucracies with "expert" leaders), promoting decency (e.g., civil censorship), pursuing happiness (e.g., the *Playboy* philosophy), improving the self (e.g., the cultivation of personality), and perfecting society (e.g., reliance on social-science norms). A converse attitude, exemplified by minorities like the Beat subculture and the avant-garde arts community, sees the questioning of official rationality as a weapon against hegemonic forces in matters ranging from behavior (e.g., resisting gender regimentation) to ideology (e.g., cultivating mysticism and using drugs to evade logic and circumnavigate reason).

Rationality and Film

Hollywood's classical filmmaking style is grounded in modern ideals of rationality, control, calculation, and manipulation. It works to incorporate images and sounds within patterns that promote narrative flow, emotional urgency, and ideological strength. At the same time, these patterns minimize all elements that might disrupt or divert the seemingly spontaneous stream of events. Folding real-world material into an all-embracing textual system has an ideological effect since it establishes a hierarchy of values, codes, and significations that accentuates some meanings, excludes others, and insists on the naturalness of those it has chosen to privilege. This totalizing process is never as successful as it would like to be, though, since the physical world is too unruly and excessive to be wholly contained by photographic images, phonographic sounds, and storytelling structures. A different set of ideological implications opens when "excess" does spill beyond standard cinematic codes, since spectators may become aware of those codes as arbitrary and constraining and begin to question them.

Despite the possibilities for liberated moviegoing that such moments may provide, the wish to homogenize experience remains deeply embedded in classical film style, which has been promulgated for decades in textbooks, film-industry manuals, apprenticeship practices, and studio traditions. Some exceptions are allowed, mainly in cartoons, musicals, and comedies. But most Hollywood filmmaking rests firmly on "notions of decorum, proportion, formal harmony, respect for tradition, mimesis, self-effacing craftsmanship, and cool control of the perceiver's response" (3–4), in David Bordwell's accurate summary. All these qualities are compatible with the project of reproducing social, cultural, and political norms claimed as natural and common-sensical by the prevailing power structure.

Writing in 1947 about television, also dominated by classical style, Frankfort School authors Max Horkheimer and Theodor W. Adorno observed that the "alliance of word, image, and music is all the more perfect . . . because the sensuous elements which all approvingly reflect the surface of social reality are in principle embodied in the same technical process, the unity of which becomes its distinctive content." This technologically produced unity represents "the triumph of invested capital" and becomes the "meaningful content of every film, whatever plot the production team may have selected" (124). (This observation foreshadows Marshall McLuhan's famous statement that the medium is the message.) Horkheimer and Adorno go on to state that cultural consumers in industrial society must necessarily accept what manufacturers hold out to them—namely, real-world material forced into a predigested form. The culture industry thus uses classical cinema as a means of containing, leveling, and rationalizing experience through modes of production and consumption that threaten no harm to dominating social forces.

The implication is that culture manufacturers are themselves tools of the system, and indeed, the authors state that these manufacturers operate under the sway of "the power of society." This power "remains irrational, however we may try to rationalize it; and this inescapable force is processed by commercial agencies so that they give an artificial impression of being in command" (Horkheimer and Adorno 124–25). To extrapolate from Horkheimer and Adorno on this point, one reason for classical film's obsession with narrative and consistency may be an unconscious reaction against the dangerous forms of irrationality that are embedded in social and state power.

Embracing the Irrational

An alternative response to this oppressive brand of irrationality is to turn it back on the social system that sustains it—which is just what the core Beats and other avant-gardists sought to do during the postwar period. Their weapons included Kerouac's spontaneous prose, Burroughs's cut-up texts, and Ginsberg's improvisatory poetics, all of which were designed to bypass the reasoning ego and uncover new wellsprings of mental and spiritual energy.[19]

Evidence of this reaction abounds in Beat writings. "I have come to believe now that life is not *essentially* but *completely* irrational," wrote Kerouac to John Clellon Holmes in a 1949 letter. "I should like anybody to challenge this CLEAR idea. I have seen proof of this. . . . It's all very beautiful because it isn't moribund, this 'irrationality' I speak of" (Knight and Knight 91–92). Burroughs adopted the method of cutting and folding pages because of its efficiency in disrupting reason, causality, linearity, and logic. "Consciousness *is* a cut-up; life is a cut-up," he declared (1993, 61), lauding montage as a writing tool. Ginsberg's evocation of "angelheaded hipsters" and "best minds . . . destroyed by madness" was part of his lifelong answer to conundrums raised for him by Carl Solomon, the mental-institution companion to whom "Howl!" is dedicated. These questions, as crystallized by a later commentator, include: Is maladjustment a sign of mental health in modern society? Do psychiatrists really like everything about contemporary American life? If not, why do they make conformity such a crusade? Aren't notions of "common sense" and "wholesomeness" merely reflections of temporary social biases?[20] Such queries strongly evoke Foucault's critique of social norms as products of interaction between knowledge and power. Looking at the core Beat writers as a group, one may roughly say that Ginsberg represents its more ecstatically transcendental wing; Burroughs represents its darker, more hysterical dimension; and Kerouac commutes between the two positions in different periods of his career. What they share is a preference for the sensuous fecundity of intuition over consensus culture and its insistence on defining and enforcing the claims of rationality.

This stance recalls the contention of Frankfort philosopher Herbert Marcuse that "the aesthetic dimension" brings intellect and senses together, in effect "strengthening sensuousness as against the tyranny of reason" and ultimately calling for "the liberation of sensuousness from the repressive domination of reason." Aesthetics thus seeks "a liberation of the senses which, far from destroying civilization, would give it a firmer basis and would greatly enhance its potentialities" (179–81). Here is a well-reasoned vote for the power, virtue, and usefulness of unreason.

*I*rrationality and Film

Aims similar to those of the Beats, approached with a similarly audacious range of methods and techniques, have animated avant-garde filmmakers who echo key aspects of the Beat sensibility in their work. Stan Brakhage underscores the importance of nonrational discourse (and, implicitly, the "play impulse" that Marcuse praises as a facilitator of moral and physical freedom[21] [182]) in the very title of his book *Film at Wit's End*, dealing with eight experimental filmmakers who have engaged with the nonrational in various ways. Jerome Hill, for example, "shares with [Brakhage] the sense that the subconscious is supreme in making a work of art." Christopher MacLaine, whom Brakhage links specifically with the Beat sensibility, may or may not have "thought of himself as 'the Artaud of San Francisco,' but he certainly did have an affinity with him: he courted madness and he finally got it." Bruce Conner's films make self-reflexive comments that "are always built of contradictions within contradictions—or perhaps we should say contravisions within contravisions. . . . His work is consistently filled with . . . contrary imagery, and more than that, imagery that elicits immediate contrary reactions in the psyche of practically everyone" (1989, 26, 116, 143).[22] Brakhage's own work is famously antagonistic to constrictive notions of logic, rationality, and logos, which are seen as arbitrary hurdles between the artist and the necessary preoccupations of art, namely, "birth, sex, death, and the search for God." In this context it is worth recalling one of Brakhage's most resonant statements:

Imagine an eye unruled by man-made laws of perspective, an eye unprejudiced by compositional logic, an eye which does not respond to the name of everything but which must know each object encountered in life through an adventure in perception. How many colors are there in a field of grass to the crawling baby unaware of "Green?" How many rainbows can light create for the untutored eye? How aware of variations in heat waves can that eye be? Imagine a world alive with incomprehensible objects and shimmering with an endless variety of movement and innumerable gradations of color. Imagine a world before the "beginning was the word." (1963, n.p.)

The kind of experience evoked here has been described by film theorist Annette Michelson as "quintessential vision, innocent, uncorrupted by the conventions of a perspective inherited from the Renaissance and built into the very lens of the camera." The cinematic representation of such vision may appear to the spectator as situated not in the rationally constructed world but rather "inside the eye," where it strives "to present itself perceptually, all at once, to resist observation and cognition" (1971, 176). Brakhage's linkage of such autotelic creation with the *ur*-perception of infancy recalls Kerouac's words in *Desolation Angels* when he writes:

Ah, if there was another sight besides *eye* sight what atomic other-levels wouldn't we see?—but here we see moons, mountains, lakes, trees and sentient beings only, with our eyesight. . . . O what peace and content I feel, coming back to my shack knowing that the world is a babe's dream and the ecstasy of the golden eternity is all we're going back to. . . . I lie on my back in the dark, hands joined, glad, as the northern lights shine like a Hollywood premiere and at that too I look upside-down and see that it's just big pieces of ice on earth reflecting the other-side sun in some far daylight. . . . "It's only recent," I realize, looking at the world, some recent cycle of creation by The Power to joy in its reminder to its selfless self that it is The Power—and all of it in its essence swarming tender mystery, that you can see by closing your eyes and letting the eternal silence in your ears. . . . (28–29)

It is unlikely that Kerouac knew Brakhage's work. Yet rarely has a Beat writer, or any writer, come so close to the experience of watching such

Brakhage films as *Mothlight* (1963), *My Mountain: Song 27* (1968), parts of *Dog Star Man* (1961–64) and *The Art of Vision* (1961–65), and *The Text of Light* (1974), with their silent-movie stillness and their radical recuperation of hypnagogic closed-eye vision. The most unwittingly Brakhage-like of the core Beats is surely Kerouac, the intuitive impro- viser who concluded the spontaneous "17th Chorus" of his *Mexico City Blues* (17),

> And I remember the Zigzag
> Original
> Mind
>
> of Babyhood
> when you'd let the faces
> crack & mock
> & yak & change
> & go mad utterly
> in your night
> firstmind
> reveries
>
> talking about the mind
> The endless Not Invisible
> Madness Rioting
> Everywhere

Rejecting the Word

Brakhage's aesthetic, and its counterparts in the work of other experi- mental filmmakers from Maya Deren on, have antecedents quite indepen- dent of the Beat movement. Michelson identifies this cinematic tradition as an American extension of '20s European avant-gardism,[23] citing the effort of Surrealism and Expressionism to undermine narrative and "situ- ate film in a kind of perpetual present . . . tending . . . to devour or elimi- nate expectation as a dimension of cinematic experience" (1971, 175–76). The core Beats also inherited a great deal from the Surrealist and Expres- sionist traditions, and much of their work shares the project of escaping the temporality of logos-bound reason and entering an eternal Now of rarified immanence and transcendence.

"WHAT SCARED YOU ALL INTO TIME? WHAT SCARED YOU ALL INTO YOUR BODIES? INTO SHIT FOREVER?" asks Burroughs, not at all rhetorically, in a 1960 letter to Ginsberg that illustrates this point. Burroughs then proposes some answers (Burroughs and Ginsberg 1963, 65):

THE WORD. THE-THEE WORD. IN THEE BEGINNING WAS THE WORD. SCARED YOU ALL INTO SHIT FOREVER. COME OUT FOREVER. COME OUT OF THE TIME WORD THE FOREVER. COME OUT OF THE BODY WORD THEE FOREVER. COME OUT OF THE SHIT WORD THE FOREVER. ALL OUT OF TIME AND INTO SPACE. FOREVER.... THERE IS NO WORD TO FEAR. THERE IS NO WORD. THAT IS ALL ALL ALL....[24]

In this rejection of the word and of the materialities (time, space, body, shit) imbricated with it, Burroughs recalls Brakhage's insistence that verbality be subordinated to imagery on the ground that, as the filmmaker explains it, "there is a pursuit of knowledge foreign to language and founded upon visual communication, demanding a development of the optical mind, and dependent upon perception in the original and deepest sense.... Allow so-called hallucination to enter the realm of perception ... accept dream visions, day-dreams or night-dreams, as you would so-called real scenes...."[25] And conversely, in another section of the same text, "Language has become at worst our burial ground" (Brakhage 1963, n.p.).

Such statements veer far away from the rationality-bound ambitions of mainstream fiction and cinema, with their logical narratives, carefully coded conventions, and heavy investments in temporality, sequentiality, and linearity. Accordingly, both the Beats and the avant-garde filmmakers developed new methods for pursuing their oppositional goals. Burroughs applied nonrational montage principles to the printed page, believing this practice would evoke an unprecedented unity of time, identity, and perception.[26] Buddhism offered some of the Beats not only a guide to new sorts of behavior but also a means of seeking pure streams of thought wherein memory and expectation would be gloriously moot.[27] Kerouac found in bebop a doorway to exquisitely impermanent levels of intuition and irrationality, as Ginsberg indicates when he describes how Kerouac became aware of the sound of the language, and got swimming in the seas of sound and guided his intellect on sound, rather than on dictionary associations with the meanings of the sounds. In other words, another kind of intelligence . . . another kind of reason, a reason founded on sounds rather than a reason founded on conceptual associations. If you can use the word reason for that." (Weinreich 57)

This ideal of grounding verbal perception in material sound rather than referential meaning—recalling Antonin Artaud's interest in glossolalia and musication—has clear resonance with Brakhage's ideal of liberating vision from human-made rules of perspective, compositional logic, and logocentric thought. "The very narrow contemporary moving visual reality is exhausted," Brakhage writes, calling for a cinema that privileges sensuality over referentiality. "The belief in the sacredness of any man-achievement sets concrete about it, statues becoming statutes, needing both explosives and earthquakes for disruption. . . . The 'absolute realism' of the motion picture image is a human invention." It is for this reason that, in order for "magic in art" to be realized, "the intellect must always be baffled and back-stepping at each successive moment, and must always be ultimately baffled, or the successive spells can never be cast and the ultimate realm never established" (1963, n.p.). Brakhage's own techniques for dodging conventional realism, referentiality, and rationality include the construction of image sequences founded on intuitive association rather than linear causality, and recourse to a hyperkinetic image flow invested with such speed and diversity that recollection becomes highly problematic and anticipation is rendered utterly beside the point. The frequent result of such practice is what Kerouac might have recognized as a radically visual experience akin to swimming in seas of sight and guiding the intellect on *photogénie* rather than ordinary experiential logic.

Other filmmakers have sought different but related goals through such means as cutting up existing cinematic texts (e.g., Bruce Conner and Anthony Balch), voiding the frame of figurative content (e.g., Harry Smith and Ernie Gehr), voiding the frame of all content whatever (e.g., Peter Kubelka and Tony Conrad), and using nonlinear structures to defamiliarize subjects, characters, and narrative ideas (e.g., Ron Rice and Ken Jacobs). Although these artists have widely divergent aims, agendas, and methodologies, they and many of their contemporaries have shared the Beat goal of dethroning linearity and narrativity, and anchoring their works in new "modalities of consciousness" (Weinreich 57) that will liberate thought by extending it not only beyond language but beyond all humanly generated conceptions of reason and rationality.[28]

This project was especially audacious at a time when Hollywood film, mainstream literature, and other conventional means of expression were tied to a sociocultural milieu in which order and consensus were fetishized; a cult of rationality was enforced by what C. Wright Mills called "the malign ascendency of the expert"; and knowledge, again in Mills's words, was "no longer widely felt as an ideal [but] as an instrument . . . of power and wealth, and also, of course, as an ornament in conversation" (354, 352). Like the Beats who shared his desire for more vital ways of life and thought, Brakhage showed formidable courage in embarking on his unpopular, anti-instrumental, pararational artistic project even though, as he well recognized,

This is an age which has no symbol for death other than the skull and bones of one stage of decomposition . . . and it is an age which lives in fear of total annihilation. It is a time haunted by sexual sterility yet almost universally incapable of perceiving the phallic nature of every destructive manifestation of itself. It is an age which artificially seeks to project itself materialistically into abstract space and to fulfill itself mechanically because it has blinded itself to almost all external reality within eyesight and to the organic awareness of even the physical movement properties of its own perceptibility. . . . The ultimate searching visualization has been directed toward God out of the deepest possible human understanding that there can be no ultimate love where there is fear. Yet in this contemporary time how many of us even struggle to deeply perceive our own children? (1963, n.p.)

Theoretical Frameworks

Dialogism, Carnivalism, and Movies

I'll bet you thought you had a brilliant idea in imposing a revolting absti-
nence on me with regard to the sins of the flesh. Well, you were mistaken.
You brought my brain to the boiling point. You caused me to conjure up
fanciful creatures which I shall have to bring into being.
                    —Marquis de Sade, in a letter to his wife, 1783[1]

■ American life in the '50s was clearly less bland and homogenized than some observers have made it sound. Even as consumerism, consensus, conformity, and cold war vigorously asserted their priorities, every development in these directions was contested by some kind of skeptical or even hostile equivalent. Some of these oppositional forces were pushed effectively into the margins of American consciousness, for example, the tendentious products of avant-garde cinema. Others, such as provocative stances and unorthodox works by the core Beat writers, were able to gain fairly high visibility—although attitudes other than intellectual curiosity and cultural respect often determined the means (condescending photo spreads in magazines, parodies on television, etc.) by which this visibility was achieved.

In any case, the '50s emerged as a time of diverse and conflicting discourses among diverse and conflicting interests. The continuing tension between "official" rationality and pararational alternatives; between homogenization and diversification; between classical and avant-garde sensibilities—these and many other dissonances marked postwar America as an abundant field of dialogic contestation, to borrow a term from cultural theorist Mikhail Bakhtin, whose concepts of dialogism and carnivalism are extraordinarily useful in illuminating the many facets of the Beat and avant-garde enterprises.

Relativity, Open-Endedness, Loopholes

Bakhtin's concept of dialogism refers not merely to dialogue between communicating people or competing ideas but to the acknowledgment and celebration of relativity, mutability, and instability as necessary characteristics of all human interaction. More broadly, it points to difference, contradiction, and open-endedness as inherent and productive aspects of the human condition itself. Confronting fixed systems of thought with a liberating "loophole" philosophy,[2] dialogism embraces uncertainty as a basic condition of consciousness, which itself is an ever-shifting result of the ever-unstable relationship between self and other.

It would be presumptuous to claim Bakhtin as an unwitting champion of the Beats and the postwar avant-garde. Still, his conviction that thought "knows only conditional points" (1986, 162) indicates a rejection of bureaucratized and consensus-bound social systems and a sympathy for the kind of radical eccentricity that the rebellious Americans praised. The ideal he nurtures is polyphonic multiplicity rather than collective rationality. "Authoritative discourse," he warns,

> permits no play with the context framing it, no play with its borders, no gradual and flexible transitions, no spontaneously creative stylizing variants on it. It enters our verbal consciousness as a compact and indivisible mass; one must either totally affirm it, or totally reject it. It is indissolubly fused with its authority—with political power, an institution, a person—and it stands and falls together with that authority. . . . Therefore the distance we ourselves observe vis-à-vis this authoritative discourse remains unchanged in all its projections: a playing with distances, with fusion and dissolution, with approach and retreat, is not here possible. (1981, 343–44)

Since questioning contexts, blurring boundaries, playing with positions, valorizing spontaneity, fusing and dissolving discourse, and other destabilizing activities were central to the Beat and avant-garde agendas, Bakhtinian thought can shed much light on them. Burroughs's cut-up texts, Ginsberg's poetic riffs, and Kerouac's spontaneous prose are all (a) expressions of assertively eccentric personalities, (b) explorations of conventionally overlooked artistic terrains, and (c) provocations aimed at the homogenized domain of "authoritative" literature. Just as self-expressive, aesthetically sophisticated, and socially tendentious are Brakhage's attacks on Renaissance perspective and compositional correctness, Kenneth Anger's celebrations of socially suppressed sexualities, Ron Rice's rambling journeys into radical narrative forms, and other filmic projects determined to raise a ruckus.

Challenging the Audience

A key aspect of much Beat writing and avant-garde filmmaking is the challenge it poses to its audience by deploying unfamiliar codes of communication—often serving unfamiliar modes of consciousness—and thus demanding that the reader/spectator play an active role in perceiving and responding to it. To use a distinction formulated by Roland Barthes, these works are not "readerly texts" marked by classical values of unity and transparency; instead they tend to be "writerly texts," requiring alert creativity from the reader or spectator.[3]

By demanding this imaginative interplay, such works place high value on (dialogic) exchange of ideas rather than (monologic) imposition of meaning. Their refusal to reproduce common patterns often gives them a lively, challenging quality lacking in more conventional works. When successful, they support the Bakhtinian view that "true understanding" must be dialogic in nature, since "meaning belongs to a word in its position between speakers; that is, meaning is realized only in the process of active, responsive understanding" (Volosinov 102). This analysis is supported by critic James T. Jones's suggestion (made without reference to Bakhtinian theory) that Kerouac openly calls for his audience to turn their reading into a creative act at certain moments and to engage in dialogue with Kerouac's own consciousness. Such a moment occurs in the "218th Chorus" of *Mexico City Blues* when the poet writes, "O come off it, the vast canopial / Assemblies wait for yr honest spontaneous reply. / What shall it be?" Something similar happens when the "235th Chorus" ends with "Oh me, Oh my, / Hello—Come in—." Kerouac seems to be addressing a visitor, quite possibly the reader, offering a friendly welcome to enter and become part of the poem, its composition, and the river of thought that it represents (Jones 156).

Bakhtin acknowledges that under some conditions, "speech communication is completely formed and has a fixed, frozen character." Such cases are not typical, though, because in living language the "interrelationships between speakers are always changing, even if the degree of change is hardly noticeable" (Bakhtin and Medvedev 1985, 95). This state of flux is continual and open-ended, Bakhtin asserts. "Even *past* meanings,

> that is, those born in the dialogue of past centuries, can never be stable (finalized, ended once and for all). . . . At any moment in the development of the dialogue there are immense, boundless masses of forgotten contextual meanings, but at certain moments of the dialogue's subsequent development . . . they are recalled and invigorated in renewed form (in a renewed context). Nothing is absolutely dead: every meaning will have its homecoming festival. (1986, 170)[4]

*B*op

This insight acquires special power in connection with progressive culture of the postwar period, when various forms of quotation, citation, and recuperation—direct instances of the recollection, renewal, and reinvigoration of meaning—became important tools for innovative writers and filmmakers. A model for both groups was bebop jazz, which took a major aspect of its creative identity from the practice of spinning out new melodies over an underlying pattern of chords from preexisting (and usually well-known) compositions.

The growing popularity of improvisation spurred the spread of this technique. The bop movement reflected the desire of musicians for a freedom and individuality that were not possible in prewar big-band jazz, which was a Europeanized style grounded in classical and romantic traditions, allowing limited scope for improvisation since a large number of players could coordinate their efforts only if their parts were composed and orchestrated in advance. Jazz remained a collaborative art as bop gained ascendancy, but orchestras gave way to small combos—three to six players were common, although nonets and larger groups did not disappear—in order to maximize flexibility and intercommunication. Ensemble passages completely "through-composed" served mainly to punctuate flights of individual improvisation, rather than the other way around.

To provide each musical number with a rhythmic and harmonic framework that would tie the improvisations together, boppers developed the practice of borrowing a piece already familiar within the jazz community and then abandoning its melody, modifying its rhythms, and using what remained as the foundation for their own creative flights. The underlying piece was thus drastically reconfigured but was not completely dismissed as a work in its own right, since its chord structure—obviously liked by the musicians who chose it—was continually present in the "new" bop number built on top of it. Instead of pretending that preexisting material was a negligible factor in their music, bop performers embraced it as an enriching form of "quotation," even throwing melody-fragments from extraneous pieces into their improvisations.

Bop numbers thus weave diverse strands of material into heterogeneous and often surprising fabrics. Dialogically explored by interacting musicians, long-familiar chord progressions and melodic ideas reveal hitherto neglected possibilities, allowing a "homecoming festival" for bypassed musicological meanings that prove to be emphatically alive.

Polyphonic Film

Like the boppers, the Beats and postwar avant-gardists reacted against the unitary neatness of authoritative discourse. Rejecting classical cinema, experimental filmmakers turned to alternative strategies, many of which involved dialogic interactions among diversified elements—and a fondness for recuperating lost or overlooked materials from the past—that are analogous to developments in postwar jazz.

One useful tactic was the cultivation of found-footage cinema, in which images are lifted out of preexisting movies and edited to form entirely new works. An influential example is Bruce Conner's first film, *A Movie* (1958), in which an extraordinary variety of images are arranged into a montage that conveys both (a) a sense of centrifugal, barely-under-control anarchy and (b) a series of carefully evoked emotions ranging from humor and absurdity to dread and sadness. The affinity between Conner's visual sensibility and modern jazz ideas is still more direct in his 1961 film *Cosmic Ray*, in which superimposition (simultaneity) is added to montage (contiguity) as a source of polyphonic structure, and the jazzlike music of Ray Charles provides an organizing pulse for the work as a whole. In both of these films, and numerous others by Conner, the revitalization of preexisting materials—and the affirmation of their value as ever-renewable elements in ever-unfinalized dialogues—is a primary source of energy and complexity.

A different approach to a somewhat similar goal is found in Ken Jacobs's film *Blonde Cobra*, which uses performance footage of avant-garde actor Jack Smith, shot by Bob Fleischner in 1959 and later edited by Jacobs into a highly unconventional form that includes lengthy passages of Smith's verbal antics accompanied by a blacked-out screen. (In another unorthodox maneuver, Jacobs calls for a radio to be played at certain moments in the room where the film is being shown.) The raw material of *Blonde Cobra* is a series of shots meant to capture Smith as a performer and personality, and this focus of the work remains after Jacobs's manipulations; hence, this film is not as drastically transformative as Conner's found-footage movies, which place their images in completely new contexts. Still and all, *Blonde Cobra* is another vivid illustration of the three-fold commitment made by some postwar filmmakers: a commitment to dialogic interchange with the past; to images that have been overlooked or rejected because they stray from mainstream paths; and to citational, recuperative art that revivifies discarded or forgotten material and allows its meanings to have the homecoming of which Bakhtin spoke.

Other major filmmakers who engaged in related projects include Stan VanDerBeek, whose 1959 animation *Science Friction* manipulates printed cut-outs into a criticism of technology and a condemnation of war, and Brakhage, whose 1961–64 epic *Dog Star Man* places a broad array of found images (taken from sources as varied as a family-photograph collection and a laboratory microscope) into point-counterpoint relationships with his own footage. (The scope and ambition of this highly concentrated work are so large that a longer "unraveled" version, running about four-and-a-half hours, is entitled *The Art of Vision*.) Also noteworthy in this context is the Austrian musician and filmmaker Peter Kubelka, who exercised a strong influence on American avant-gardists with his 1960 work *Arnulf Rainer*, constructed from rhythmically alternating frames of pure black and white. Here the recuperative activity consists not of creatively "recycling" preexisting images but of taking aesthetic ideas from arts that predate cinema—architecture and music—and placing these into dialogue with fundamental principles of film. These principles are deployed in nonfigurative ways that foreground not the representational capacities of film, but rather the expressive capability of the basic cinematographic apparatus itself.

Beat Quotation, Creation, Recreation

The core Beat writers were strongly influenced by the practice of bop "quotation" and by the spontaneity and self-inventing vitality that they prized in jazz improvisation. Kerouac thought of his work as "spontaneous bop prosody" and used his writing to rediscover in words, memories, and ideas the sort of resonances suggested by Bakhtin in his remark on contextual meanings that are never truly dead but only forgotten or overlooked. This aim is especially clear in such early works as *Doctor Sax: Faust Part Three* and *Visions of Cody*, two of Kerouac's most complex achievements. *Doctor Sax*, published in 1959, incorporates a seething heteroglossia of styles, references, and discursive practices ranging from novelistic narrative and childhood fantasy to poetry, newspaper headlines, snatches of cartography and scripted dialogue, a lengthy tale-within-the-tale, and segmented scenes from a "gloomy bookmovie" based on Kerouac's early life. *Visions of Cody*, published in 1972 but written during a visit to Burroughs in Mexico City twenty years earlier, contains not only novelistic descriptions, autobiographical musings, poems, and drawings but also a long section composed of meandering conversations between Kerouac and Neal Cassady (here called Jack Duluoz and Cody Pomeray, respectively) as transcribed by Kerouac from tape recordings made by Cassady and himself in the manner of jazz soloists improvising with voices and words rather than instruments and notes. These two novels have substantially different priorities and tones: The latter is more closely attuned to adult experiences and real-world events, while the former is a complicated flight into childhood and adolescent mentalities fueled by private and even hermetic fantasies. Yet together they form a tapestry of creation and recreation that rivals Brakhage's achievement in *Dog Star Man*—interweaving the revivified past with the compulsive present so energetically that a sense of spontaneous discovery remains intact despite the time and labor (Kerouac's writing and transcribing, Brakhage's shooting and editing) that obviously went into the construction of such densely creative works.

Kerouac's accomplishment here is echoed by Ginsberg in numerous works from the same period, such as the magnificent *Kaddish*, dated 1957–59 and incorporating an electrifying flow of childhood memory, early-adulthood reflection, religious invocation, and even animal sounds, all within a cascade of long-line verse that manifests a heady influence from jazz (the poet's admiration for certain saxophone players is well known) along with an expansive verbality based on Whitmanesque models. Burroughs reveals a similarly recuperative sensibility in his early semi-autobiographical novels, such as *Junky* and *Queer*, and in the more broadly experimental works that followed these, such as *Naked Lunch* and *The Soft Machine*; the former are based directly on personal memory, while the latter make use of previously written texts that have been cut, edited, and reordered in processes roughly analogous to the changes wrought on preexisting songs in the formation of bop numbers.

Of all the core Beats, however, Kerouac maintains the strongest sense of recuperation, reinvention, and recirculation in his work. This statement is true of individual novels such as those cited above and of the over-arching "Duluoz legend" formed by his primary works as a whole. Regina Weinreich, one of the critics who has addressed his entire *oeuvre*, characterizes the Duluoz legend not as a linear saga but as a repetitive cycle (11–12).[5] Within this cycle, key events are revisited and rethought at different times in the author's history; each time they take on a newly conceived "truth," much as a jazz player's favorite themes take on fresh contours with each new improvisation. Events depicted in this way exist in the momentary present even as they recapitulate the past and speed instantaneously into the future. Kerouac's inventions thus have the mingled spontaneity, nostalgia, and evanescence that characterize the most intuitive jazz—at once temporal, timely, and timeless.

Unitary Discourse in the '50s

In all the film and literary works considered here, and in others by different artists with more or less related goals, elements from various social, cultural, and semiotic categories—old/new, real/fictitious, literal/allusive, linear/nonlinear, and so on—enter interactions that clear away encrustations of accepted meaning, generating new and unexpected significations. The lively allusiveness and unpredictability of such works bear out Bakhtin's statement that when carriers of meaning engage dialogically with one another—whether these carriers are words, discourses, languages, or entire cultures—they take on new awareness of their instability, relativity, and temporality.

What lends sociocultural importance to this aspect of Beat writing and experimental film is its opposition to the monologism (i.e., unity and authority) of much mainstream expression in the postwar period. To describe an entire sociocultural milieu as monologic would of course be a monologizing action in itself. As already noted, however, powerful forces were working hard in '50s America to shift social, cultural, and political values as far as possible toward consensus-bound homogeneity. The consensus would be sustained by a complex of rationalizations drawn from psychology, sociology, economics, political science, and other disciplines, marking a victory in the long historical process of making rationalism and anthropocentrism the primary bases for sociocultural coherence.

As discussed above, the notion of "conformity" was central to postwar discussions of this situation, which was widely recognized (and frequently deplored) even as it continued to prosper and evolve. One of the most pungent indictments of conformist ideology was set forth by Robert Lindner in 1956, pointing out conduits for the "socialization" that he saw as a ubiquitous social threat:

> *You must adjust* . . . This is the motto inscribed on the walls of every nursery, and the processes that break the spirit are initiated there. In birth begins conformity. . . .
>
> *You must adjust* . . . This is the legend inscribed in every schoolbook, the invisible message on every blackboard. Our schools have become vast factories for the manufacture of robots. . . .
>
> *You must adjust* . . . This is the command etched above the door of every church, synagogue, cathedral, temple, and chapel. It constitutes a passport to salvation, an armor against sin: it sums the virtues and describes the vices. . . .
>
> *You must adjust.* . . . This is the slogan emblazoned on the banners of all political parties, the inscription at the heart of all systems that contend for the loyalties of men. . . .
>
> *You must adjust* . . . This is the creed of the sciences that have sold themselves to the status quo, the prescription against perplexity, the placebo for anxiety. For psychiatry, psychology and the medical or social arts that depend from them have become devil's advocates and sorcerers' apprentices of conformity. . . . (167–73)

Other voices were equally passionate even if they did not share Lindner's orational tone. "Groupthink is becoming a national philosophy," declared William H. Whyte Jr. in 1952, suggesting his own term for the interrelated phenomena of adjustment, conformity, and what David Riesman called "other-directed" behavior. Distinguishing modern groupthink from the perennial human failing of "mere instinctive conformity," Whyte defined the newer arrival as "a *rationalized* conformity—an open, articulate philosophy which holds that group values are not only expedient but right and good as well." Such thinking conceives of humanity as "Social Man—completely a creature of his environment, guided almost totally by the whims and prejudices of the group, and incapable of any real self-determination of his destiny" (1952, 114–17).

Leveling the Arts

Visual artists, authors, and other "creative" persons were not seen as immune to such leveling influences, especially when they came into contact with contemporary practices of standardization and mass dissemination. "The contemporary American novel is part of the contemporary world, which is perhaps more uniform than any period since the Middle Ages" (33), wrote literary critic Ihab Hassan in the early '60s. Playwright, screenwriter, and novelist Elmer Rice commented in 1952 that when one looks at "the new channels of communication—motion pictures, radio, television—it is not surprising to find that the industrialization of the writer is almost complete." In all economic areas, he continued, the tendency "is toward concentration of ownership and control. The field of communications is no exception. . . . It is no exaggeration to say that a few hundred men have effective control over 95 per cent of what is read, seen, and heard in newspapers and magazines, and on the motion-picture and television screens." Insisting that such "monopolization of control operates against diversity of outlet and variety of expression," he went on to summarize society's message for the contemporary writer of books, movies, and other works: "You not only have to write right, you have to think right, perhaps even prove that you don't think wrong" (13–14, 62–63).

These words reflect well-focused anxiety over centralized power and also a keen awareness of the McCarthyist crusade. Following on the heels of the House Committee on Un-American Activities, which launched its aggressions in the late '40s, this campaign had been requiring proof of "non-wrong" thinking for about two years when Rice's essay was published, and still had a couple of years to go before its heyday would be over. One senses the same atmosphere in Maxwell Geismar's 1954 statement that artists had entered a period of social and political conformity—of timidity, fear, and suspicion. Ours is also an epoch of shifting social foundations in which the freedom, not only to dissent politically or socially, but even to criticize, has in turn become suspect. Those forces of self-appointed censorship in our past, those forces of ignorance and superstition, have gained a semiofficial status in our society and have gathered to themselves a semilegal sanction. This *is* a new and serious mode of spiritual repression which can lead easily from the social and political area to the religious, and so back again, in a vicious circle, to the most personal sort of opinions. It threatens the life atmosphere of American thought and American art.

For, if an artist has not yet felt the lash of official condemnation, he has already been sensitized to the less tangible but equally ponderous and oppressive forces of intellectual regularity in our present cultural atmosphere. Think for yourself—but think like everybody else. (26)

Ironically, what such observers often seem to be describing is a set of phenomena that add up to something like the dearth of "individualism" and the enforcement of "group orientation" and "collective mentality" that many Americans feared with paranoid intensity as products of Marxist philosophy and Soviet social engineering. Here were those evil things, conceptualized in terms that emphasized their worst possibilities, yet encountered as natural products of the "marketplace of ideas" championed by supporters of Western capitalism and free enterprise. While such non-Marxist authors as those quoted above would not have approved of these phenomena in their Soviet incarnations any more than in their American versions, the writers show little awareness of how much their society was mimicking the very sociopolitical system to which it considered itself most diametrically and unalterably opposed.

The Carnival Tradition

Bakhtin cuts through distractions on these issues with his distaste for monologism in social as well as artistic forms—surely including such phenomena as group adjustment, rationalized conformity, and centralized power. He vigorously questions the Enlightenment, since the "image of the contradictory, perpetually becoming and unfinished being could not be reduced to the dimensions of the Enlighteners' reason" (1984b, 118), no matter how hard the Enlighteners tried to accomplish this. That image was equally difficult for the group-adjusters and power-centralizers of the postwar United States to understand—or to tolerate, if less rigidly social-ized persons sought to embrace it. This fact helps explain the hostility that often confronted Beat and experimental-film artists who placed at the (shifting) core of their (eccentric) activities a belief in the unfinalizability of their work and of themselves. It also helps explain their fondness for such devices as nonlinear montage and cut-up texts, improvised camera-dances and spontaneous typewriter-songs, cascades of instinctive imagery and howls of intuitive incantation. All were aimed at subverting and in-verting the proprieties of a world perceived as suffocating in the prison of its own orderly thoughts.

Such subversions and inversions are vividly illuminated by Bakhtin's notion of carnivalism as a tradition with deep roots in Western art, cul-ture, and society. Among the defining traits of carnival is a suspension of "hierarchical structure," allowing people to work out, "in a concretely sensuous, half-real and half-play-acted form, a *new mode of interrelation-ship between individuals,* counterposed to the all-powerful socio-hierarchi-cal relationships of noncarnival life." Connected with this "familiariza-tion" are "*mésalliances*" and "*profanation*: carnivalistic blasphemies, a whole system of carnivalistic debasings and bringings down to earth, carnivalistic obscenities linked with the reproductive power of the earth and the body, carnivalistic parodies on sacred texts and sayings, etc." Carnivalistic life is "life drawn out of its *usual* rut [and] to some extent 'life turned inside out,'" revealing a vision of "'the reverse side of the world' ('*monde à l'envers*')." Hence, carnival thinking is often concerned with "the utilization of things in reverse" and with "*eccentricity*, the vio-lation of the usual and the generally accepted . . . " (1984a, 122–26).

Official Life, Carnival Life

The usual and the generally accepted were just what the Beats, the avant-gardists, and certain innovative figures in mainstream film wished to reverse, violate, and suffuse with eccentricity during the postwar era, for their own good and for that of society at large. Bakhtin suggests that in many ways a typical person of the Middle Ages lived two lives:

[O]ne was the *official* life, monolithically serious and gloomy, sub-jugated to a strict hierarchical order, full of terror, dogmatism, reverence, and piety; the other was the *life of the carnival square*, free and unrestricted, full of ambivalent laughter, blasphemy, the profanation of everything sacred, full of debasing and ob-scenities, familiar contact with everyone and everything. (1984a, 129–30)

American postwar culture felt bound to cultivate only what Bakhtin would call the "official" version of life, bolstering it with rationalistic ar-guments while discouraging pararational or "free and unrestricted" incli-nations by means ranging from outright suppression to subtler methods of containment and marginalization. Carnivalesque sensibilities were not eliminated by this discouragement, to be sure; still, the "life" they repre-sented was inaccessible to the majority of citizens. Proper members of the bourgeoisie enacted a modern version of the medieval subject's "official" routine, fulfilling socially approved patterns of work, family, and civic re-sponsibility. The long-suffering protagonist of Alfred Hitchcock's 1956 *The Wrong Man*, based on a real person of the '50s, remains a splendid specimen of this breed: His work life is dutiful and mechanical, even though his potentially carnivalesque profession is playing jazz in a night-club; the most free-and-unrestricted pastime he allows himself is pretend-ing to bet on horse races; his daily routine is so rigid that he barely needs to speak with the people he deals with on his way home; he is so indoctri-nated with respect for authority that he scarcely questions the police who wrongfully arrest him; and so on.

Rejecting this existence as vigorously as they knew how, the Beats and a limited number of like-minded rebels attempted to live more carnivalis-tically than this well-meaning Everyman could ever conceive of doing.[6] A key project of the Beats was to cultivate what Bakhtin called the "im-age of the contradictory, perpetually becoming and unfinished being" within their own consciousnesses. Among the forms this project took were Kerouac's embrace of spontaneous creativity, Ginsberg's nurturing of a transcendent visionary sensibility, and Burroughs's decimation of linear thought patterns as a means of liberating the self from outwardly (and inwardly) imposed matrices of power and control.

Of these writers, Burroughs has articulated such matters most exten-sively, in both his fiction and nonfiction writings. The very form of his most characteristic prose reflects his vision of an explosively unfinalized and self-contradictory world inhabited by an equally unfinalized and self-contradictory self; critic John Tytell states this well when he observes that Burroughs's authorial eye "moves swiftly, cinematically, uninterested in formal transitions or artificial connections, concerned primarily with capturing the sense of chaotic flux, the terror of disaster" in order to evoke "an atmosphere of conflicting particles" within a novelistic world that "projects a relativity of endless exfoliation" (112, 114).

Dialogism and Dualism

Bakhtin's enthusiasm for dialogics leads him to a poor opinion of dialectics, which he finds desiccated and reductive by comparison. He also looks down on sexual attitudes that foster a "monadization" or "diadization" of eroticism (Stam 161). Along similar lines, Burroughs despises dualism, which he finds as ubiquitous as it is disastrous for any kind of meaningful freedom. In a world of unworkable formulas, he says, possibly the most unworkable of all "is the whole concept of a dualistic universe. . . . Dualism is the whole basis of this planet—good and evil, communism, fascism, man, woman, etc. As soon as you have a formula like that, of course you're going to have trouble." At times, Burroughs appears to accept a sort of cosmic monologue as the only workable alternative to dualistic dysfunction, as when he says, "I don't think that there is really room for more than one person, that is, one will, on any planet. As soon as you get two you get trouble" (Odier 96–97). Such a statement appears to be profoundly monologic until one recognizes the exaggerated impossibility of a science-fictional "one planet, one will" solution to human problems, and the carnivalesque sarcasm (mingled with *épater la bourgeoisie* mischievousness) that undergirds its hyperbole.

When he builds his mythological world in fiction, moreover, Burroughs's choice of Rabelaisian modes—parody, grotesquerie, the comedy of excess, laughter in the face of death—indicates the closeness of his writing to important aspects of Bakhtin's thought.[7] Liberation is a key notion for both writers, and they carry their concepts of it to heroic extremes, suggesting the boundary-free, radically unfinalized, supremely undefined self as an ultimate product of the carnivalesque sensibility.

It is within this framework that the theorist and the novelist do eventually part company. Bakhtin finds possibilities for interconnectedness and open-endedness in the free-and-familiar play of interacting conscious-nesses. Burroughs finds them in the impossible yet (for him) seductive fantasy of a single free-and-unrestricted self inhabiting its own planet. Burroughs's ideas have dystopian aspects, moreover, that fly away from Bakhtin's basically optimistic perspective—and Burroughs revels in these, making them a perverse carnivalization of carnivalism itself. He sees du-alism as a continual source of conflict and misery. His outrageous con-tempt for women ("I think they were a basic mistake, and the whole du-alistic universe evolved from this error" [Odier 116]) illustrates the perils of a carnivalism that allows for rejection of difference and otherness. And his embrace of apocalyptic sadism treats violent domination as a free-and-familiar game. The title characters of his novel *The Wild Boys* may repre-sent the wretched of the earth, but their inescapable energy and gleeful savagery make them a demonic nightmare of feral viciousness.[8]

While the flamboyant extremes of such a vision may provide a certain catharsis, Burroughs makes this catharsis more harsh and vengeful than purgative and liberating; and his sardonic laughter is designed as much for subjugation as for emancipation. Yet his fantasies have positive value none-theless, particularly when viewed in the context of his overall challenge to postwar American thinking, which he brazenly parodies and relentlessly contradicts. He is carnivalesque in a deeply dystopian way, but within the homogenized confines of a Rational Society, his brand of dizzying desta-bilization is as salutary as it is shocking.

The End of the Amateur Limb

Pointing to a significant cause of carnivalesque notions among the Beat crowd, Brakhage connects the attitudes of young people in the mid-dle '40s to the wartime disruptions they endured.[9] Many of them had effectively "missed their adolescence. They had been taken suddenly and thrown abroad into a war when, in a saner world, a saner time, they would have been enrolling in college or passing through other civilized rites of adolescent passage. Crucial years of their growing-up were missing" (1989,117). Carolyn Cassady bears this point out: "Small wonder I was confused as to which [recent acquaintance] was or wasn't in college. . . . School and age no longer matched" (29).

Like many of their Lost Generation predecessors in the World War I era, the core Beats found (or stumbled into) a variety of activities linked somehow with the war; these ranged from Kerouac's stint with the Merchant Marine to Burroughs's escapades in joining and then escaping the American military machine. Although none were thrust into overseas combat, as the "trench poets" of the First World War had been, all were touched by the war, and of course many of their contemporaries were engulfed in it. What the Beats and like-minded youngsters had in common, Brakhage implies, was a sort of brash teenage mentality that found delayed and perhaps heightened release after wartime repressions ended. Brakhage finds much that is charming in this mentality. Others, such as Richard Hofstadter and Leo Marx, who led an early '60s attack on the Beats as an "adolescent" group (McNally 270), were decidedly uncharmed. So was the young Jonas Mekas, who in 1955 criticized the "markedly adolescent character" and "adolescent frustrations" of experimental filmmakers whose works reflected "juvenile pessimism" and "young senile" personalities (Sitney 1970, 21–22).

Brakhage makes a persuasive case for *The End*, made by Christopher MacLaine in 1953, as the most vigorous embodiment of this mentality in film. In this and other MacLaine movies, Brakhage says,

> anyone who does not look self-conscious is the rare exception. The apparent amateurishness of his filmmaking is deliberate; one might say that he went clear out to the end of the amateur limb. And it was exactly this amateurish look that fascinated him. He is always making love to these photographed women with his camera ineffectually, and obviously so. His heroes are always pale, tormented neurotic young men who cannot quite limp down to the beach or even masturbate effectively. (1989, 119)

Referring to MacLaine's film *Beat*, made in 1958, Brakhage applauds the skip-frame photography of a person "who behaves as though she were free and lovely. . . . But she is like a turtle trapped in a cage, going around the four corners of an intersection. One can look at this as humorous or as unbearably horrible. If you can regard it as both delightful and horrifying, you are close to the balance that makes MacLaine an artist" (1989, 119)—and a filmmaker not quite arrived at adulthood, one might add, at least by conventional '50s standards.

MacLaine was not the only experimental filmmaker to reveal a ripely adolescent mentality during the postwar period, of course; one thinks of

Vernon Zimmerman and the slightly later George Kuchar, among others. But his most characteristic works represent the '50s as a time when delayed maturity walked hand in hand with the spirit of carnival.

Hollywood Carnival

Given the symbiotic relationship between mainstream society and mainstream cinema during the postwar years, it is not surprising that carnivalism was hard pressed for expression in Hollywood, except for the sort of "managed carnivalism" found in formula entertainments and mass-market diversions. Yet such an enduring aspect of Western culture could not be entirely suppressed or co-opted, especially if one sees in carnivalism a "safety valve" function that is useful to entrenched power structures, allowing limited eruptions of antiestablishment feeling that help sustain domination and control over the long run. Certain innovative filmmakers, such as Hitchcock in *Psycho* (1960) and *The Birds* (1962) and Sirk in *All That Heaven Allows* (1955) and *Written on the Wind* (1956), treated Hollywood conventions to audacious revisions and ironic interrogations. When successful, these amounted to a carnivalization of cinema itself, since they injected doses of the improper, the grotesque, and the sardonic into movies that audiences expected to find traditional and reassuring.

Movie comedians of the period developed humorous stories and characters, of course, but some went a step farther by carnivalizing film's own language. The most important is Jerry Lewis, whose carnivalism leaps forth on two levels: the cultivation of bizarre behaviors, preposterous speech patterns, and absurd twists on conventional logic in his on-screen persona, and a subversion of comedy-film norms in his work as a director. His performances have received much comment, some of it reflecting the spirit of his own humor, as when the *Harvard Lampoon* annually gave him a mock award called the "Arrested Development Oblation" in the early '60s. As a director he shows an interest in filmmaking that reflects back on itself and a tendency to replace the *presence* of humor with the *idea* of humor—using sly conceptual jokes in place of blatant sight gags, for instance, as when the hero's incompetent airplane-flying in *The Bellboy* is not milked for laughs or even depicted on the screen, but is suggested by a sound effect and a reaction shot (Coursodon and Sauvage 189–200). (This method shows the influence of Lewis's mentor, Frank Tashlin, who also pioneered in this area.)

Pointing out cinema's long connection with carnival, Robert Stam notes that American film grew up with both literal and metaphorical links to the sideshow, the fairground, and the penny arcade (113). Still, the popular-entertainment side of cinema has often been resisted by critics, just as the penny-dreadful and dime-novel aspects of literature have traditionally been scorned by serious observers of that field. This fact helps explain why Lewis's appeal to large American audiences (until his decline in the late '60s) was resented by most American critics, notwithstanding the interest given to the same movies in France and some other countries. None other than Burroughs is one such critic, judging from a journalist's report: "[B]eing told that he, [David] Cronenberg, and Jerry Lewis have each been elected members of the French Order of Arts and Letters is nearly enough to send him on another heroin jag. 'We need to vote him out, then,' shouts Burroughs" (Krutnik 12).[10]

Another naysayer is *auteur* theorist Andrew Sarris, who states (in one of a dozen "skeptical observations" on Lewis's work) that the comedian "appeals to unsophisticated audiences in the sticks and to ungenteel audiences in the urban slums; he is bigger on Forty-Second Street, for example, than anyplace else in the city. Most urban reviewers limit even his most ambitious efforts to the most routine reviews, and the weekly and monthly reviewers barely acknowledge his existence" (1968, 242).[11] Yet the same observation could be used *un*skeptically to argue for Lewis's status as a genuine carnivalizer whose work appeals to "unsophisticated" and "ungenteel" audiences precisely because it subverts the sort of highbrow seriousness that Sarris seems to be buying into wholesale.

In sum, carnivalism persisted in postwar America despite the era's unfriendly climate of rationalism and rectitude, just as it has persisted in countless periods and places marked by all sorts of sociocultural conditions. "The carnival sense of the world," Bakhtin insists, "possesses a mighty life-creating and transforming power, an indestructible vitality" (1984a, 107). To stay strong, however, this vitality must be continually reborn and renewed. In the postwar era, an important arena for this revivification was the proudly outrageous activity of "immature" artists like the Beats, the avant-gardists, and Hollywood's seriocomic clowns.

Americanness and Classical Film

Bakhtin did not write directly about mass communications, but mass-media products can be fruitfully examined in light of his warning that "official" thought tends to push out the diversity of ideas that healthy societies ought to reflect.[12] Not only Hollywood movies but the entire territory of mainstream visual communication—including television, photography, and picture magazines—fell into monologic habits during the postwar years, absorbing and reproducing the very norms and ideologies that Beats and avant-gardists sought to denigrate, demystify, and detoxify through the rude rebelliousness of their work.

Belonging

Looking at popular photography, for instance, one is struck by how consistently it portrayed Americans as "parts of a huge network of entities, institutions, and communities that nurtured and encouraged them to become healthy, normal citizens" (217), as critic James Guimond accurately puts it. Serving up endless images of families in supermarkets, cheery corporate employees, voters wearing "I Like Ike" buttons, and their friendly neighbors, picture magazines almost invariably depicted them as people who "belonged" to a good society that deserved all the allegiance they could muster.[13] Rendered so monologically, with misfits and miseries carefully eliminated from view, this vision proclaimed the rightness of Americanness and the consensus mentality that lay behind it. While photo-essays made during the '30s sometimes expressed liberal or even radical views regarding the "real America," by the early '40s this form of journalism had fallen into hackneyed patterns, pushing patriotic notions as simplistic and misty-eyed as the flag-salute montages that closed the day on television channels. *Life* and *Look* were among the respected magazines that expressed such feelings, shaped by editors who excised uncomfortable facts or presented them as problems to be solved by civic-minded social scientists (213–14).[14]

Many a Hollywood film endorsed Americanness in similar ways. *My Son John*, directed by Leo McCarey in 1952, is one of the purest examples, losing no opportunity to promote the unquenchably patriotic virtues of its middle-class main characters. The film portrays a "typical American family" that positively glows with propriety, rectitude, and ordinariness: Dad and Mom live upright lives as a schoolteacher and a homemaker, and two of their three sons are flying off to Korea for brave service to their nation. Yet all this virtue notwithstanding, the clan has been sullied by the inexplicable conversion of its oldest son to communism. Even as his brothers wing their way to the Asian front, John schemes to advance his

Soviet-sponsored cause through deceit, treachery, and subversion. His parents love him and take pride in his professional status as a rising official of the United States government. Still, they recognize his unhealthy state from telltale remarks he makes during a family reunion and from his sarcastic responses to jingoistic statements by his American Legionnaire father. Proof positive comes from an agent of the Federal Bureau of Investigation, who barges into the family's home so sneakily and aggressively that it rattles even the patriotic sensibilities of Mom and Dad. They don't much like the FBI man's tone, but he soon demonstrates the necessity of his tactics by convincing Mother that her worst suspicions about John are all too true. In the end, the parents are spared the unhappy duty of handing their son over to the Feds—which they are all set to do, if necessary—since John abruptly sees the light, thanks to a sudden realization of his mother's long history of selfless devotion. He writes a confession and promptly gets killed in a car accident while on his way to deliver the admission of guilt at a college commencement ceremony. Unhappily, both of his audiences—the people *in* the film and the people *watching* the film—have to hear his windy speech despite his death, since he has dictated it into a tape recorder. The playing of this tape to a multitude of capped-and-gowned Americans constitutes the last important scene of the film; it is accompanied by many of Hollywood's signifiers for an earnest religious occasion, with rapt faces gazing at an empty podium as ethereal beams of light stream down from above.

It is not by accident that Robert Walker plays the communist in this movie, just two years after appearing as the insane killer of *Strangers on a Train*, the popular Alfred Hitchcock thriller about a psychopath who wants to "trade murders" with a man he has met by chance. Viewers of *My Son John* could be expected to perceive (and dread) the title character's wicked political leanings all the more readily, given Walker's recent association with loony Bruno of the Hitchcock film. Coincidentally, this connection was enhanced by Walker's own death shortly before the shooting of *My Son John* had ended; faced with a handful of incomplete scenes, the filmmakers appropriated footage from *Strangers on a Train* to fill in the gaps. This oddity of the movie's production history underscores an "intertextual" effect the filmmakers were surely aware of throughout their project, since the Walker/John/Bruno linkage is exploited from the early moments of the picture.

Also revealing is the movie's depiction of the FBI agent. He first appears as an innocent stranger who has a minor automobile collision with

John's parents. Arriving at their home to discuss his repair bill, he strikes up a conversation with John's mother, expressing great admiration for her family while showing more curiosity than seems "natural" under the circumstances. When he eventually reveals himself as a government agent, the parents voice indignation at his stealthy way of insinuating himself into their lives; but they calm down when his mission turns out to be based on a correct assessment of John as an enemy of the free world. What is noteworthy here is the willingness of the parents—and the film—to excuse and even justify what amount to police-state tactics on the agent's part, just as long as he has a "good reason" for his behavior. As indicated above, the threat of enforced (over)conformity was decried by postwar commentators such as Rice and Geismar, whose warnings indicated that American society could fall into patterns not unlike some that were feared as outgrowths of the communist system. The demonization of communism in Hollywood films was one component of the obsessive "Americanness" campaign that helped foster authoritarian thinking in American culture.

Classicism and Ideology

My Son John is one of countless films that show the classical Hollywood style in action. This style did not make its way into every single corner of '50s film, and even the sponsor-driven television medium could produce not only product-peddling diversions but also the jolting experiments of an Ernie Kovacs, the anarchic gags of a Sid Caesar, and occasional bouts of Lenny Bruce's wild humor. Still, the Hollywood establishment nearly always matched predictable style with fastidious content that hewed to the limited range of possibilities (familiar genres, cycles, star vehicles, and the like) to which audiences were accustomed. Large areas of experience were excluded from movies, such as "obscene" matters like excretion and copulation; or they were marginalized, such as depictions of American hunger and poverty; or they were reduced to carefully calculated formulas giving the impression of engagement and concern—as in "problem dramas" about racial and religious difference—while minimizing challenge, discomfort, and controversy. Such tactics helped classical Hollywood maintain its reputation as a source of unproblematic entertainment steeped in consensus-supported values. But they did little to educate spectators, provoke fresh thought on current problems, or heighten awareness of alternative views on social or political conditions.

The Smiling Side of Life

In this way American films resemble much popular fiction of the post-war era. Geismar calls the mid-'50s a time when "conformity has settled down over the nation," when adventurous writers like Ernest Hemingway and William Faulkner "cannot really function," and when "our intellectuals have somehow combined with the advertising sloganeers and the chambers of commerce to disparage or deny the peculiarly American social, moral and artistic achievements of the twentieth century." In an essay on author Herman Wouk and the popularity of such novels as *Marjorie Morningstar* and *The Caine Mutiny* in journalistic circles, Geismar asserts

> that both *Time* and *Life* are laying down a program for a new slap-happy optimism mingled with a proper respect for whatever exists and a species of domestic drama that will avoid all bad language and all serious human issues. We are back again to that "smiling side of life" which the Victorians believed to be the true American side, though we have been through a sewer of corruption since then, and are now sitting on top of a volcano. This new literature will be based on the principle of "Woukism." The object will be to persuade millions of people that they are completely different from all the other people whom they are exactly like. "Peace, Prosperity, and Propaganda" will be the grand theme of the new literature, and all deviants from the norm, whether biological or aesthetic or ethnic, will be tolerated so long as they do what they are told. . . . I suspect that the final impact of the atomic age has had the effect of a lobotomy upon the national spirit. Don't look now, but we're all dead. (14, 37, 44–45)[15]

By and large, this literature and the classical Hollywood cinema (which, not surprisingly, produced major film versions of both Wouk novels that irritated Geismar so much) were excellent allies for each other. They also aligned themselves with other forces that sought to sustain conformity and consensus—from the child-rearing, educational, religious, political, and psychological establishments decried by Lindner to the "social engineering" establishment that Whyte accused of enforcing group-think.[16] Much critical writing on the period bears out this conclusion, sometimes deliberately and sometimes while seeking to convey a different message. Looking at the postwar years from a standpoint only slightly removed from them, Marcus Klein wrote in the late '60s that the "state of the culture since World War II, as it affects fiction, might be described entirely in terms of negatives and losses. Or the time might be described not even as a period of the breakup of things, a condition that would clearly invite new energies, but as one of dissolution and dubiety." Klein looks for hope in the continuing willingness of authors to throw "an assertion into the void" and to engage in the "general action" of "making manifest a token of existence where no institutions are to be taken for granted." Yet he cannot help observing that postwar literature is less than vigorous in a wide variety of areas. Only a limited amount of "serious fiction" has been written on such social problems as poverty and crime, and when such books *are* written they tend to be "distant anachronisms" that "expose" what is "already . . . very familiar" to most readers. Fictions about minorities often "have little to do with minorities as an issue" but rather "universalize" their subject. Fictions about nuclear terror suffer from "redundancy," since all they can do is "vivify" a subject that is quite vivid to begin with. More generally, "social facts are regarded at best—in the best part, probably, of contemporary fiction—as an overbearing confusion, and at worst they are dismissed" (15–18). It appears, therefore, that authors are confronting the most troubling aspects of their age with little but vague "assertions" and "tokens of existence" that evade the hard realities of collective failure.

What Is Liked in the Middle West

The monologic nature of this literary epoch seems plain, and it was shared by most of the period's mainstream cinematic production. This opinion was certainly held by philosopher Bertrand Russell, who republished in 1958 a comment he had originally written in 1935, stating that perhaps

> the greatest of all forces for uniformity in the modern world is the cinema, since its influence is not confined to America but penetrates to all parts of the world, except the Soviet Union, which, however, has its own different uniformity. The cinema embodies, broadly speaking, Hollywood's opinion of what is liked in the Middle West. Our emotions in regard to love and marriage, birth and death are becoming standardized according to this recipe. To the young of all lands Hollywood represents the last word in

modernity, displaying both the pleasures of the rich and the methods to be adopted for acquiring riches. I suppose the talkies will lead before long to the adoption of a universal language, which will be that of Hollywood. (Satin 174)

It was within and against this atmosphere that the Beat writers and the postwar cinematic avant-garde emerged; and it was the unruly, often boisterously dialogic spirit represented by those artists that the literary establishment and the classical Hollywood cinema instinctively opposed.

Repression and Productivity

If power were never anything but repressive, if it never did anything but to say no, do you really think one would be brought to obey it?
—*Michel Foucault,* Power/Knowledge

This is one of the most important aspects of the monopoly of vested interests: They must stimulate sex, and make sex difficult to obtain. In that way, they keep people always thinking about it, always worrying about it, and it keeps them from causing trouble.
—*William S. Burroughs,* The Job

Why and how did alternative discourses manage to arise in the postwar era—including Beat literature, experimental film, and studio productions by innovative figures who brought offbeat sensibilities to Hollywood? One explanation is that carnival energies can be repressed for only so long before they burst into some kind of activity. Another is that consensus and conformity not only *repress* transgressive impulses but *produce* these by articulating them (however negatively) as focuses of knowledge and power. The most sophisticated theorist of this view is Foucault, who sees modern society as a widely diffused network of subtly controlling interests, integrated by a powerful bureaucracy that manipulates individual behavior through social-science practices and ideas.

Control Machine and Master Switch

Burroughs shares the notion of society as a spread-out network of manipulative forces. "The control machine is simply the machinery—police, education, etc.—used by a group in power to keep itself in power and extend its power," he says (Miles 1993, 172). Kerouac, who had a streak of social and political conservatism quite different from anything in Burroughs's makeup, nonetheless etched in *The Dharma Bums* a portrait of postwar suburbia—and media power—that throws conformity and control into frightening relief:

> . . . pass house after house on both sides of the street each with the lamplight of the living room, shining golden, and inside the little blue square of the television, each living family riveting its attention on probably one show; nobody talking; silence in the yards; dogs barking at you because you pass on human feet instead of on wheels. You'll see what I mean, when it begins to appear like everybody in the world is soon going to be thinking the same way. . . . Only one thing I'll say for the people watching television, the millions and millions of the One Eye: they're not hurting anyone while they're sitting in front of that Eye. . . . I see [Japhy Rider, the novel's hero] in future years stalking along with full rucksack, in suburban streets, passing the blue television windows of homes, alone, his thoughts the only thoughts not electrified to the Master Switch. (104)

This vision can also be traced to Kerouac's short story "CITYCitycity," based on observations of '50s suburbia. It portrays citizens regimented and controlled by a powerful mass-media enterprise called Multivision, as well as by computers, tranquilizing drugs, and "Deactivation," a surgical procedure causing "general psychic pacification" (Stephenson 176).[17]

Power and Pleasure

The repressions of modern society do not steadily diminish human activity, however. Power is not simply "a law which says no," Foucault argues. Rather, what makes power acceptable and effectual is the fact that "it traverses and produces things, it induces pleasure, forms knowledge, produces discourse" (1980, 119). And the knowledge formed can never be separated from the interests that engendered it.

Once again, Burroughs is the Beat writer whose positions reflect these ideas most closely. Agreeing that knowledge is inseparable from power, he uses as a recurring motto the statement, "Nothing is true—everything is permitted," attributed to his important character Hassan i Sabbah, also known as the Native Guide.[18] Glossing this statement, Burroughs remarks that "if we realize that everything is illusion, then any illusion is permitted. As soon as we say that something is true, real, then immediately things are not permitted." Good and evil are only determined "according to your needs and the nature of your organism. . . . I think it's naive to predicate any absolutes there; it only has reference to the conditions of life of a given organism or species or society." In postwar Western culture, as elsewhere, power inflects knowledge according to its material interests. So it is not surprising that "[i]ntellectual uniformity is more and more necessary as the contradictions and failures of the society become more and more apparent. It has reached the point now where it's practically a criminal offense to express a sensible opinion" (Odier 97, 75, 69).

Censorship

The issue of censorship makes a good proving ground for the idea that repression—in this case, the prohibition of explicit sexuality, excretion, profanity, and so forth, in '50s movies—serves to provoke the very representations it purports to deplore. Since the mid-'30s, the Hollywood studios had obeyed a self-imposed Production Code that spelled out fixed guidelines for material related to sex, violence, drugs, and other sensitive areas. These rules were increasingly bent during the '50s, however, as studios tried to reinvigorate box-office profits and compete effectively with television, which was heavily regulated because of its direct penetration into the home and its limited number of available franchises. Accordingly, various public and private groups sought to impose their notions of propriety through protests, boycotts, and pressure campaigns, as similar groups had done at other times. The studios proceeded with understandable caution in opening new doors; and their timidity was reinforced when an occasional overdose of permissiveness led to a burst of anger from some segment of the public.

Many intellectuals shared the popular view that screen representations were too powerful for their creators to be given free reign. The sociologist Ruth A. Inglis asserted in 1947 that "[m]ovies for mass audiences cannot possibly be free. This is simply a fact, and wishing it were not so will not change it" (155). In the same year Byron Price, a journalist who served as national Director of Censorship during World War II and later became vice president of the Motion Picture Association of America, wrote a plea for "free press, unfettered radio, and uncensored films." Yet he managed to accompany this libertarian statement with an assertion that the nation's "laws against political subversion, libel, slander, blasphemy, and pornography are universal and no one can quarrel with them. These laws can always be invoked against any newspaper, any broadcast, or any motion picture which outrages the moral standards of civilized society" (138). The vagueness of these "moral standards" and "civilized" values evidently did not occur to the commentator, whose wealth of establishment credentials—he was executive news editor of the Associated Press and assistant secretary-general of the United Nations, in addition to his other posts— perhaps hindered his qualifications as a dispassionate observer of free mass-media enterprise.

Given such statements, it is not surprising that the '50s era is often seen as thoroughly anxious and oppressive with regard to sexuality. Further evidence is readily available in media products of the period. An image that sums up much about postwar American sex is found in Nicholas Ray's film *Rebel Without a Cause* (1955), as the adolescent Natalie Wood character tries to give her father an innocent kiss even though he considers her "too old" for this behavior. Her attempt to maintain a physically affectionate father-daughter relationship, even though she is now sexually mature, elicits from the father a reaction of explosive discomfort at the presence of such energies (however contained and controlled) within his very home. Surely this man would enthusiastically support the laws, boycotts, moral standards, and civilized values cited above, if only to fortify his defense against the forces of sexual pleasure that are so impertinently threatening to mow down the patriarchal control he obviously exerts in his household. And surely he is a representative member of the respectable mainstream society that formed both the subject and the audience for most classical Hollywood films.

This cinematic moment also points in another direction, however, since its very familiarity indicates the inescapable nature of the sexual energies signified by the closeness of the daughter's breasts and the father's face as they quarrel at the dining-room table. These energies are themselves a product (biologically and culturally) of the middle-class family, and the attempt by such families to disavow them is precisely what charges them with such intensity. True to Foucault's argument, '50s efforts to deny sexuality resulted in *production* of sexuality, in forms ranging from the voluptuous physicality of Marilyn Monroe to the coy evasiveness of sex-education films. Such efforts have a venerable lineage, but reached a high point in conjunction with the cold-war fears and suburban ideals of the postwar era.

Raging Sin

This emergence of sexual discourse from sexual prohibition was recognized by many contemporary writers, although they did not always recognize the implications of their observations. "In America, sex is sinful everywhere, and it rages everywhere," wrote James Collier, clearly mindful of the Kinsey report's revelations. "There is no other country in the world—and possibly in the entire history of the world—where sexual practice is so at odds with the sexual code." And again, stated simply but succinctly, "A suppression of sex inevitably leads to a fascination with the subject" (3, 5). Censorship inevitably "attracts attention and adds interest to what it conceals," noted Ernest van den Haag, a psychoanalyst. "An image may be censored because too prurient. But things also become prurient because censored" (Hughes 124). Addressing this issue through a worst-case example—the proliferation of "sadistic pornography" that is "socially worthless" by any standard—Paul Goodman writes, "But here is a dilemma: *what if the censorship itself, part of a general repressive antisexuality, causes the evil, creates the need for sadistic pornography sold at a criminal profit?*" (Hughes 43).

Referring to less flagrant breeds of pornography, a later commentator notes how tolerance and intolerance may work side by side in American culture. Despite persistent attacks on sex-related printed matter, sociologist Ned Polsky says, masturbatory material has always been tolerated to a degree—for instance, it is spared the pornography label if it is packaged with nonerotic material, as in *Playboy* magazine. Alongside such dissemination, however, society keeps up a stream of official denouncements aimed at other pornographic stuff (196–97).[19] This pattern had ironic reverberations for such Beat writers as Ginsberg and Burroughs, who found their work gaining attention and sympathy as a result of censorship assaults and obscenity trials that will be discussed below. Also affected were mainstream filmmakers with a feisty streak, who found similar publicity value in public conflicts over sexual representation. A well-known example is Otto Preminger, who mischievously insisted on using the words "virgin" and "mistress" in the racy dialogue of his 1953 comedy *The Moon Is Blue.*

In sum, the '50s have not gone unrecognized as a time when efforts to control and repress sexuality resulted in an expansion and at times a veritable explosion of sexually marked consciousness. The oppressive side of this equation is articulately presented in a 1956 statement by Lindner:

> The real situation regarding sex today is a kind of travesty on human nature. The drive that underwrites almost the whole of behavior and the continuation of the species is, from cradle to grave, the object of every conceivable repressive force. Although it naturally becomes manifest shortly after birth with pleasurable sensations in the organs of generation and allied erotogenic zones, any attempt to respond to such sensations is subject to censorship. During the years of bodily growth and sexual maturation, shame and guilt are attached to all forms of erotic play, while illogical, mythical fears, anxieties and punishments are made to attend the slightest exercise of the functions involved. When, at last, at a relatively advanced age, social, religious and legal institutions relax somewhat their prohibitive attentions . . . the instinct and its executive organs . . . are still allowed only a modicum of employment—and that merely along highly specific lines. (39–40)

On the production side of the equation, one need only remember that in literature the '50s saw the rise to fame of Kerouac's kinetic liaisons, Ginsberg's pansexual celebrations, and Burroughs's caustic fantasies of orgasm and death, and that in cinema this decade was the heyday of Monroe, Jayne Mansfield, Mamie Van Doren, Diana Dors, and others— including men like Rock Hudson and Elvis Presley—who traded in overt expression of exaggerated sexuality. Or at least their sexuality *seemed* overt and exaggerated. Its notoriety may actually be another index of the period's repressiveness, since the performances of such stars were really quite euphemistic by later standards.

Atomic-Age Eros

> Me—most popular girl in school, and my boyfriend was the most popular boy. We were a perfect pair, everybody said. Perfect pair. I was the perfect

idiot. I did everything for him, and he did everything to me. You know, love
does more harm than all the atom bombs, and they're trying to ban the
bomb. Poor bomb. At least it looks pretty when it breaks up. Hey, doctor.
Do you suppose that I'm the victim of fallout? Romantic fallout?
—Psychiatric patient in The Disorderly Orderly,
directed by Frank Tashlin, 1964

The beginning of the atomic age brought newly accentuated fears over sexuality. One result, identified by social historian Elaine Tyler May, was a heightened fetishization of marriage as a means of containing and controlling sexual energies. May also notes that a new wave of female fashions replaced the "boyish freedom" of the '20s and the "shoulder-padded strength" of the '30s and early '40s with "quasi-Victorian crinolines and frills, along with exaggerated bust lines and curves which provided an aura of untouchable eroticism" even as "the body itself was protected in a fortress of undergarments" (155, 165–66). May's aim here is to document sexual anxiety and control, but one also finds indications that sexuality was intensified by the mechanisms she cites. For one thing, a renewed emphasis on the sexual component of marriage—as distinguished from, say, the "companionship" or "home economics" aspects—was an obvious byproduct of the marriage fetish that was meant to confine sexuality within a limited domain. (One thinks of the public *frisson* generated by the "private" marriages of Monroe and Mansfield, widely discussed events that figured significantly in their careers.) For another, eroticism that is "untouchable" remains eroticism all the same, especially with those exaggerated bustlines and curves (abetted by stays, girdles, and padded brassieres) to reinforce its allure. May herself acknowledges that the fortress of undergarments promised "erotic excitement in the marital bed" even as it warded off sexual contact in other situations; and she notes that the postwar drop in the average marriage age may have been caused partly by efforts to restrict sex to married couples. A study of more than four thousand adults found a majority believing that people who do not marry are sick, immoral, selfish, or neurotic (166). Sex may have been frightening in the '50s, but it was also craved and venerated. If marriage was the place to have it, then everyone should get married—and, finances permitting, people of younger and younger ages should enter this temple of carnality as soon as possible.

Further illuminating such areas, Richard Dyer puts Monroe's impact in context by suggesting that in the United States of the '50s, "sex was seen as perhaps the most important thing in life," as evidenced by various publishing events of the period including the Kinsey reports on men and women (1948 and 1953, respectively); the first issues of *Confidential* (1951) and *Playboy* (1953); and the popularity of such novels as *From Here to Eternity* (1951), *A House Is Not a Home* (1953), *Not as a Stranger* (1955), *Peyton Place* (1956), *Strangers When We Meet* (1953), *A Summer Place* (1958), *The Chapman Report* (1960), and Mickey Spillane's thrillers. (It is interesting to note how many of these books were made into much-discussed Hollywood movies.) He further cites Albert Ellis's survey *The Folklore of Sex* (1961), which demonstrates that between 1950 and 1960 references to sex increased more than two-and-a-half times in the American media. Not only producers of avant-garde and specialized movies (e.g., "hygiene pictures") but also mainstream filmmakers participated in this upswing, allowing bolder treatment of sex and a loosening of prohibitions (24–26). Monroe herself broke taboos regarding nudity in film and photography, but Dyer notes that one need not look to exceptional commodities like her "Golden Dreams" calendar to detect the '50s surge in sexuality. Comedies, romances, and musicals defined the problems of hero and heroine in terms of virginity rather than love and understanding, and a preoccupation with the meaning of "going far" suggested sexual actions as a key to understanding the heterosexual couple itself. The twin images of the liberated playboy and the mysterious or mystifying woman became organizing principles for sex-related thought and feeling, "united by the notion of 'desirability' as the female sexual characteristic that meets the needs of the playboy discourse" (26–27).

Dyer exaggerates when he nostalgically suggests that pre-'50s films habitually define their protagonists' problems in terms of love and understanding; terms of domination and manipulation are often more like it. And his designation of "desirability" as a "characteristic" that meets discursive "needs" seems vague (and circular) since the term "desirability" applies to any characteristic that meets any need whatever. Dyer is fundamentally correct, however, in his argument that the American '50s constitute something of a high point when it comes to sexuality being seen as a source of truth about human existence. This idea is borne out by the endless fascination with Monroe, who was first voted the top female box-office star by American film distributors in 1953 (25, 27). Molly Haskell groups her with Presley, Jerry Lewis, and Doris Day, calling them stars with "an unreal quality, images at once bland and tortured. They were all *about* sex, but *without* sex." The notion of innocence, Haskell states, was no longer as charming in American culture as it might have been in the past but was starting to appear "a little unhealthy, what with breast fetishism combining with Lolita lechery" in Monroe, the "ultimate sweater girl/daddy's girl" (235).

Figures like Monroe and Presley did not emerge as isolated stars with unique screen personae, moreover, but bore relationships to one another that intensified their social and cinematic importance. James Naremore points to this fact when he contrasts "utterly straight" heroes of the '40s—such as John Wayne, Clark Gable, and Gregory Peck—with Marlon Brando, Montgomery Clift, James Dean, Presley, and Monroe, all "brooding, ostensibly inarticulate types who suggested a scandalous sexuality and who signalled American entertainment's drift toward adolescent audiences." Brando's accent in the 1961 western *One-Eyed Jacks*, which he both directed and starred in, is apparently modeled on Presley's inflections, Naremore interestingly suggests, "and he and Presley together virtually taught Dean how to play the quintessential sexy teenager of the fifties." Thus it appears that Dean's work in *Rebel Without a Cause* borrows a number of elements from *On the Waterfront*, including use of a woman's compact that echoes Brando's use of a woman's glove in the earlier film. Presley's equally strong influence on *Rebel Without a Cause* is "only slightly less apparent, perhaps because Warner Brothers was nervous about the implications of rock and roll; whenever the rebellious kids turn on a radio, we hear a big band" (195).

Big-band music also dominates *The Wild One*, made in 1954 by producer Stanley Kramer and director Laslo Benedek, with Brando as the motorcycle-riding antihero. There is a little boppish scat-singing in one barroom scene, however, when jazz from the jukebox and clownish vocalizing by bikers are put into ironic counterpoint with an elderly bartender's complaint that modern people don't know how to talk anymore but only "grunt" at each other. The bartender is against television, too, because "pictures" also contribute to this trend.

Nervousness about new currents in popular music and youth culture was appropriate on Hollywood's part, judging from Beat associate John Clellon Holmes's observation that the '50s were a time of much youth-centered anguish in grown-up circles. Parents, civic leaders, law officers, and even literary critics were "outraged" by a long list of phenomena, he found in 1958. These included "the adulation of the late James Dean," in which they saw "signs of a dangerous morbidity," and "the adulation of Elvis Presley," in which they saw "signs of a dangerous sensuality." The notion that young people's almost exclusive interest was "the discovery of something in which to believe," the writer concluded, "seems to them to fly directly in the face of all the evidence." One route to a better understanding of this generation, Holmes felt, lay in more sensitive observation of performances by the likes of Dean, who "spoke to [young people] right through all the expensive make-believe of million-dollar productions," and Brando, who seemed to say in scene after scene of *On the Waterfront* that "[m]an is not merely a social animal, a victim, a product. At the bottom, man is a spirit." The much-debated Method acting of Lee Strasberg and the Actors Studio was keyed to this proposition, Holmes asserted, making this "preeminently the acting style of the Beat Generation" (Donaldson 369–70, 372–74).

Part

LITERATURE, PHOTOGRAPHY, FILM

Two

From American
Jukebox to Biologic
Theater

Social Criticism

Photographic Discourse

Moral overtones overtake this machine.
                    —Robert Frank, in a letter to Allen Ginsberg

NAKED Lunch—a frozen moment when everyone sees what is on the end of every fork.
                    —William S. Burroughs, Naked Lunch

■ One need not turn to the postwar era's most seductive mass-media products, such as Hollywood's biggest hits, or to its most eccentric literature, such as scandalous Beat books, to find fascinating instances of conformist value-mongering on one hand or individualistic norm-flouting on the other. As noted earlier, the world of photojournalism presented a social vision as charged with monologic tendencies as anything concocted by the Hollywood film industry. Yet the work of certain photographers—including some with solid establishment credentials—presented alternative visions with very different priorities.

The works of Robert Frank and William Klein—both of whom later turned to film and both of whom shared conscious attitudes with members of the Beat movement—are worth examining for their portrayals of dominant sociocultural values and also for their creative reactions against those values. In addition, Frank and Klein are of interest for the midway position they carved out for themselves between the image-production industry, represented by Hollywood and the large-circulation picture magazines, and the artisanal tradition of art-for-art's-sake expression, embodied by avant-garde cinema and such authors as Kerouac and Ginsberg in the years before they started publishing on a regular basis.

Cars and Jukeboxes

For all his skill in maintaining this midway position over the years, Frank has shown a preference for working as independently as circumstances allow. Arguing that his *oeuvre* falls into "the Beat-Hipster idiom," critic George Cotkin labels him "the existential photographer *par excellence*," citing his persistent sense of being an outsider and his wish to be more an observer than a participant. Pursuing an emphatically personal and emotional vision, the Frank of *The Americans* avoided firm connections to the places, persons, and events that he encountered in his work. Kerouac believed the photographer's "in-motion attitude and style" made him "shadow-like and at times invisible" to his subjects. His tilted horizon lines, hazy prints, use of lightweight equipment, and on-the-go spontaneity contributed to his self-constructed image, which is clearly similar to that of the Beats (Cotkin 21–22).

In this context, it is interesting to consider an aspect of Frank's work that ties in with a widespread fascination of the '50s in general and the Beats in particular: the discourse of machinery, especially the automobile and the jukebox that figure so frequently in *The Americans*, the most important and influential of Frank's books. Frank had a steady interest in cars, which appear in many of his major photographs. He often takes a critical stance toward their near-ubiquitous presence, their relentless transformation of the American landscape, and the many establishments (service stations, garages, drive-ins, etc.) that accommodate them. At the same time, however, Frank as social critic—the peripatetic loner, the dispassionate observer, the questioner of dominant values—is inseparable from Frank as practical artist and responsible professional. He takes part in the very culture that he documents and criticizes, and he is not averse to finding personal utility in artifacts that he simultaneously invests with symbolic and metaphorical meanings. Hence, he made the epic journey that produced *The Americans* in an automobile, even as he chronicled the dubious effects of automobiles as molders and mirrors of the American scene; and while he often associates cars with decadence and isolation, at other times he presents them in a positive or at least nonjudgmental light. Like the Beat writers, he leans toward the free-and-familiar ambivalence of the public realm, often embodied (as in some of Kerouac's key work) by the road and its inhabitants.

Frank's dual relationship with cars also indicates his ability to strike a productive balance between insider and outsider status vis-à-vis society at large. Balancing his career between commerciality and independence, Frank may be seen as a creative consumer at the supermarket of sociocultural alternatives, insisting on the possibility that a photographer can, in art historian Jane Livingston's words, "work artfully on assignment and still maintain an absolutely uncompromised creative stance in relation to a higher, 'personal' artistic achievement" (306). Klein did something similar, combining a successful career in magazine photography with a strong critique of the consumer culture to which the magazines contributed.

Frank and Kerouac

There is no more powerful summation of the '50s era than the eighty-odd images included in *The Americans*. This book was shot in 1955–56, published in 1958 in a French edition, and then printed in 1959 in an American edition for which Kerouac wrote the introduction.[1] The photographs are as methodically sequenced as the shots in a carefully edited film. Some of their primary concerns are "universal" phenomena, including contrasts and conflicts between gregariousness and isolation, religion and secularity, youth and age, life and death. Still, many of the most insinuating images reflect specificities of American life in the first decade after World War II. Again, ambivalence and oscillation are clearly evident.

Kerouac's introduction is more an impressionistic overture than an exposition or explanation of Frank's approach. Key words, tropes, and descriptions are arranged like melodic elements in a piece of music; the result conveys Kerouac's gut-level excitement at recognizing a sensibility very similar to his own, confronting a vast range of American experience with the sort of energy, enthusiasm, and spontaneity that he sought in his writing. While the exuberance of Kerouac's poetic prose is best taken as a sign of pleasure at finding his sensibility validated by another artist—it is no accident that he works the phrase "on the road" into the very beginning of his essay—certain aspects of the introduction point to important elements of Frank's collection. The opening sentence mentions not only the road but also three other leitmotifs of the photographs that follow: the automobile, the jukebox, and the funeral. Of the most resonant components in *The Americans*, only the flag is missing from the informal catalogue in Kerouac's first paragraph.

Kerouac appears to hold two related conceptions of the photograph-series as an expressive form. One conception recalls Christian Metz's view that the series of shots in cinema is analogous to the series of spoken sounds in language. The other conception recalls André Bazin's idea that photographs are direct "tracings" of reality, since light from real objects has imprinted the film. In keeping with this double view, Kerouac describes Frank's photos both as a poem and a poetic *subject* for some future author who will describe "every gray mysterious detail, the gray film that caught the actual pink juice of human kind." Pursuing his notion of photography as a mirror of reality, Kerouac also sees Frank's pictures as objective records of the things they show, such as diversified faces that "don't editorialize or criticize or say anything but 'This is the way we are in real life . . . '" (Frank 1959, 6).

*T*he Photographer as Interpreter

When allowed to speak for itself in the subsequent pages, however, Frank's work indicates that he does editorialize, or at least that he sees himself and his camera as interpreters that impose meanings and judgments on everything they confront. One piece of evidence for this conclusion is his method of labeling images with phrases indicating a spatial area not visible within the photograph; the existence of this unseen space then inflects and articulates the space that *is* visible. The collection's first photograph introduces this practice. The words "Parade—Hoboken, New Jersey" identify the image of two partially obscured human figures framed by windows and an American flag punctuating a grimy brick wall; if these people are indeed watching a parade, the carnivalesque festivity of that "offscreen" event makes a grimly ironic counterpoint to the uninviting image that does appear within the frame. A companion photograph appears much later in the book. It is labeled "Bar—Detroit," yet it depicts only the wall space *over* this bar, on which the camera again captures two figures (this time George Washington and Abraham Lincoln in reproduced portraits) that are both joined and separated by a desperate-looking American flag. Once more, a verbally evoked extraphotographic space derives meaning *from* and contributes meaning *to* the visual area within the frame.

In other pairs of images and titles, the label merely identifies the place and circumstances of the photo or (more interestingly) indicates that a limited part of an environment is standing in for a larger whole, as when political posters and a pool table represent a "Luncheonette—Butte, Montana," and when a flag-accompanied tuba player signifies a "Political rally—Chicago," leaving the viewer to imagine the rest. Frank's use of words to expand the meanings of his photography serves to criticize Kerouac's assumption that his pictures are direct extensions of reality, conveying "the actual pink juice of human kind." It also casts doubt on Kerouac's insistence that authentic literary artists should "write without stopping, without thinking, just go."[2] Frank's work suggests that the artist is always a mediator and that no texts—however "spontaneously" created—are free of the contexts brought to them by producers and consumers alike. Another statement of this message is found on the last page of *The Americans*, where alternative versions of the final image are presented, again acknowledging the arbitrary nature of the photographer's role as chooser and definer of the pictures we see.

Tragic Poets of the World

Looking more directly at Frank's images of '50s America, one is struck by how persistently he contests the views of consensus intellectuals, popular magazines, and Hollywood films. Susan Sontag notes that while European photography has historically tended toward subjects considered picturesque, important, or beautiful, American photographers have often taken a "partisan" route, revealing things that need confronting, deploring, and fixing. American photographers thus have a more ambivalent connection with history, and a relationship with geographic and social realities that is both more hopeful and more predatory than that of their European counterparts. They also incline toward randomness in their choices more than many European photographers do. Frank's collection indeed projects a feeling of random encounter, yet it is certainly not "random" enough to expunge awareness that social criticism courses through it; and Sontag is correct to state that for Frank's tradition of photography (as for Kerouac's tradition of writing) the appearance or claim of randomness is actually a mask for "a mournful vision of loss" (1990, 63, 61, 67). Such a vision makes itself felt throughout *The Americans* as Frank laments the lies and confusions of American society in a sustained elegy that justifies Kerouac's placement of him "among the tragic poets of the world" (Frank 1959, 9).

Views of the United States as a heartily democratic society, for instance, are refuted by the supercilious facial expressions of the "City fathers—Hoboken, New Jersey," and by the phallic arrogance of the "Convention hall—Chicago" power brokers; indeed, the shot of a florid speech-giver in "Political rally—Chicago" suggests a single-image *Citizen Kane* with its eloquent graphics and telling reflexivity. The virtues of capitalism are not easily gleaned from the conspicuously consuming subjects of "Hotel lobby—Miami Beach" or "Cocktail party—New York City." Both the outgoing flashiness and the lurking emptiness of much mass-produced culture are captured in image after image of jukeboxes that seem intended not to enrich imaginations or provide spirited diversions but to spur mindless consumption and mask the dullness of wretchedly conceived architecture. The automobile, celebrated so convincingly in the buzzing dynamism of Kerouac's early prose—and regarded by so many Americans, especially young ones, as a sign of the good and liberated life—often becomes an ambulatory site of loneliness and death.

Racial Misery

Most stunning of all are the images of racial misery that parade through the volume, documenting black despair and the white dominance that causes it. Cotkin accurately notes a key connection between Frank and the Beats here, observing that "Beat writings pulsate with the liveliness of jazz; blacks are walking expressions of uninhibited sexuality, of disdain for social convention. They are open to the possibilities of freedom in an age of domination and the bomb" (26). He does not reveal the extent to which Beat writing on African-Americans is sentimentalized and nostalgic, however. And while he takes care to exempt Frank from such shortcomings—saying the photographer did not try to mythologize African-Americans or celebrate their culture simplistically—it is important to go a step farther, underscoring the urgency that marked Frank's awareness of obstacles between black people and their right to authenticity and freedom.

Frank did feel African-American life benefited from its status of not-belonging to a dominant society that was killing itself with compulsory consumerism, fraudulent political ideals, and other brain-deadening ills. Yet that society was killing its minority members in ways still more effective, efficient, and tragic. Frank's most powerful representation of racial horror is the image labeled "Trolley—New Orleans," in which the photographic tension between spontaneity (the found situation, the momentary snap) and deliberation (on-site decisions, later darkroom manipulations) conjoin to produce an image of extraordinary graphic sophistication and social awareness. (Its power was recognized by Aperture, which placed it on the cover of its original edition of *The Americans.*) Five windows of the trolley are visible to the camera. The three on the left reveal white faces—one rendered inscrutable by a superimposed reflection; the next glaring at the camera with undisguised ill will; the last two belonging to unhappy-looking children who seem fated to become as armored and hostile as their white companions. The other two windows ("the back of the bus") hold black faces—a man with an expression of open-hearted sadness and a woman gazing at a point outside the camera's range. The gestic qualities of this image are immediately accessible and lastingly resonant. Its graphic dimensions are similarly rich. Each compartmentalized window-world is divided from the next by a white bar, while over each head hovers a pane of light-reflecting glass that could almost be seen as a comic-book-style "thought bubble" conveying the dimly perceivable, barely conceivable mind-set of the individual below it. At the bottom of the frame is a wall of blank riveted metal, as implacable as the culture that produced such a situation and such a scene.

Frank's depiction of black experience balances his view of generalized American alienation by pointing toward liminal possibilities for more authentic living. It also offers a symbolic vision of failings in the American dream, coupled with a documentary record of African-American subjugation. While it is true that "Frank's whites are enslaved as well, prisoners of the staleness of modern, consumer America," as Cotkin says (31), it must be stressed that the photographer's deepest compassion goes to the dark-skinned occupants of the diseased culture portrayed in his pages. His view of coexistent black and white problems is not merely balanced but is rather polemical in the best sense of that term—and vastly more sophisticated than anything in Kerouac's novel *The Subterraneans,* with its feverish tale of black-white romance, not to mention the woefully inadequate depictions generally served up by Hollywood.

Limits of the Pictorial

One other point that must be made about Frank's work is that for all his concern with observation and commentary related to the sociocultural scene at large, he does not exempt pictorialism itself from scrutiny. The visual aggression of his numerous flags, magazine covers, public signs, and especially jukeboxes (which function as pop sculptures within the bleak spaces that surround them) is amplified in his articulate use of subjects connected with film and television. Examples include the televised man declaiming to a deserted room in "Restaurant—U.S. 1 leaving Columbia, South Carolina," and the oblong screen flinging its hazy image to a mass of automobiles in "Drive-in movie—Detroit."

Purposefully, however, these are followed by three images suggesting that visual figuration can only murkily imply the stirrings of consciousness (and subconsciousness) that arise in extreme human situations. One shows an African-American priest carrying a cross along an overgrown bank of the "Mississippi River, Baton Rouge, Louisiana." Another shows a dark composition of "St. Francis, gas station and City Hall—Los Angeles." The third, most evocative of the trio, shows a lightstruck view of "Crosses on scene of highway accident—U.S. 91, Idaho." Similar in their meticulous mystery are pictures of a mournful "Funeral—St. Helena, South Carolina" and a ghostly "Chinese cemetery—San Francisco." These lead to the void-centered image of the tuba player at a political rally; a pointlessly picture-crowded "Store window—Washington, D.C."; a depopulated "Television studio—Burbank, California"; and a monstrous neon arrow in "Los Angeles" directing an isolated pedestrian to a destination as ominously undiscernible as it is socially constructed and arbitrarily assigned.

Klein's Urban Centrifuge

Klein's photographs of New York in the '50s etch a somewhat different portrait of American life but find a similar wealth of social and cultural traits worthy of pungent (if mainly implicit) criticism. Japanese commentator Hiroshi Hamaya has linked Klein's first collection, the ironically titled *Life Is Good & Good for You in New York* (1956), with David Riesman's cautionary works *The Lonely Crowd* and *Abundance for What?* This connection is valid, since the photographer and the sociologist indeed share a fear that contemporary urban experience produces dysfunction, decay, and despair. Hamaya also identifies in Klein's work a refutation of the "melting pot" metaphor that has often been applied to urban American life. More appropriate, the critic suggests, is a "centrifuge" metaphor connoting "fascinating and disillusioning powers [that] represent centripetal force and centrifugal force, respectively" (*William Klein*, 1991 Catalogue, n.p.).

Klein's photographs support this proposition. The interplay of multi-directional vectors, physical and perceptual, is almost palpably evoked by his well-known photograph "Four Heads, Thanksgiving Day, New York, 1954," which conjoins tight framing, grainy texture, and limited depth of field to convey the sense of isolation-within-proximity that Riesman's phrase "lonely crowd" was formulated to express. Something similar happens among the intersecting planes of "Grace Line, New York, 1955," and in certain photos taken by Klein in non-American cities.

His most ferocious observations of '50s American life, however, are often found in portraits of individuals and very small groups. There is nothing subtle about the message of "Gun 1, New York, 1955," for instance, with its snarling youngster aiming a pistol directly at the camera while an even younger boy gazes at the weapon with awe and respect. Nor is it hard to interpret Klein's habit of separating heads from bodies, whether by blurring the head (e.g., "Dance Brooklyn, New York, 1955"), eliminating it from the frame (e.g., "Candy Store and Checkered Wall, New York, 1954"), or highlighting it while obscuring the body beneath (e.g., the bluntly titled "Severed Head, New York, 1955" and "Heads Cut, Palladium Ballroom, New York, 1955," and also the stark "Black and Hand, Harlem, New York, 1955"). Here the photographer uses dissection of the material body to suggest disintegration of the sociopolitical body, constructing a Bakhtinian parody of "proper" photographic figuration (e.g., the conventional portrait image) that is as modernistically aggressive as it is grimly carnivalesque.

Sontag contends that "people of good will" desired the consolation and distraction of a "sentimental humanism" in the '50s, and suggests that photography with such a message rules out "a historical understanding of reality" (1990, 32–33). In their most important work of the decade, Klein and Frank refused to serve this desire. Instead they produced imagery that may resemble "a sad poem," in Kerouac's phrase, but does not relinquish a quest for historical understanding of the social realities it scrutinizes and frequently deplores. Like the Beats, the most inventive avant-garde filmmakers, and the line of Whitmanesque artists who preceded them all, these image makers found the United States an invigorating site of personal adventure and aesthetic stimulation. More successfully than the Beats, however, they usually kept their own energies and preoccupations from obscuring an awareness of American failings that was rigorous as well as melancholy.

A Woman's Face

> Let's swing a camera down on Cody and catch him hurrying up the ramp like Joan Rawshanks in the fog, but Gad he would outrun the camera!— he would astound the lighting with his furlibaes, eye-flutters, show-offs, piper jigs and "shining eyes"; he wouldn't even make the son of the villain he's so dishonest looking . . . fah! He is a hero, a champion, he wrote "Laura"; he married Frank Sinatra; he gave David Rose his very first kiss, or was it Thor Heyerdahl Axel Stordhal. Kon-Tiki! A man committed suicide because he couldn't write a song like that. I am amazed by this in America.
>
> —Jack Kerouac, Visions of Cody

When he poured out that moment of stream-of-consciousness fantasy—actually a fantasy-within-a-fantasy, in a novel of vast and mirrored complexity—Kerouac made a multifaceted linkage among: (a) his hero Neal Cassady/Cody Pomeray, (b) the actress Joan Crawford/Joan Rawshanks, and (c) his vision of her as histrionic-historical-hysterical icon of (d) a Hollywood that has not "won us with its dreams" but has rather "enhanced our own wild dreams, we the populace so strange and unknown, so uncalculable, mad, eee . . . " (1993, 286).

Like the Beat writer whose introduction graced his most important book, Frank was also fascinated by the movies (and incidentally by Crawford) as a vivid producer/product/production of American culture. A striking statement of Frank's interest in these areas is found in a mid-'50s photograph called "Detroit Movie House," not included in *The Americans* and therefore given less attention by critics than it deserves.[3] Picturing the front of a garish "picture palace," it stresses the centrality of box-office concerns (the movies as show *business*) by the simple expedient of focusing primarily on the theater's box office, which doubles as a luridly mounted advertising collage including about twenty still pictures from the current revival attraction (*A Woman's Face*, 1941) plus a huge blow-up of Crawford's own face (photogenically) contorted in an attitude of (conventionalized) fear that is (melodramatically) punctuated by the star's (gracefully) upraised hands framing her (voluptuous) mouth. It is hard to imagine the representation of a woman's face being more emphatically constructed, displayed, and marketed. Yet there is another woman's face in the photograph, as well: Above and to the right of Crawford's hyperbolic effigy, surrounded by smaller stills that cover the rest of the box-office facade, one sees the ticket seller literally caged within her booth. Gazing past a "now showing" logo and a price-of-admission sign (Adults 50¢/ Children 15¢), she wears an expression commingling boredom, sadness, a shade of wistfulness, and perhaps a hint of semiconscious pride at being included in this sensational spectacle, which heralds a *more* sensational spectacle on the silver screen within. Hers is the least assertive woman's face on view, but its dead-center position within the frame signals Frank's genuine and compassionate interest—in the woman herself, and in her status as poignant representative of the strange, unknown, "uncalculable" populace of which Kerouac wrote in such ringing Whitmanian terms.

(Also visible, at the very bottom of the box-office display, are two shoved-aside stills from a more recent film apparently showing with the Crawford vehicle. Mickey Rooney obviously cannot compete with his glamorous Hollywood colleague, even when he stars in such a timely nuclear-age attraction as *The Atomic Kid*.)

Splendid Entertainment for the Entire Family

> Pull my daisy
> Tip my cup
> All my doors are open
> Cut my thoughts for coconuts
> All my eggs are broken
> Hop my heart song
> Harp my height
> Seraphs hold me steady
> Hip my angel
> Hype my light
> Lay it on the needy
>
> —"The Crazy Daisy"

In 1959, the same year when Aperture published *The Americans* in its American edition, Frank made the transition from still photography to cinema with *Pull My Daisy*, codirected by Alfred Leslie and featuring Kerouac as narrator, commentator on the action, and supplier of all of the characters' voices regardless of age and gender. (The sole exception is a brief nursery rhyme spoken in a child's voice—probably that of Frank's son Pablo, who plays the little-boy character in the film.) The narrative is based on the third act of an unproduced Kerouac play called *The Beat Generation*, written at Lillian Hellman's request when Kerouac was much in demand after *On the Road* was published (McNally 262). The film's title was changed from *The Beat Generation* to *Pull My Daisy* because, to the distress of Kerouac and his associates, MGM had just co-opted the former title for Albert Zugsmith's forthcoming exploitation movie on Beat life and other California skullduggery. The new title came from a whimsical song performed by Anita Ellis during the opening credits.[4] Composed by David Amram, who also appears in the film as jazz musician Mezz McGillicuddy, it sets a jaunty 1949 poem by Kerouac, Ginsberg, and perhaps Cassady[5] to a lively tune and spiky, surprising harmonies that intermittently underscore the film's insouciant mood. (Amram recorded it at least once more, with vocalist Lynn Sheffield and his own quintet in 1971.) Further signifying the film's Beat sensibility are writers Gregory Corso, Peter Orlovsky, and Ginsberg as on-screen performers.[6]

For all its obvious Beat credentials, however, the film displays only limited amounts of such Beat-notorious qualities as alienation, anarchy, and spontaneity. Most of it has the appearance of a careful, even studied, attempt to capture the spirit of a mildly unconventional time and place; what glimmers of outrageousness it does show are inscribed more fully in the profilmic action than in the cinematic style of the work, which includes a certain amount of childish horseplay and whimsical wordplay without deviating from a unified single-day structure and a meandering but basically linear story. The story focuses on a working-class poet and his family, their "beatnik" friends, a visit from a "bishop" who causes everyone to assume more or less good manners—for a while, at least—and the eventual escape of the other male characters into the New York night.

Among aspects of the film pointing to a less-than-revolutionary agenda is its unquestioned male bias. Visually, the female characters (the poet's wife Carolyn, the Bishop's mother and sister, the woman identified in the credits as Girl in Bed) are relegated almost entirely to the background by Frank's camera work and Leslie's staging. Verbally, the Kerouac voice-over reinforces this bias at key moments, including the start and finish of the film. The narration begins, "Early morning in the universe. The wife is getting up, opening up the windows. . . . " This passage flaunts a "poetic" conjunction of the cosmic and the quotidian, but actually inscribes universal daybreak as an occasion for women to begin straightening their homes ("There's her husband's coat on a chair—been there for three days—neckties and his tortured socks") while getting their children dressed, fed, and off to school ("And she says, Come on now, got to go to school, learn all about geography and astromomology and pipliology and all them ologies, and poetology, and goodbyeology"). The ending symmetrically recuperates this theme: Carolyn explodes at Milo's cavalier behavior during the Bishop's visit ("All that time you give 'em wine and beer and give 'em all these beatniks in the house"), and Milo belligerently kicks a chair before summarily leaving the apartment with his friends for new all-male adventures, passing by a hanging rose-shaped lamp as Kerouac utters a final burst of hand-clapping jive:

> And the rose swings. She'll get over
>   it.
> Come on, Milo. Here comes sweet
>   Milo, beautiful Milo.
> Hello, gang.
> Da da da da da.
> And they're going dada da da dada da
>   da da. . . . Let's go. 'sgo, 'sgo. . . .
> Off they go.

Extensive research into the production of *Pull My Daisy* by Canadian film historian Blaine Allan bears out the impression that the movie is more planned and structured and less random or improvised than legend would suggest.[7] Even the original decision by photographer Frank and painter Leslie to enter filmmaking was arrived at in a considered way, partly spurred by Leslie's belated idea that the divorcement of Hollywood studios from the theaters they owned (a divestiture forced in the late '40s by court-ordered antitrust action) had opened new possibilities for non-Hollywood films in commercial movie houses. Although the partners intended to break away from dominant Hollywood styles, Leslie told Allan that he wished to develop not a radical film avant-gardism nor a hipsterish home-movie aesthetic, but rather "a realigned framework of what had been the so-called commercial cinema" complete with real box-office potential (Allan 1988, 189).

Nor was either filmmaker a complete novice at motion-picture pro-

duction. Leslie had experimented with the medium as early as the mid-
'40s,[8] and Frank had begun exploring cinema during the later stages of his
Americans project, using film at one point to reshoot subjects he had previously captured in still photos. The model for their joint project was early
short-film production by members of the *Nouvelle Vague* (presumably such
recent works as François Truffaut's *Les Mistons* and Jean-Luc Godard's
Tous les garçons s'appellent Patrick, also known as *Charlotte et Véronique*,
both completed in 1957) and also Roberto Rossellini's episodic *Paisan*
(1946), which combined multiple stories into a viable theatrical package.
In the end, their idea of collaborating on a trilogy of consecutive shorts
was never realized, since their Zero Mostel project (*Mr. Z*, about a man
obsessed with mannequins) did not materialize and *The Sin of Jesus* was
filmed as a solo venture by Frank, emerging as a heavy-going narrative that
shares only a limited number of stylistic traits (studied compositions, an
offbeat narrative approach) with *Pull My Daisy*. Still, awareness of *Pull My
Daisy* as one projected element of a three-part theatrical package is important if one is to understand the film's mixture of avant-garde components
(e.g., loosely strung narrative, expressionistic sound track) and traditional
elements (e.g., basically linear structure, steady tripod-mounted cinema-
tography). Although the film was financed in a non-Hollywood fashion—
Frank and Leslie started with money of their own, then Wall Street broker
and future filmmaker Walter Gutman kicked in and coaxed investments
from others—the filmmakers hoped their effort would eventually play in
movie theaters and attract sizable audiences. Leslie appears to have been
particularly interested in dreaming up attractive marketing strategies.
He drew a poster (displaying a foot and knee viewed from a subjective
position), placed an advertisement in the entertainment trade newspaper *Variety*, and plagiarized an advertising slogan from a theater marquee:
"At all times a splendid entertainment for the entire family—no sex—no
violence." (This platitudinous statement was presumably offered in an
ironic spirit, although Allan does not indicate such an attitude in his account of Leslie's public-relations tactics.) Leslie also hoped a recording
tie-in might emerge from the movie. Inspired by the Drifters' rock hit
"There Goes My Baby," he approached the hugely successful songwriting
team of Jerry Lieber and Mike Stoller to ask if they would contribute to
the film; but Frank discouraged their participation. Leslie said later, "If
there was anything that I could have dreamed up that could have been
merchandised, including little statues of Allen and Gregory, I would have
done it" (Allan 1988, 201–2). Rarely has a figure so closely associated

with experimental film sounded so much like a member of Steven Spiel-
berg's business staff.

About three hours of 16-mm footage was shot by the directors and
their hired assistants for the twenty-eight-minute *Pull My Daisy*. The
shooting was accomplished during fourteen eight-hour workdays (between January and April, 1959) in Leslie's loft on Fourth Avenue in Manhattan; some additional material (most notably the sermon delivered by
the Bishop to his flock) was shot later to flesh out the film's structure.
Postproduction stretched over the next few months, and the budget came
to around $15,000 (Nicosia 583). Once the footage was edited, Kerouac
performed his voice-over, improvising it to piano music played by Amram
as the film was projected for him. (Kerouac alone heard this music,
through earphones.) The voice-over was recorded three separate times,[9]
and the final sound track incorporates portions of all three takes, edited
to match the on-screen action (including lip movements) fairly closely
most of the time. (Amram has praised Kerouac's work as a quasimusical
element of the film: "Jack's narration was almost like a great jazzman . . .
he played around the [musical] chords or played around the situation, improvising on certain things, and made a beautiful tapestry out of nothing" (Clark 176). Although a good deal of carnivalistic play reportedly
took place during the shooting, the finished film rarely has an anarchic
appearance, and even its crazier on-screen behavior (as the poets parody
a western movie, for instance, or as Ginsberg gyrates on the floor while
Kerouac does a goofy riff about Guillaume Apollinaire) is captured in
shots that are coherently, often soberly composed. Amram has said that
Leslie was "an amazing director—even if he didn't know what he was
doing, it would all come out," and actor Richard Bellamy has stated that
Leslie (who concentrated on staging) and Frank (who focused on cinema-
tography) consulted about each scene before it was begun, and that every
shot was designed to facilitate ready repetition (Allan 1988, 195). The
completed movie reflects this careful approach; horseplay too zany or irrelevant for inclusion was filmed but not included in the final cut. Thus was
an aura (and legend) of Beat irreverence shaped (and contained) by a savvy
consideration of filmic professionalism and audience appeal.

Such irreverence and professionalism also coexist in Frank's still-
photography work, which (as suggested above) develops particularly artful tensions between found material/spontaneous snapping on one hand
and camera virtuosity/darkroom refinement on the other. *Pull My Daisy*
thus emerges as a project fully in keeping with the preceding phase of

Frank's career. While it is substantially different from *The Americans* in its (mostly) single-set confinement and linear (if wandering) narrative line, it again allows him (as primary molder of the film's cinematographic content) to play subject-matter spontaneity and aesthetic/semiotic complexity off each other while constructing a record of a time, a place, and an ethos that are as thoroughly American as the beat-hipster idiom itself. A prime example is the scene portraying the Bishop's sermon. Filmed on a bitterly cold day in a warehouse district beneath the Manhattan Bridge (Allan 1988, 197), it incorporates genuine movie acting by a half-dozen cast members who look like they are actually participating in a churchly experience, and show no visible signs of discomfort at the freezing weather or amusement at the nonsermon being cantankerously delivered by Bellamy as the clergyman. Yet even as Frank presided over the realistic approach of this scene, along with codirector Leslie and camera assistant Gert Berliner, he managed to introject a visual component that has no logical place within the diegesis yet (a) carries a metaphorical meaning that conveys much about Frank's view of the American scene and (b) introduces an element of deliberately unmanageable, even aleatory motion into the mise-en-scène: a large American flag that waves in the breeze alongside the Bishop's podium, comically obscuring him as he speaks, and suggesting that patriotism and piety are promoted in ways reflecting more interest in the amplitude of their display than the appropriateness of their presence or the effectiveness of their symbolism. This moment establishes the most vigorous intertextual link between *Pull My Daisy* and *The Americans*, associating the former with all the visual complexity and semiotic passion that made the latter (in which the flag was a major leitmotif) such an explosive event in the world of art photography. More than any other single element in the film, it confirms *Pull My Daisy* as a privileged point of intersection among Beat, photographic, and experimental-film sensibilities.

*T*he Well-Equipped Pad

> But the shabby Beats bungle the job [of rebellion] in arguing, sulking and bad poetry.
> —Subhead on Life article, "The Only Rebellion Around"

> ... bah, bum bunk like the rest of it all, pure puke.
> —Neal Cassady on the Life article

It is an ironic addendum to the foregoing that Leslie's interest in the commercial prospects of *Pull My Daisy*—not only immediate financial gain but also the larger goal of reshaping "commercial" cinema—led to an indirect association between the movie and one of the most notorious late-'50s attacks on Beat life. Leslie and the film's production company, G-String Enterprises, recruited photographer John Cohen to document the shooting process, hoping his pictures might produce extra income for the project. Cohen took photographs on and off the set and then earned several hundred dollars, according to Allan, by selling a number of the pictures to *Life*, which had encountered resistance in its own attempts to photograph Beat writers[10] (1988, 192, 189). Two of the photos ended up accompanying Paul O'Neil's derogatory *Life* article, "The Only Rebellion Around." The author commences his text by likening the Beat Generation to "a few fruit flies" infesting "the biggest, sweetest and most succulent casaba ever produced by the melon patch of civilization," this being the United States in 1959. Nor are these "contented . . . blissful fruit flies . . . raised by happy environment to the highest stages of fruit fly development." Rather, they are "some of the hairiest, scrawniest and most discontented specimens of all time," not only refusing "to sample the seeping juices of American plenty and American social advance" but also rudely scraping their feelers "in discordant scorn of any and all who do." The subsequent tone of the article is suggested by the dividers marking off its major sections; these range from sarcastic ("Squares are tragic saps") to ominous ("A fix at the altar") to simultaneously prim and prurient ("The rare pad-sharing chick"). The final paragraph is pithy and pugnacious: "A hundred million squares must ask themselves: 'What have we done to deserve this?'"

Beneath these concluding words, and labeled "Languishing in His Pad," is a photograph (originally taken for *Paris-Match* by Charles Bonnay) of Ginsberg lying on a messy bed and stroking a Siamese cat. (The caption notes that Corso and Orlovsky share Ginsberg's unkempt quarters, thus assailing two additional Beats with the implied charge of guilt-by-messiness.) Two earlier pages carry Cohen photos with direct *Pull My Daisy* connections. "Beatdom's Grand Old Man" shows Kerouac and an unidentified female friend (actually Dody Muller) as they watch the shooting from a scaffold on which Kerouac perched during some of the filming process. "Horsing Around" shows Ginsberg playfully making a "scary face" at Corso on the *Pull My Daisy* set, while Corso "makes a motion as if to shoot him." Although this image is carnivalesque rather than menacing, it helps support Kerouac's somewhat paranoid but not wholly gratuitous conviction that the establishment press was determined to link the Beats with violence. Three additional pictures not connected with *Pull My Daisy* purport to represent the Beat scene in general.[11] "Beat Hangout," the most publicly oriented photo, shows San Francisco's popular Coffee Gallery at a crowded moment. "Ex-Dope Addict," the most poignant and atmospheric picture, depicts Burroughs sitting gloomily on the edge of a (neatly made) bed in a (hopelessly dingy) room identified as "what has become known as the Beat Hotel" in Paris. "Inspected at Princeton," the most semiotically sophisticated shot, portrays neatly but casually clad "Beat Poet Mike McClure" talking with student "well-wishers" before a reading of his work. This photo cleverly arranges the well-wishers on one side, McClure and what appear to be his companions on the other. The well-wishers most prominently on view stretch eagerly toward McClure like a trio of clean-cut gargoyles, constituting a near-parody of '50s-establishment types with identical crewcuts, jackets, and (on two of the three) eyeglasses; clustered with them are two professor types with mature faces and (in one case) a pipe, lending tweedily respectable Ivy League connotations to this half of the frame. By contrast, while McClure himself looks as well groomed and responsible as anyone else, the photo groups him with two scruffy men; one sports dark glasses and a beard, and the other has uncombed hair and such poor manners that his back is turned to the camera. McClure may be able to infiltrate the halls of academia, the picture implies, but "well-wishers" should not be fooled into thinking the Beats as a group are similarly presentable. In a final bit of verbal anchorage with clearly partisan connotations, the last line of the caption takes a parting shot at McClure and his poetry: "Actual reading was greeted with booing."

The *pièce de résistance* of the *Life* spread, however, is its introductory photograph. It is labeled "The Well-Equipped Pad," and represents a Beat domestic scene that contrasts revealingly with the Beat-sympathetic imagery of *Pull My Daisy*, which also takes a "slice of Beat life" as its subject. Taken by Bert Stern, the picture spills over one-and-a-third pages, showing what the caption describes as "[a] Beat's entire 'pad' or household" with "all the essentials of uncomfortable living." Interestingly, the photo is clearly identified as "re-created in studio shot using paid models." One reason for this identification may be that anti-Beat articles had become a veritable genre by the late '50s,[12] and there was no need to conceal the fictional trappings of a discourse that flourished (as Foucault would quickly have recognized) more on the reinforcement of popular expectations than on claims of literal truth or accuracy. But it is also likely that the willingness of *Life* to label this fiction as such was an early symptom of the sweeping (if temporary) shift in mass-media ethics that came about as a result of the era's quiz-show scandals. "The Only Rebellion Around" appeared in an issue dated just four weeks after quiz-show star Charles Van Doren was questioned by a congressional committee about his coached appearances on the *Twenty-One* television program; the scandal had appeared prominently in the press, and public interest was high.[13] In the wake of this upheaval, network and local television went through a truth-in-marketing phase: Reenacted scenes in commercials and documentaries were identified as "dramatizations," actors in aspirin commercials stopped wearing physician-style white coats, and so forth. Picture magazines and other media outlets did not escape the ripples of this development, which called for "studio shot" photographs and the like to declare themselves as what they were.

The carefully arranged components of "The Well-Equipped Pad" are marked with numbers corresponding to an itemized list in the caption. The first and last are human beings: "1. Beat chick dressed in black" and "22. Beat baby, who has gone to sleep on floor after playing with beer cans." Dead center on the list is "11. bearded Beat wearing sandals, chinos and turtle-necked sweater and studying a record by the late saxophonist Charlie Parker." Other items range from "naked light bulb" and "typewriter with half-finished poem" to "Beat poetry leaflet (*Abomunist Manifesto*)" and "coal stove for heating baby's milk, drying chick's leotards and displaying crucifix-shaped Mexican cow bells." The list is sometimes innocuous ("hi-fi loudspeaker"), sometimes coyly neutral ("marijuana for smoking"), and sometimes openly negative ("ill-tended plant") in its attitudes toward the things it catalogs; but the anti-Beat devil is in the details of the photograph itself. Faces are one good index of its bias. There is a surly scowl on the face of "bearded Beat" as he scans the back of his Charlie Parker album jacket. There is an ambiguous mixture of attractiveness and purposelessness in the expression of "Beat chick" as she gazes into the camera with espresso cup in hand. There is no look at all on the countenance of "Beat baby," who sprawls face down like a forgotten corpse on the opposite side of the room.

Many of the objects in "The Well-Equipped Pad" are similar to those encountered in *Pull My Daisy*—alcoholic drinks, musical instruments, modest furnishings—but their recontextualization in *Life* transforms them from trappings of a vaguely free, mildly hedonistic home to signs of unalloyed decadence and irresponsibility. Carolyn, the most conventional and propriety-seeking member of Milo's circle in *Pull My Daisy*,[14] is characterized as a lovable, ignorable drag on male energy and enthusiasm. In the household depicted by the *Life* photo, the "chick" is cooler than her screen counterpart, showing no evidence of Carolyn's impatience with alcohol, her conscientious mother love, or her desire for a little tidiness and order. If the household shown by *Pull My Daisy* has only a tenuous grasp (through Carolyn) on bourgeois responsibility, there is *no* responsible adult in the home shown by the *Life* photographer—as the figure of the baby, disregarded and neglected in its exhausted sleep, most vividly and alarmingly conveys. What the Stern photo and the Frank-Leslie film *do* share, beyond a basic interest in Beat living, is promale bias: Just as Carolyn does the cooking and cleaning in her home, "Beat chick" is standing near the stove (actually a hot plate on top of a crate) and apparently preparing coffee for "bearded Beat" to consume. Finally, it is interesting to note the bareness of the Beat man's bed and the presence of a cat near the sleeping child in the photo; the bed's unattractiveness and the cat's possible dirtiness anticipate the Ginsberg photo displayed at the conclusion of the same article. Messy sleeping arrangements, animals roaming where they will— what else would one expect from a "cult of the Pariah" that, in O'Neil's colorful words, "yearns for the roach-guarded mores of the skid road, the flophouse, the hobo jungle and the slum? . . . "

The Beats as Rebels

Attitudes of the Beat Generation toward American society were echoed in the photography of Frank and Klein, among other innovative *oeuvres* of the '50s. Attitudes of society toward the Beats were similarly echoed in the famous "Rebellion" photo spread and plenty more like it. The ideological groundwork for the Beat mind-set was itself partly prepared by a phenomenon linked with photography, and not a particularly enlightened one: the drumbeating for male freedom that filled the pages of *Playboy* magazine. Those who considered themselves Beats rejected middle-class patterns in more sweeping terms than the *Playboy* philosophy did, throwing away steady jobs along with the suburban families that Hefnerism called into question (Ehrenreich 52–53). Still, the Beats were seen as conformist and even conservative by some critics, who asked whether the Beat subculture represented a true alternative to the status

quo or merely another cleverly disguised reflection of it. This implication—especially with regard to alleged Beat conformity—is a major sub-
text of the "Rebellion" photos.

Adopting unusual clothing styles and speech patterns was certainly
not a strong enough maneuver to change the American scene, as Goodman and other commentators recognized. Rather than substituting free-
and-familiar *communitas* for organized *societas*, to use terms from anthropologist Victor Turner, these gestures simply replaced one set of folkways
and mores with another that was perhaps a bit more flexible but appeared
to pose normative strictures of its own. Acute critics noted that such
bourgeois trappings as the business suit, the taste for alcohol, the clichés
of Madison Avenue, and the Protestant work-and-progress ethic were par-
alleled by such bohemian counterparts as the work-clothes outfit, an interest in drugs, jargons influenced by jazz and African-American speech, and
a longing for Zen Buddhist peacefulness and harmony. No mainstream
powers were seriously threatened by any of this, so it was safe to conclude
that conventional society could take this rebellion in stride. Even the characters in Kerouac's novels, usually based on people he knew, seemed peril-
ously similar to ordinary citizens with their up-and-down home lives, aspirations to literary success, and grumpiness about personal problems.[15]
Small wonder that *Mad* magazine kiddingly portrayed the Beats as ultra-
conformists in the purest '50s style, sporting indistinguishable beards and
identically sloppy clothing that locked them into patterns of appearance
(and, by implication, of thought and behavior) every bit as rigid as those
of the "squares" they so scathingly spurned.

Individual Insurrection

The portrait of the Beats painted by critics as diverse as Goodman and
the *Mad* humorists is incomplete, however, and supplementary points
must be made. To begin with, the charge that the Beats failed to mount a
meaningful challenge to the mainstream consensus may be rooted in for-
getfulness of the simple fact that there was only a limited quantity of
Beats to spread the movement's ideas. Membership in the Beat community
never totaled more than a few thousand—constituting a far smaller group
than, say, the slightly later Hippies, whose sheer numbers facilitated major
shake-ups of American life. As for matters of style and presentation of self,
most Beats were the opposite of flamboyant, for reasons of both sensibility
and finance. Only a handful were published writers; most wore working-

class clothing that would seem distinctive only to the narrowest middle-class perception; and most startling of all in the face of familiar stereo-types, only a minority were bearded (Gitlin 45–46).

Nor were they geographically clustered around New York City's fabled Greenwich Village, despite legends associating them with that area. If the early Beats did have a favorite locale, it was Times Square, where cheap cafeterias and amusement arcades seemed more authentically human to them than the gentrified Village, which they already considered a symbol of commercial exploitation[16] (Charters 2–3). Later there was a substantial Beat presence in San Francisco, but it was supplemental to a literary "re-naissance" that predated the Beats' arrival.

In sum, the Beats—and other mavericks of a similar bent, including film experimentalists—were not uniformed guerrillas organizing violent assaults on mainstream ideology, nor did they intend to be. Rather, the most influential among them were radically individualistic thinkers who fought consensus and conformity more by eluding or transcending these than by mobilizing militant allies for some sort of head-on sociocultural battle.

If they posed little direct threat to major institutions and power hold-ers, it was largely because they waged their struggle on a capillary level, in Foucault's terminology. Still, their ideological challenges became widely known, despite such obstacles as their own marginality and the strangle-hold on popular communication held by corporate entities with reasons for reinforcing the consensus mentality. Recognition came less readily to most independent filmmakers, who faced the Hollywood system's over-whelming power; yet at least a small number of cinematic rebels were also able to carry on their activities and make sporadic forays into popular awareness.

Beat and avant-garde activities may have provoked no uprisings, then, but they certainly provoked a lot of thought. And much of this thought was refreshingly skeptical toward a normalized society that tried to neu-tralize even its own minority of establishment-certified critics by labeling them "eggheads" and treating their analyses as interesting curiosities—about which a well-informed person ought to know, but upon which a responsible person should not even dream of acting. The most effective Beat writers and experimental artists cut through the anxious haze that "lonely crowd" and "hidden persuaders" theorization had produced in the popular imagination, and held up to the mainstream a peculiar but de-fiantly real alternative to its deadening habits. Most observers refused to take this alternative very seriously, but the issues raised by their encounter with it were not easily dismissible. This background helps explain the Beats' success in moving from what Gregory Stephenson (2–3) calls the underground period of their historical trajectory, from 1944 to 1956, into the public period, from 1956 to about 1962—the latter characterized by far-reaching public awareness of the Beats and their "nonconformist" sensibility.[17]

Angelical Ravings

The discontent of the Beats was far more profound than criticisms of their "apathy" or "conservatism" indicate, and at times the rhetoric of their protest was forceful enough to be noticed for its aggressive and transgressive characteristics as well as its ideological content. One example out of many is Ginsberg's poem "Howl," which played an important role in sparking the first blaze of attention for the Beats and their message. Ginsberg wrote it in 1955 during a period of turmoil in his life, when depression over a psychiatric crisis of his friend Carl Solomon (to whom the work is dedicated) joined with long-term guilt feelings over his own authorization of a psychosurgical procedure for his mother. He wrote the first and lengthiest section of the poem in one sitting, breaking with his usual habit by composing it directly on a typewriter, instead of writing by hand. Encouraged to innovate by the conviction that this work was merely experimental and would never be published, he also left behind the short-line style he had recently been using, substituting a long-line format influenced by Walt Whitman and Christopher Smart, two favorite poets of the Beat writers.[18] In addition, he used a triadic ladder structure drawn from William Carlos Williams and an improvisatory expansiveness inspired by two sources: the spontaneous writing that Kerouac had been practicing, and luxurious saxophone lines that Ginsberg had been impressed by in jazz nightclubs. Other sections of the poem were written and revised in days and months to come, until the work as a whole was crafted exactly as Ginsberg wished (Schumacher 200–207).

While it is obviously informed by Ginsberg's personal state at the time when it was written, "Howl" also incorporates a forthright social and political critique. Indeed, a later (1982) comment by Ginsberg places "the right historical situation" first on his list of prerequisites for the composition of such a "spontaneous" outcry (Schumacher 207).[19] In this phrase he refers to his personal "history," of course, but also to the world political

situation, which he (like many of his peers) perceived as grim in the mid-
'50s. In view of the cold war, the Korean war, and nuclear escalation, notes
Michael Schumacher in his Ginsberg biography, "the idea of America's
feeding its children in sacrifice to a fire god was a frightening, realistic
image to the poet—thus, Moloch, the destroyer of the human spirit, the
black heart behind the collapse of civilization." This interpretation is supported by Ginsberg's own words in a 1954 letter to Kerouac, where he
wrote, "the possibility now after Indo China and Ike's admission that U.S.
contingency policy would be replaced by a weaker more limited policy of
cold war—are we losing? Is the Fall of America upon us? . . . So the possibility of a prophetic poem, using ideas of politics and war and calling on
love and reality for salvation . . . " (Schumacher 208–9). This is not to
claim that Ginsberg's idea of political poetry is conventional in the sense
of calling for a logic-based analysis of political problems; in a 1959 comment on politicians, he states that his poetry "is Angelical Ravings, & has
nothing to do with dull materialistic vagaries about who should shoot
who"[20] ("Notes for *Howl and Other Poems*" [Allen and Tallman 321]). Yet
it is certain that "Howl" has a distinct and deliberate relationship with the
national and international politics of its day.

The public unveiling of "Howl" in a celebrated 1955 reading at the
Six Gallery in San Francisco also took place in a clearly political context.
"We were locked in the Cold War and the first Asian debacle—the Korean
War," said the Beat-associated writer Michael McClure in a retrospective
comment on the reading. "We hated the war and the inhumanity and the
coldness. The country had the feeling of martial law. An undeclared military state had leapt out of Daddy Warbucks' tanks and sprawled over the
landscape. As artists we were oppressed and indeed the people of the nation were oppressed. . . . We knew we were poets and we had to speak out
as poets." Listening to Ginsberg's verse, the vocally moved listeners at
the Six Gallery knew "that a human voice and body had been hurled
against the harsh wall of America and its supporting armies and navies and
academies and institutions and ownership systems and power-support
bases" (Charters xxvii–xxviii). Again, this is hardly the stuff of "apathy"
and "conservatism," notwithstanding the charges leveled by some critics
against Beat priorities.

"Howl" took on an additional political function, moreover, when it
ran into censorship problems that were hardly unanticipated by Ginsberg
and his colleagues. "I am almost ready to tackle the U.S. Govt out of sheer
self delight," Ginsberg informed his father (Louis Ginsberg, himself a rec-

ognized poet) after learning that his prospective publisher, poet Lawrence Ferlinghetti, had consulted the American Civil Liberties Union about providing legal representation if the poem's British printers had difficulty getting it through United States customs. The second printing of *Howl and Other Poems* was indeed confiscated for alleged obscenity; the ACLU announced its intention to challenge the seizure; Ferlinghetti printed an offset edition of the book to establish a presence for it in the United States; and there ensued a long and tangled series of incidents that eventually culminated in victory for Ginsberg and his allies—a landmark event in an era when, as Schumacher notes, Elvis Presley's body movements were controversial; "sick" comedian Lenny Bruce was just gearing up for battle; books by Henry Miller and D. H. Lawrence still had to be smuggled into the United States; and Hefner was fighting obscenity charges over photographs of nude women (228, 252–59). Stating that the book was not obscene, the ruling by Judge W. J. Clayton Horn showed an awareness that it was not conventionally prurient and also a recognition that "Howl" had a political dimension, since a portion of it indicts "those elements in modern society destructive of the best qualities of human nature; such elements are predominantly identified as materialism, conformity, and mechanization leading toward war" (Miles 1989, 232). This political dimension was an explicit factor in the judge's finding that "Howl" was not "without redeeming social importance" and that the defendants in the trial should therefore be found not guilty.

Further Provocations

Although all of the core Beat writers, including Ginsberg, have produced works in which a specifically political dimension is muted or apparently absent, most have also produced works that are more openly politicized than "Howl" is. Such later Ginsberg poems as "Wichita Vortex Sutra" and "Pentagon Exorcism" have been cited in this regard by Schumacher, who asserts that the aspect of "Howl" most accurately foreshadowing Ginsberg's future activity as a political gadfly is simply the "prophetic voice" established in its first line. The suggestion is that other elements of the poem cannot be productively read as harbingers of the aggressive political stance that Ginsberg was to assume at a later time. But even if Ginsberg was not yet ready in 1955 to integrate headlines, news items, dates, and names into his poems—as he was to do in later works— Schumacher himself nonetheless acknowledges that the focus on individuals in "Howl" generates not only a personal but also a political statement, since Ginsberg implies that such individuals *en masse* add up to an oppressed society. This implication accords with Ginsberg's overall decision to position himself (as narrative voice of the poem) not "off to the side as an impartial observer" (Schumacher 209, 202) but squarely amid the oppressed individuals of whom he was writing. Sociopolitically as well as literarily, this was a bold gesture to make during the '50s period.

Other instances of social protest and political criticism by key Beat writers form a broad spectrum of explicit and implicit expression. At one point on this spectrum would be portions of Burroughs's novel *Junky*, characterized in 1959 by Beat critic Alan Ansen as a combination of narrative and lecture packed with "facts in season and out, medical, legal, anthropological," all portraying a flattened-out society that "is Riesman's lonely crowd with the factitious warmth of convention replaced by the real if forbidding warmth of—junk" (27–28). At another point on the spectrum would be Kerouac's performance at Hunter College in Manhattan during a 1958 panel discussion. Kerouac was a special case among the core Beats, since he had a self-absorbed political sense that harbored a streak of anticommunist, pro-"traditional values" patriotism; he grew more curmudgeonly in projecting this as he grew older and more alcoholic. Yet his views were so mercurial, and he flaunted them in so cavalier a fashion, that they bore stronger witness to his belief in ornery self-definition than to any cogent ideological agenda. In any case, when he was in top argumentative form, what emerged from his oratorical flights was a spontaneous and unfinalizable outrageousness that was radically liberating in form if not always in content. At the Hunter event, he eclipsed two of the speakers, novelist Kingsley Amis and anthropologist Ashley Montague; and he positively discombobulated newspaper editor James Wechsler, an old-line liberal, by aiming taunts at "big smart know-it-all Marxists and Freudians," by celebrating "the glee of America, the honesty of America," by accusing Wechsler of believing in "the destruction of America," by declaring, "I vote for love," and by doing all this in a manner that sociologist Todd Gitlin has described as drunken, rambling, "sliding saxophonically . . . across the registers," and peppered with Zen-inspired nonsense (55–56).

Provocations like these by Burroughs and Kerouac are eccentric in their means and personal in their motivations, driven largely by individual contingencies such as the former's drug dependence and the latter's religious preoccupations. Yet they have a keen sociopolitical edge, since they are directed toward society by members of that society who have been deeply and permanently alienated from it. Much of their disaffection is traceable to their observation of the society's pathological effects not only on themselves but also on countless others who suffer worse than they from its distortions. They wrote often about these victims, who range from Burroughs's helpless addicts to Kerouac's poverty-stricken "fella-heen," such as the heroine of his 1960 novel *Tristessa*. (Kerouac's conception of fellaheen draws on historian Oswald Spengler's description of peasant-class "masters of adaptation," who have the ability to exist *in* societies without being *of* them and therefore survive when civilizations fall.[21]) Although none of this fits into traditional activism as defined before or since the Beat moment, there is a seething activism at work within it. In keeping with the Rabelaisian spirit as described by Bakhtin, a basic goal of the Beats was "to destroy the official picture of events" so as to "break up official lies and the narrow seriousness dictated by the ruling classes," and to replace what their epoch "said and imagined about itself" with something closer to "its true meaning for the people." In this way they could aid the process of "breaking up false seriousness, false historic pathos," and prepare the ground for a new perception of social and historical fulfillment[22] (1984b, 439).

Hollywood and Social Consciousness

Few would use the word "activism" in describing the political attitudes of Hollywood film during the '50s period. Still, just as charges of "conservatism" and "apathy" prove porous at best and erroneous at worst when applied to the Beats, they are similarly inappropriate when applied too sweepingly to American cinema of the postwar years.

The general consensus regarding Hollywood films of this era is that they are a sociopolitically backward lot. Film historian David A. Cook offers a rationale for this opinion when he contrasts the years between 1952 and 1965 with the immediate post–World War II period. Soon after the war, his analysis asserts, the exhilaration of victory was succeeded by a disillusioned and cynical mood that was caused not only by the trauma of the war itself but also (and at least equally) by a changing self-image within the nation. Along with less powerful components of the United States propaganda apparatus, the Hollywood studios had worked during the war to create an impression of American society as richly democratic, allowing persons from widely differing social and ethnic groups to live as harmoniously together as the multiethnic units in many combat movies. Following the war, people found it harder to locate this ideal society in real life than in the film fantasies they had so recently accepted. Conversely, they found it all too easy (if they took the trouble of looking) to discover such real-world problems as social inequity, racial prejudice, business profiteering, government corruption, and lack of opportunity for returning soldiers. In addition, the frugalities of wartime filmmaking had increased Hollywood's dependence on individual directors and writers rather than the studio-coordinated teams of the prewar period, and some of these workers were themselves disturbed by the nation's current social situation as they perceived it (Cook 463–80).

Problem Pictures

As a result, expressions of social malaise soon started appearing on movie-theater screens. Among their basic types were the late-'40s "social-consciousness" or "problem" picture, such as Elia Kazan's 1947 *Gentleman's Agreement* and Mark Robson's 1949 *Home of the Brave*, dealing in a constructive way with such social problems as racism and political corruption; the semidocumentary melodrama with social overtones, such as Henry Hathaway's 1947 *Kiss of Death* and Jules Dassin's 1948 *The Naked City*, often based on real events and shot outside the studio; and the *film noir*, such as Billy Wilder's 1944 *Double Indemnity* and George Marshall's 1946 *The Blue Dahlia*, characterized by dark, sinister treatment of dark, sinister stories that reflected an unmistakable anxiety in the American mood.

Circumstances took a sharp turn, however, when Hollywood was confronted by the federal government's House Committee on Un-American Activities, which decided in 1947 to investigate "communism in motion pictures."[23] The sentencing of the so-called Hollywood Ten for refusing to testify before HUAC and the instituting of a soon-infamous studio blacklist against "communist" sympathizers are among the events that followed. Soon such a fearful atmosphere enveloped the Hollywood community that even slightly provocative narrative material was discouraged by a new emphasis on caution, conservatism, and propriety. Also generating worry in Hollywood was the challenge of competing with a new mass medium, television, and a fresh set of economic difficulties, most notably the forced divestiture by film companies of their exhibition facilities. Everything that characterized Hollywood film between 1952 and the mid-'60s, Cook sweepingly concludes, can be understood as a response to anticommunist hysteria and the blacklist or to the advent of television and divestiture. Since films conveying serious social commentary could not be made in an epoch of rampant anticommunism, sanitized genre entertainment (with an emphasis on visual spectacle to please newly independent theater bookers and give television a run for its money) reigned supreme.

There is a good deal of accuracy in this analysis, as far as it goes, and numerous historians take similar positions, although with different emphases and priorities. Hollywood's legal and commercial woes, Gerald Mast asserts, were accompanied by a postwar American mood swing that produced antagonism toward the motion-picture industry and a resulting stream of desperately inoffensive message films. Only those that came up with some special approach, such as a distinctive visual style or a translation of social problems into "human" problems, managed to achieve lasting resonance with audiences (277, 291). Even in films by the Hollywood Ten or such a non-Hollywood picture as Herbert Biberman's 1953 *Salt of the Earth*, writes Andrew Sarris, one finds a revealing trend whereby populist puerilities replace calls for social change, and such vague concepts as "the people" or "the folk" replace the precisely defined proletariat and peasantry, putting a severe dent in any sense of forthright political commitment that might otherwise make itself felt (1978, 9, 10–11). (One might respond by observing that *all* generalizing terms, "the proletariat" as well as "the folk," are monologic; as Bakhtin notes, speech aimed at replacing diversity with unity often uses such vague symbols as "the voice of the people" and "the spirit of a people" to create the impression of a single consciousness [1986, 163; 1984a, 82].) Robert Sklar states that the pervasive fears of the anticommunist era led the film industry to avoid projects that might give anger or offense to any vocal minority; he adds that Hollywood's ingrained visual and characterological artifices were too formulaic and stylized to mesh convincingly with complex social and psychological themes in the first place (267–68, 280). One analysis finds that in 1947, twenty-eight percent of films released in the United States could be described as oriented toward social problems and psychology; by 1954, only nine percent of American movies fell into this category (Bohn and Stromgren 233–34).

Signs of Progressivity

Despite the overall factual accuracy of such assessments, however, the notion of '50s-era Hollywood films as a homogeneous mass of ideological inhibition and sociopolitical blandness must—as the best of these and other historians realize—be resisted. Social commentary and criticism were brewing within many films of the period, and while much of this was implicit rather than explicit, it could be pointed and even forceful; and in some important movies it must have been perceptible to all but willfully self-blinded spectators. Mainstream films of the '50s were typical popular-culture works, of course, in that contemporaneous audiences generally saw their attitudes as natural, normal, and commonsensical. Yet some took skeptical, even antagonistic, attitudes toward prevailing values, partaking of views that seem unmistakably progressive, or at least unaccepting of the status quo in one or more of its shapes and forms.

As noted earlier, mainstream American film certainly did not offer as emphatic a challenge to dominant values as the Beat writers did. One reason is that the provocations of the Beats continued to operate in a covert or insinuated manner (through idiosyncrasies of belief, behavior, and the negative dialectics of "dropping out" and embracing subaltern living patterns) even when their most prominent cultural productions appeared to have an apolitical or even antipolitical cast. Hollywood did not manifest any such pattern of purposeful eccentricity. Still, a significant subset of '50s Hollywood production contains an openly and at times defiantly questioning attitude toward the hegemonic milieu. This is ironic, since Hollywood was itself an important constituent of that milieu, wherein (to employ catchphrases of the time that remain suggestive today) a consensus bred by power elites and hidden persuaders strained to exert its influence over lonely crowds of organization men and their relentlessly normalized households.

Sirk and the Beats

If the '50s *oeuvre* of any one Hollywood director can be singled out as a particularly concentrated focal point for the interrogation of sociocultural values, a strong case can be made for that of Douglas Sirk, whose films during this period reflect a conscious commitment to social awareness and cultural criticism. After spending his early life in Germany and Denmark, he began his career as a painter, writer, and stage director before turning to cinema, working at Germany's renowned UFA studio, moving to France and the Netherlands in the late '30s, and eventually staying for many years in Hollywood, where his activities included an enormously productive sojourn at the Universal International studio throughout the '50s. His films of this period are not just deliberately symptomatic reflections of American sociocultural life but are actively critical in their attitudes and approaches, especially in the towering melodramas that he made with producers Ross Hunter and (in a single but exceptionally vivid case) Albert Zugsmith.

An aspect of Sirk's social criticism that has not been noted previously is its congruence with aspects of the Beat project, as articulated and practiced by Kerouac and Ginsberg in particular. This congruence is borne out by observations that some commentators and Sirk himself have made in describing his most incisive dissections of American life. Sirk is an "artist of impossible America," whose most imposing characters "are trying to escape into the air, into bars, into churches," states critic Jon Halliday in phrases with a strikingly Kerouacian ring; he also observes that Sirk provides a "counterpoint to the condition of America" in some of his films located outside the American scene. Similar points can be made with regard to works (especially early ones) in the Kerouac and Ginsberg canons, with the proviso that while Sirk tends to situate his alternative visions outside the contemporary United States, the Beats tend to seek theirs via geographical and psychological journeying within the boundaries of the American landscape. Halliday remarks that the 1953 western *Taza, Son of Cochise* and the 1957 war drama *A Time to Love and a Time to Die* possess a "sense of space and love and feeling quite distinct from the obsessive and frequently sick attachments" of the 1953 melodrama *Magnificent Obsession* and the 1956 melodrama *Written on the Wind* (10–12); this statement identifies in Sirk's cinema of the '50s a surprisingly close parallel with the difference between (a) such early Kerouac works as *On the Road* and *The Dharma Bums*, which are charged with a powerful enthusiasm for space, love, and emotion for their own sakes, and (b) such later Kerouac works as *Desolation Angels* and *Big Sur*, which are marked by sundry forms of anguish and torment.[24] Faced with the oppressive sociocultural realities of their time and with the psychodynamic contingencies bred by their encounters with those realities, the Beats and their surrogate characters often tended to replace involvements in movement, love, and feeling with psychic and physical attachments not free of obsessive and otherwise disturbed qualities; and they often sought refuge precisely in the air

of free-form travel, in bars where alcohol and drugs induced a complicated mixture of narcotized anesthesia and galvanic stimulation, and in
the "churches" of an idiosyncratic and Eastern-influenced religious urge
that hinted at respite from otherwise insupportable burdens of mind and
spirit. Not many Beats would spontaneously remind a disinterested observer of a Sirk character in a Sirkian framework; yet more than one Beat
figure (whether author or literary surrogate) has a good deal in common
with the personality or career of some Sirkian counterpart, be this a barn-
storming flyer in *The Tarnished Angels*, a sad alcoholic in *Written on the
Wind*, or a religious wanderer in *Magnificent Obsession*, among other possibilities. Indeed, the air and the bars and the churches were as central to
the midcentury American experience as were the movies themselves. It is
not surprising to find artists as outwardly different as Sirk and the Beat
writers making contact with all these discursive arenas in their own distinctive manners.

Sirk's affection for an ideal America of his own imagining—which
grew out of youthful reading and contemplation, and lingered in his mind
for much of his life—also has strong similarities to feelings expressed by
the Beats, especially Kerouac, in important works. In an interview dealing
with his 1955 melodrama *All That Heaven Allows*, for instance, Sirk says
the film is concerned with "the antithesis of Thoreau's qualified Rous-
seauism and established American society," and also (like his 1952 drama
Take Me to Town) with "the American ideal of the simple, outdoor life."
Adding authors Ralph Waldo Emerson and Willa Cather to Henry David
Thoreau as influences on his thinking, the filmmaker praises Cather's
novel *My Ántonia* for incorporating "circularity; the hero comes back to
the place where he started out from," and then he reminisces about the
American landscape by musing that he himself "sometimes still would
love to be back in the West. In Oregon, with its dark greens. In the desert,
with its yellow light. . . . It's wonderful up in the North-West, sheltering
woods, open country. Old farms. Oldness . . . " (Halliday 99–101). There
are clear resonances here with Kerouac's love of circularity in fiction—a
phrase in one of his poems, "your goal / is your starting place" (113),[25]
relates to the overall structure of his novelistic *oeuvre*—and Sirk's short-
hand description of beloved American sites could have been borrowed
from a Kerouac notebook.

While many artists have expressed similar sentiments about an ideal
America, the concord between Sirk's visions and those of Kerouac and
Ginsberg is rooted in strongly held tastes shared by the European-bred

filmmaker and the American-bred writers. For example, Sirk has said that "heaven knows I'm an admirer of Melville, the greatest in American literature, I think" (Halliday 97). Kerouac admired Melville with similar enthusiasm; biographer Gerald Nicosia uses such phrases as "brash, obsessed brilliance" and "zingy wit" (412, 406) to describe traits of Melvillian prose that Kerouac admired and tried (not always successfully) to emulate at one time or another. Ginsberg considered a "Hebraic-Melvillian bardic strain" (Morgan 288) to be a key element in his own literary heritage. Beyond this, Ginsberg considered Melville's work to be part of an "evolution of human consciousness" in which Edgar Allan Poe, Emily Dickinson, Whitman, Hart Crane, and ultimately the Beats themselves each played necessary roles (Schumacher 333).

Looking at such matters in a broad perspective, John Tytell finds the spiritual ancestors of the Beats to be such figures as Thoreau, with his "aggressive idealism, his essentially conservative distrust of machines and industry, his desire to return to the origins of man's relations to the land"; Melville, with his "adventurous tolerance of different tribal codes"; and Whitman, "optimistically proclaiming with egalitarian gusto the raw newness and velocity of self-renewing change in America while joyously admiring the potential of the common man" (4). This catalogue of artists and enthusiasms has a Sirkian ring. It should be added that the Beats' rejection of social convention and propriety and their general sympathy for underdogs, outcasts, and scoundrels—which was largely responsible for their choice of the self-descriptive adjective "Beat" in the first place—is also echoed in Sirk, as in *Written on the Wind*, where, as Rainer Werner Fassbinder has observed, "the good, the 'normal,' the 'beautiful' are always utterly revolting; the evil, the weak, the dissolute arouse one's compassion. Even for the manipulators of the good" (23). Again the correspondence between Beat and Sirkian attitudes is not difficult to detect.

The Cinema of Skepticism

While the Sirk melodramas of the '50s are unusual in their specific affinities with facets of the Beat sensibility, this body of films is only one of numerous candidates that could be used to illustrate the sociocultural awareness and commentary that run through some mainstream American cinema of the period. Other films of different types can be cited, as well as critical assessments that demonstrate how the films have been received as social and political statements. To select a few such movies and assessments as examples is not to compile an arbitrary list of random instances, on one hand, or to suggest a tentative canon, on the other; it is simply to indicate the range, variety, and resonance that were sustained in a consensus-bound age by what might be called the cinema of skepticism.

An appropriate starting point is *Force of Evil*, directed by Abraham Polonsky in 1948, three years before he was placed on the Hollywood blacklist for being an "uncooperative" HUAC witness. The movie is based on an Ira Wolfert novel called *Tucker's People*, which Polonsky has called an "autopsy on capitalism." The filmmaker took an unsympathetic view of the American consensus about free enterprise when he adapted this book into a dark-toned, persistently skeptical movie. Its main character is a lawyer (played by John Garfield, an actor with left-wing connections during a substantial portion of his career) whose lack of social vision leads him to get involved with a scheme for consolidating small-time New York criminal operations into a single conglomerate that can be run as an ordinary business. There is also a subplot involving the protagonist's brother, carrying the film's social despair into the area of family relations as well. The story has been noted for its virtual eradication of difference between crime, business, and law enforcement as morally and legally distinct enterprises, and for its conveyance of what critic Danny Peary calls an "ugly, cynical view" (158) of capitalist society.[26] The film ends with an expression of outrage at how contemporary American society can harbor flourishing fields of morally and ethically bankrupt activity, wherein a human being can be discarded as readily and irretrievably as a piece of trash or garbage.

Similarly aggressive in its sociocritical stance is Robert Aldrich's 1955 detective thriller *Kiss Me Deadly*. Loosely adapted from Mickey Spillane's novel, it treats Spillane's protagonist (Mike Hammer, played by Ralph Meeker) as more a sadistic thug than a hard-boiled hero, and culminates in an atomic explosion that sets loose all the ill-contained paranoia lurking within '50s political notions about peaceful and protective uses of nuclear energy. Referring to the film's transformation of a popular private eye into a perverse and complex figure—within a story that traces '50s-era corruption to debased cold-war politics—Sarris recognizes the political significance of Aldrich's decision to make Spillane's "right-wing hero" an unglamorous "transom-peering opportunist" (Roud 23). Ed Lowry similarly observes that Hammer's individuality, a trait normally celebrated in consensus-formed American films, is "revealed as insanity" in Aldrich's drama (Lyon 1986, 9).[27] Aldrich confirmed the political dimension of *Kiss Me Deadly* when he stated in a late-'60s interview that the film's "importance" becomes apparent when it is "juxtaposed against a particular political background," this being "those McCarthy times" of the early '50s (Higham and Greenberg 28).[28]

Other relevant films include a number of Nicholas Ray's works, including his 1955 youth drama *Rebel Without a Cause*—a paradigmatic film with obvious links to the Beat sensibility—and his 1954 western *Johnny Guitar*, written by Philip Yordan; dealing with the plight of a lonely man (Sterling Hayden) and two feuding women (Joan Crawford and Mercedes McCambridge) in a volatile Old West community, the latter has been described by critic Jeanine Basinger as a metaphorical view of the McCarthy era from the viewpoint of those who were persecuted by it (Lyon 1985, 226). A different sort of example is Alexander MacKendrick's 1957 melodrama *The Sweet Smell of Success*, written by Clifford Odets (who had strong leftist credentials) and focusing on the corrupt, corrupting practices of press agentry and manipulation of public opinion.[29] There is obvious social skepticism in *The Big Heat*, directed in 1953 by Fritz Lang, with a hero who must leave the police force and its official sanctions in order to continue his pursuit of a publicly influential criminal. Also socially critical are such John Ford films as the 1962 western *The Man Who Shot Liberty Valance*, which exposes the social hypocrisy of a lawyer whose ideals are not matched by his accomplishments in attempting to civilize life on the frontier, and the 1964 historical epic *Cheyenne Autumn*, which treats the oppression of a Native American community with a sympathy not found in traditional westerns. Orson Welles attacked various forms of corruption in such works as the 1958 police melodrama *Touch of Evil* and the dizzying 1962 *Citizen Kane* redux called *Mr. Arkadin* (known as *Confidential Report* in Great Britain). Howard Hawks satirized American materialism in such deceptively diverting works as the 1953 musical *Gentlemen Prefer Blondes* and the 1964 comedy *Man's Favorite Sport?* Frank Tashlin made satiric use of hipster-type figures—in a more innovative and socially portentous form, the hipster model helped shape the early Beat mentality—in such comedies as *The Girl Can't Help It* (1956) and *Will Success Spoil Rock Hunter?* (1957).

Obstreperous Spirit

In some instances, whole bodies of cinematic work plugged into a current of dissatisfaction, or disillusionment, or even paranoia regarding the sociocultural status quo. There was nothing passive or apathetic about the emergence of the *film noir* cycle in the '40s, for example, or what some observers regard as its culmination in the early '50s. "After ten years of steadily shedding romantic conventions," writes *noir* critic Paul Schrader, "the later noir films finally got down to the root causes of the period: the loss of public honor, heroic conventions, personal integrity, and, finally, psychic stability." The arrival of these films in the '50s was not an accident of haphazard aesthetic evolution, but represented the socially generated emergence of a self-aware variety of cinema that seemed to recognize its culminating position within an extraordinarily dark-toned film tradition.

Schrader goes on to echo the conventional view that American films after the early '50s were tame and timid compared with their predecessors in the '40s, citing the rise of McCarthy and Eisenhower as evidence that Americans were eager to see themselves in more bourgeois-suburban terms, complete with movies showing criminals in gray flannel suits, "flatfoot" patrol officers replaced by mobile units on expressways, and social criticism disguised by upbeat affirmations of the American way. Once again, however, the attempt to characterize American films of the '50s as uniformly conservative or even reactionary oversimplifies the situation by overstressing the ubiquity of consensus-dominated values. Some films by the very directors whom Schrader cites as exemplars of the middle-and-late-'50s school of post-*noir* crime drama demonstrate a continued (and very *noir*ish) sociocultural skepticism, and Schrader seems oddly unaware of this when he terminates the obstreperous spirit of the *noir* cycle (allowing for certain exceptions, including *Kiss Me Deadly*) in 1953. Examples include the suspicious attitudes toward protocols of crime and punishment in Donald Siegel's *Riot in Cell Block 11* (1954) and *The Line-Up* (1958); the pervasive morbidity in Richard Fleischer's *Violent Saturday* (1955) and *Compulsion* (1959); the feral energy of Phil Karlson's *The Phenix City Story* (1955) and *The Brothers Rico* (1957); and the violent expressivity of Samuel Fuller's *Pickup on South Street* (1953; called by Schrader a transitional film blending "the black look with the red scare") and *Underworld U.S.A.* (1961). All these works, and numerous others by different filmmakers, demonstrate that early-'50s *noir* was less of an endgame than Schrader claims and that the entry into a new, weaker crime-movie era was less definitive and permanent than his analysis suggests. In the '50s as in the preceding decade, *film noir* remained a paradoxically caustic arena of mainstream cinema wherein a broad array of characters, filmmakers, and audiences could "encourage the psychopath in oneself" just as Mailer had suggested the urban hipster must do in real-life experience (223–25).

Politics, Paranoia, and Science Fiction

Furthermore, another cycle (in this case a long-established genre ready to take on a newly relevant set of socioaesthetic meanings) was on hand to pick up whatever momentum *noir* had relinquished: science fiction, which entered an extraordinary new phase at this time. It has been widely remarked that science-fiction movies of the '50s bear a close relationship with the period's overall social and political milieu, reflecting apprehension over the cold war and also nervousness about new developments in science and technology (especially the nuclear variety) whose possibilities and implications were little understood by the public—or, some members of that public suspected, by the "experts" who claimed such understanding was their exclusive possession. Movies obsessed with invasion, infiltration, subversion, and subjugation via exotic technological devices in the hands of "aliens" became a staple of the science-fiction screen.

Noël Carroll correctly notes that early-'30s monster films (e.g., *Frankenstein*, *Dracula*, *King Kong*) often admit a sympathy for the monster that reflects (among other things) a poignant response to the Depression-era fear of finding oneself outside the boundaries of ordinary society. By contrast, monster movies of the '50s (featuring giant insects, bug-eyed space creatures, etc.) allow no such sympathy for creatures who are really unsubtle symbols of the "international communist conspiracy," seen as lacking normal human emotions and perpetually conniving at world conquest. Such films often imbue their villains with "collectivist and anti-individualist" leanings, and pit Marxist-style intellectuality against Yankee-style feeling in contests of inhumanity versus its decent, right-thinking opposite (208–9). Bearing out this analysis, evidence of a paranoid cold-war discourse in '50s science-fiction films is everywhere to be found, from basic thematic concerns to the frequent use of newsreel footage depicting real events and even the titles emblazoned on theater marquees; note, for example, that George Waggner's 1941 *Man-Made Monster* was reissued in 1953 as *The Atomic Monster* (Lucanio 150–51).

As if to ratify the atomic-paranoia aspects of this trend, moreover, the Japanese film industry turned out a large number of science-fiction pictures during the '50s (and continuing well past that decade) in which atomic accidents and nuclear radiation play a crucial role. From the sensationally popular *Godzilla, King of Monsters* (1954) to *Rodan* (1957), *Mothra* (1962), and beyond, this cycle was enormously successful in its native country, where a keen and immediate sense of nuclear anxiety would seem altogether appropriate, given the horrors recently visited on two of its cities by the United States in what remains the only wartime use of atomic weaponry. The cycle was received with similar enthusiasm in the United States itself, where the presence of second- and third-rank American performers (such as Raymond Burr and Russ Tamblyn) surely played less of a role in drawing audiences than did the resonance of the films' atomic-age tropes, at once extravagantly fearful and—rendering the impact of their violence acceptable, assimilable, and pleasurable—extravagantly fanciful.

A Failure to Affirm

In this genre as in the late-phase *film noir* cycle, the melodramas of Sirk, the psychodramas of Ray, and (some) other areas of Hollywood cinema, social unease found expression in movies that gained wide and eager audiences despite a deliberate failure to affirm the supposed consensus that all was safe, sound, and secure in a nation made strong by conformity and conservatism. Much the same went on in other artistic fields, where painters (e.g., Pollock) moved from representation of an agreed-upon repertoire of subjects to new extremes in abstraction and expressionism; jazz musicians (e.g., Parker) shifted from the audience-tested safety of big bands playing from prefabricated "charts" to a fresh emphasis on small-combo improvisation and idiosyncratic individualism; certain theatrical troupes (e.g., the Living Theatre) broke down the division between art (constructed commodity) and audience (passive consumer) traditionally signified by the proscenium arch; and the Beat writers pioneered a new kind of literature marked by an anguished individualism whose oppressions and frustrations were seen as byproducts of the culture at which its analyses and outcries were aimed.

Of the two socially revealing film cycles discussed above, '50s *noir* and science fiction, *noir* carries more similarities with the Beat project, since *noir* most successfully evades, or at least modifies, the monologizing tendencies of postwar hegemonic forces. The reason is that style and politics are ultimately inseparable, and *noir* reacts against the uniformity of consensus-bred values not only in its social vision (depicting a cold, dangerous

urban world) and choice of subject matter (charged with danger, duplic-
ity, betrayal) but also in its stylistic approach: dark in tone, fragmented in
structure, labyrinthine in plot, and often assuming a complex and unconventional orientation in space (unexpected cuts and camera angles) and
time (narrative lines with frequent flashbacks and complicated chrono-
topes).

These traits accord with nontraditional and nonlinear stylistic practices used by all the core Beat writers, notably in such Kerouac works as
Doctor Sax and *Visions of Cody* and such Burroughs fictions as *Naked Lunch*
and *The Ticket That Exploded*. The emergence of such mutually reflective stylistics in realms as different as mass-audience cinema and avant-
garde literature is plainly not accidental. Rather, it points to the presence
of discursive tendencies quite opposed to (or at least nonsupportive of)
the monologizing forces produced and reinforced by promoters of consensus and conformity. From its inception as a more or less discrete style in
Citizen Kane (1941), the *noir* approach ranks with the most dialogically
inclined varieties of American cinema, building nontraditional chrono-
topes that incorporate tones, tropes, spatial configurations, and temporal
convolutions that are significantly more diverse, multivalent, and prone to
"loopholes" than are the diegetic compounds normally encouraged by
classical Hollywood style. Many of Burroughs's works are particularly
congruent with *film noir*, portraying (along with other ingredients woven
into multilayered patterns) a *noir*-like world of personal intrigue, urban
harshness, and societal-political violence. Some of his early writing is directly influenced by detective fiction of the sort that influenced many *noir*
screenplays; his 1985 introduction to his early-'50s novel *Queer* acknowledges this when it describes protagonist William Lee in *noir*-like terms as
"disintegrated, desperately in need of contact, completely unsure of himself and of his purpose," and when it remarks of the narrative itself, "that
hallucinated month . . . takes on a hellish glow of menace and evil drifting
out of neon-lit cocktail bars, the ugly violence, the .45 always just under
the surface" (xii). Later works mix similar elements with additional materials, many of them also influenced by popular-literature genres such as spy
fiction and, especially, science fiction.

Burroughs's science fiction tends to be vastly dissimilar from mainstream science fiction of the '50s, however, and this fact also reveals much
about the period's sociocultural dynamics. Science-fiction films of the '50s
(like most science-fiction films of other periods and many films in the related horror genre) are fundamentally monologic in form, texture, and

content. Conventions tend to be rigid, characters tend to be stereotypical, and plots tend to operate within a limited sphere determined by a limited number of common themes and variations. This description is confirmed by science-fiction critic Patrick Lucanio's observation that most '50s alien-invasion films are constructed as classical texts in which characterization is dominated by calculated, cause-and-effect progressions centering on a hero who employs not intuition but methodical evaluation, who acts thoughtfully rather than impulsively, and who finds solutions grounded in logic and reason. All this happens within scenarios that are structured in a sensible, cause-and-effect manner, visualized in a mise-en-scène that reflects the real historical world. Even the most frequently encountered deviation from this set of generic patterns, labeled "the Prometheus variation" by Lucanio, follows a similarly predictable group of norms; its hero, for instance, tends to be ordinary, moral, hardworking, and pragmatic. Nor can we see the classical science-fiction text and the Prometheus variation as dialogically (or even dialectically) intersecting voices. Like the twin thematic aspects of '50s science fiction—hope and aspiration on one hand, death and destruction on the other—the basic text-types are "complementary opposites that make for a sturdy balance," as Lucanio states it (22–23, 53); in Bakhtinian terms, they operate in the synchronized harmony of monologism rather than the many-voiced polyphony of dialogism. Other accounts of science-fiction film also recognize signs of monologism at work. John Baxter, for instance, observes that science-fiction movies resemble horror movies with their "largely interchangable [*sic*] stories, distinguishable from one another only by subtle differences in visual style and approach" (10–11), and Penelope Houston comments that in science-fiction films of the early '50s "[h]uman agency now counts for little, and the rocket, the atomic weapon, the electronic gadget, the cybernetic brain machine—expressions of science considered almost as an abstraction—have taken charge" (Baxter 8).[30]

These descriptions bear out science fiction's role in reflecting and reinforcing a discourse of logic, reason, and linearity as the basis for a self-constructing and self-justifying Rational Society wherein assertions of authority rest on claims of indisputable, commonsensical truth. Contrasting with this orthodoxy are Burroughs's fictions, which are not always science fictions but often draw wholly or partly on discourses taken (often with savage sarcasm and sardonic disdain) from science-inspired fantasies. These may involve war between the Nova Police and galactic villains called the Nova Mob; time traveling and instantaneous physical transformations;

squishy monsters and interplanetary addictions; and figures like the "Controller of the Crab Nebula on a slag heap of smouldering metal under the white hot sky [channeling] all his pain into control thinking" (1980, 67). Or they may conjure up any number of other characters, scenarios, and ideas woven into a richly dialogic concatenation of fantasy, speculation, and myth that is not so much interwoven in a coherent tapestry as swirled around a spinning centrifuge, disrupting the possibility of monologism through its fragmented form as well as its outrageous content. It is no wonder that the consensus-dominated society that tolerated the politely fantastic visions of Hollywood science fiction took not only umbrage but also legal and police action against the dark-hued dialogism and uproariously subversive carnivalism that characterize Burroughs's hallucinatory view of the stifled present, the electrifying future, and the human body inscribed with the murky results of its own bad-cop tendencies toward spiritual and technological self-mutilation.

Beats, Films, and Liminality

Has there been a revolutionary transformation that wasn't made by a crazy, visionary affirmation of what was not there? The bigger the change, the crazier the vision, the more reckless the faith.
—Joel Kovel, "Cryptic Notes on Revolution and the Spirit"

Limning Behavior in Play and Culture

■ Public performances involve elements of ritual, play, and presentation of self to others. They also involve what theorist Richard Schechner calls the main characteristic of performance: restored behavior, defined as living behavior treated the way a film director treats a strip of film. If all goes right during a performance, Schechner asserts, "the experience is of synchronicity as the flow of ordinary time and the flow of performance time meet and eclipse each other. This eclipse is the 'present moment,' the synchronic ecstasy, the autotelic flow, of liminal stasis." Experts at reaching this balance include shamans, con operators, acrobats, and artists—one thinks of Kerouac spontaneously typing, or Brakhage dancing with his camera—but nobody can keep it long (112–13).

The so-called behavior strips of performance activity can be manipulated in any number of ways. Since the behavior and the person are separate, the former can be variously stored, transmitted, reworked, and transformed as the latter contacts, recovers, remembers, or invents the strips and then rebehaves according to them. Persons behaving tend either to merge with the behavior strips, as in Stanislavskian acting, trance activity, and the highly intuitive shooting of some avant-garde filmmakers; or to exist alongside them, as in Brechtian theatrics and the comparatively distanced activity of a Burroughs carving a printed text with a pair of scissors.

Central to restored behavior is the idea that the self can act "in" or "as" another self, since the social or transindividual self is fundamentally a role or a set of roles. Stated in personal terms, restored behavior is the individual behaving "as if I were someone else," or "as if I were beside myself," or "as if I were not myself." The someone else may also be "me in another state of feeling or being," as if there were more than one "me" in each person—which in fact there is, according to psychoanalytic thought. Effective performances thus share a "not me-not not me" quality and an awareness of behavioral territory that exists between established identities. In this sense, Schechner writes, "performing is a paradigm of liminality. And what is liminality but literally the 'threshold,' the space that both separates and joins spaces: the essence of in-betweenness?" (35–37, 113, 295).

Kick in the Eye

Phenomena associated with restored behavior are found not only in public performance but also in other activities linked to ritual, play, and self-presentation. Filmmaking is one of these. Cultural anthropologist Victor Turner recognizes this fact when he likens cinema to ritual, noting the large amount of time and organization that are necessary for its complicated network of significations to take shape. At the end of this process, the original ideas and screenplay of a film have been absorbed into a multigenred, multicoded, collectively orchestrated product representing a distillation of all the processes that have acted upon the starting material. For the filmmaker, Turner suggests, the achievement of "creative 'flash' or *satori*" is realized through the plural reflexivity of the artistic process, whereby the energies of the participants are channeled into a work of "public liminality and social creativeness" (31–32). Such a work is at once the product of behavior and the representation of behavior-once-removed, hence its ready association with threshold or "not me-not not me" experience.

Bakhtin sheds further light on this expressive mode when he discusses "dialogue on the threshold," a literary genre with a "tendency to create the *extraordinary* situation, one which would cleanse the word of all of life's automatism and object-ness, which would force a person to reveal the deepest layers of his personality and thought" (1984a, 111).[1] Here again, the threshold is associated with expressive possibilities that emerge under in-between or transitional circumstances. Liminality and *satori*, then, are states of consciousness and behavior accessible not only to those who visibly present themselves as performers but also to all who engage with the ambivalence and in-betweenness of threshold or "not-not not" experience. Included may be makers of literary works, such as the Beat writers; makers of entertainment or "art" films, such as Federico Fellini, whom Turner cites; and makers of "poetic" or "personal" films. The latter works, produced on an artisanal rather than an industrial scale, may escape mass-market economic imperatives and thereby retain a playfulness and intimacy that enhance their qualities of ritual, reflexivity, and liminality—making them possible roadways toward active attainment, or at least intuitive awareness, of the *satori* of which Turner speaks. Kerouac defines *satori* as "the Japanese word for 'sudden illumination,' 'sudden awakening' or simply 'kick in the eye'" (1988, 7).

Expressive Eccentricity

In a culture where hegemony seeks justification through appeals to reason, rationality, and authority, threshold experience and liminality become highly charged areas because of the relativism, allusiveness, and elusiveness that they place in opposition to officially sanctioned discourses. Individuals who contested dominant values in the '50s, such as Beat writers and avant-garde filmmakers, often staked out their liminal positions in ways that were highly visible and conspicuously performative, making anticonformist statements not only through the content of their work but also through the cultivation of eccentric habits and the development of artistic modes that inverted "proper" styles, subjects, and articulations.

By contrast, dominant strains within the literary establishment and the Hollywood cinema tended to position themselves as guardians of reasonable discourse and common-sense ideas, protecting the status quo through "classical" norms derived from decades of direct experience with "popular entertainment" and centuries of inherited wisdom regarding "human nature." The postwar opposition between Beat-experimental sensibilities and mainstream-conservative sensibilities was marked by profound disagreement over relativism, ambiguity, and liminality as factors that are productive and liberating—or, contrarily, destructive and obfuscating—in human experience. Hence, the interaction between mainstream and Beat-influenced culture may be illuminated by looking at their respective treatments of sociocultural topics connected with liminal or threshold areas of experience, such as creativity, altered states of consciousness, and marginal behaviors. First, however, it will be worthwhile to trace the origins of liminal experience in psychoanalytic terms—not as a digression but as a useful way of approaching Beat-related thought through its roots in early childhood experience—and to note important links between liminality and play, an indispensable component of the carnivalism that is such an important part of the Beat and avant-garde sensibilities.

Transitional Objects, Transitional Phenomena, Paradox

Psychoanalytic theorist D. W. Winnicott attributes great importance to "transitional objects" and "transitional phenomena" in early childhood development. Transitional objects—for example, a piece of cloth or blanket—are those discovered and used by the infant as a defense against anxiety. Transitional phenomena include such behaviors as holding an object in the mouth, babbling, or making musical sounds.

These objects and phenomena are transitional since they constitute the infant's first "not-me" possessions and experiences. Ultimately they lose meaning as they are diffused over the intermediate territory between "inner" psychic reality and "outer" material reality—that is, over the field of cultural activity. This leads to the emergence of such experiences as play, dreaming, fetishism, and mendacity, representing both positive and negative possibilities (3–5).[2] Among the most vital is artistic creativity, which (notably in the free-associative forms often favored by Beats and avant-gardists) draws on intuitive links with experiences long relinquished as accessible memories.

The concept of an intermediate area between subjectivity and objectivity can be used to give a psychic "location" to play and cultural experience. This intermediate area provides most of the infant's experience, and a connection with it is retained throughout life in the intense perceptions linked with art, religion, and creative work. Since the intermediate area is rich in paradoxical forces, rapport with it is facilitated by a willingness to accept paradox (14). Again one finds clear connections with the Beat and avant-garde sensibilities, which have often made strong investments in the value of paradox. Examples range from the ludic juxtapositions of Surrealist and Dadaist work to the Beat and experimental-film fascination with indeterminate states—between conscious and unconscious (e.g., Kerouac's *Book of Dreams*, Brakhage's hypnagogic visions), mind and body (e.g., Ginsberg's bodily inflected poetry, Jacobs's performance-based movies), and sense and nonsense (e.g., Burroughs's cut-up texts, Conner's discombobulations of found footage).

There is much playfulness (although a *purposeful* playfulness) in many of these works, confirming that play marks an important link between intermediate experience in infancy and cultural activity in later life. Play and culture both originate in the potential space between "me-extensions and the not-me." This is an outgrowth of early experience between parent and child—in a "hypothetical area that exists (but cannot exist) between the baby and the object (mother or part of mother) during the phase of the repudiation of the object as not-me, that is, at the end of being merged in with the object" (53, 100, 102, 107–8).

Winnicott not only recognizes but also positively embraces the paradoxical implications of a hypothetical area that both exists and cannot exist; and he relates these to the equally paradoxical notion of a transitional object serving as an instrument of conjuncture and separation at the same time. It is the baby's growing confidence in the parent, and therefore in the dependability of other persons and things, that makes possible a separation of the not-me from the me. Yet simultaneously, "it can be said that separation is avoided by the filling in of the potential space with creative playing, with the use of symbols, and with all that eventually adds up to a cultural life." The links between conception-subjectivity and perception-objectivity, between separation and denial-of-separation, between the existence and nonexistence of a hypothetical space in which these mutually negating operations are both conjoined and kept apart—all these come together in a paradox that calls for acceptance rather than resolution (109, 151).

In its ready accommodation of paradox and ambiguity, this theoretical position (like the art that it helps to explain) acquires the rich ambivalence and in-betweenness of play itself. And it suggests—in the fecundity of its very irresolution—the profound limitations of a sociocultural stance (such as that of mainstream America in the '50s) that attempts to justify claims of authority by appealing to the absolutes of an ideal rationality.

*P*lay and Carnival

Turner likewise sees play as a "liminal or liminoid mode." Echoes of Bakhtinian carnivalism abound in his observation that play "makes fun of people, things, ideas, ideologies, institutions, and structures; it is partly a mocker as well as a mimic and a tease" and a "reflexive interrupter" (168).[3] Leaning toward the volatile, explosive, and subversive, play is anything but monologic or authoritarian, hence the determination of cultural institutions to contain it. In its very craziness, it reveals "the possibility of changing our goals and, therefore, the restructuring of what our culture states to be reality" (167–68).

Turner and Bakhtin clearly share a fascination with carnivalistic experience as a route to liminality, liberation, and enjoyment of the potential space between me-extensions and the not-me. Outside the realm of liminality one encounters what Turner calls *societas*, the social entity marked as structured, organized, compartmentalized, and hierarchical. Liminality gives access to the opposite of this: *communitas*, a domain of unfettered possibility and undifferentiated, ecstatic one-ness among those who share it. Here one senses the boundlessness and unfinalizability associated with states of meditation, prayer, intoxication, the (hypnagogic) threshold between wakefulness and sleep, sexual passion, and other situations in which self-identity loses its customary supports (Schwartz-Salant and Stein 41).[4] These states are manifested not only in firsthand liminal experience but also in artworks partaking of liminality, from movies with closed-eye imagery to writing intoxicated with the ecstasies of transcendent revelation or flamboyant sexuality. In complex modern societies, as sociologist Bernice Martin notes, "the functional equivalent of liminality is above all the arts. Once literacy and a rich vocabulary of visual, aural and dramatic expressions exist, then society has a permanently available, 'liminoid' resource in which all the tabooed, fantastic, possible and impossible dreams of humanity can be explored in blueprint" (51).

Beat Writing as Liminoid Performance

All the core Beat writers were deeply interested in exploring tabooed and fantastic material and their own possible and impossible dreams; and all pursued this quest by cultivating liminality in such forms as play, ritual, self-observation, and restored-behavior activity.

By synthesizing characteristics of the autobiographical protagonists in works by major Beat authors, including Kerouac's Jack Duluoz, Burroughs's William Lee, and Ginsberg's angelheaded hipsters, Gregory Stephenson has constructed a composite Beat hero. The typical exploits of this hero involve estrangement from society, sufferance of a psychic wound, embarkation on a quest involving transgression and visions, confrontation with personal demons and disintegration of the self, and an epiphany that results in transformed consciousness and a return to the world. Stephenson appears to be describing a liminal experience when he states that psychic transformation and the movement from a Beat state to a beatific state have "significant affinities both with the rites of individual initiation as practiced in tribal societies and with the shamanistic enactment of redemptive rites for the tribe as a whole and for the world" (178).[5] Yet the profoundly personal nature of the Beat myth suggests that Turner's distinction between the liminal and the liminoid—the former being collective in nature, the latter more pluralistic and experimental—has particular relevance in this context. As practiced by the Beats and their reflexive protagonists, the quest for psychic transformation is not an organized or even semiorganized activity, as it would become in the '60s-Hippie counterculture presided over by gurus, pop stars, and leaders versed in the manipulation of mass media. Rather, it is an inwardly focused journey, during which persons test private knowledges "by redefining popular notions of sanity and extending the borders of social prudence" (259), as John Tytell puts it. The psychic space occupied during these activities is therefore less liminal than liminoid, in the sense intended by Robert L. Moore when he notes that in desacralized modern culture, "a quest for transformative space together with a lack of ritually created boundaries usually leads to the boundaries provided by the socially marginal or by actual movement through natural or sacred geography. Liminoid space is . . . not so much constituted by boundaries as it is *on the boundary*" (24).

The ideological boundaries of the postwar United States—authoritatively designated, rationally justified, and ubiquitously dispersed via powerful norms of sanity and prudence—are precisely what the Beats sought not merely to challenge, nor even to transgress, but to obliterate from consciousness. Their project was realized through acts of inner transformation that were as radically self-generating as they were profoundly individualistic, necessitating social marginality (e.g., embrace of working-class disempowerment, relinquishment of conventional sanity) as well as movement through geography both natural (the highways of *On the Road*, the jungles of *The Yage Letters*) and sacred (the oceanic deliria of *Big Sur*, the deracinated space-time of *Nova Express*).

If the literary works of the core Beats constitute a sort of metaperformance aimed at confronting ideological hegemony, their working methods reflect a similar intention. Schechner's notion of synchronic ecstasy evokes the spontaneous joy and joyous spontaneity they sought. They approached these by turning literary creation from an act of cognition and cogitation to one of playfulness and performance, centered not in the rational areas of the mind but in those having access to the threshold realm of "not me-not not me" identity associated with liminoid exploration of restored behavior. They drew precedents and procedures from sources as diverse as Zen paradox, Surrealist and Dada subversiveness, and Arthur Rimbaud's call for a systematic derangement of the senses. Within the parameters of this grand experiment, the Beats developed creative techniques as various and distinctive as the works that resulted from them.

Ginsberg, Physiology, and the Vision-Haunted Mind

Ginsberg, the most insistently public figure of the core Beats, began the major phase of his career when he discovered in writing "Howl" that his "imaginative sympathies" could be grasped more readily through emotional improvisation than through rational reflection. "I thought I wouldn't write a *poem* but just write what I wanted to without fear," he later said of this insight, "let my imagination go, open secrecy, and scribble magic lines from my real mind. . . . writ for my own soul's ear and a few other golden ears." He composed the work using rhythms from urban street corners and saloons, showing particular interest in African-American speech patterns along with sports announcers, late-night disc jockeys, and sounds of jazz, weaving these into what amounts to a Bakhtinian heteroglossia. The result was a style that Ginsberg described in cinema-tinged terms as

> a tragic custard-pie comedy of wild phrasing, meaningless images for the beauty of abstract poetry of mind, running along making awkward combinations [of images] like Charlie Chaplin's walk, long saxophone-line chorus lines I knew Kerouac would hear *sound* of—taking off from his own inspired prose line, really a new poetry. (Miles 1989, 187–88)[6]

The experience was exuberant as Ginsberg gathered momentum, "continuing to prophesy what I really knew, despite the drear consciousness of the world" (Miles 1989, 188). His use of the word "prophesy" in this self-description points to the spiritual, even messianic, leanings he already felt during the early stages of his career.

As years passed, Ginsberg became increasingly interested in physio-logical conditions as factors in poetic composition, spurred by his involve-ment with mantra chanting, Buddhist meditation, blues singing, and spontaneous oral poetry. Years of private writing and public reading con-vinced him that different forms of poetry are connected with different parts of the body and that to achieve a complete employment of self in art, the poet must bring thought and physiology into alignment.[7] It was interests such as these that led Ginsberg to his technique of "auto poesy," starting in 1965 when he began exploring the tape recorder as a "new ax for composition," as he described it to Gregory Corso at the time (Miles 1989, 381). Not only the verbiage—generated by direct oral activity rather than writing or typing—but also the structure of a poem could be realized with tape-recorder assistance, as Ginsberg discovered when he found that his clicking of the machine's on-off switch roughly corre-sponded to the beginnings and endings of distinguishable thoughts and, thus, indicated possible line breaks. Lines in the "Wichita Vortex Sutra" were arranged in this way, to cite one of his most celebrated works; their divisions were determined, Ginsberg said, "according to their organic time-spacing as per the mind's coming up with the phrases and the mouth pronouncing them" (Schumacher 466).

Many critics have focused on these aspects of Ginsberg's work. Schu-macher, borrowing a phrase from Beat associate Philip Whalen, calls the auto-poesy experiments one of Ginsberg's first conscious attempts to make his poetry a true "graph of the mind" (466). Stephenson stresses Ginsberg's use of somatic expression as a route to spiritual insight, stating that "acceptance of the body is essential for Ginsberg, for the senses can be a way to illumination. The body is where we must begin" (57). Tytell likens the performative, spontaneous, impetuous aspects of Ginsberg's method to Alfred Jarry's insistence that "true hallucination is the sus-tained waking dream" and to the Surrealist demand for what André Breton called a "subconscious irrationality" manifested by an outpour-ing of monologue "unencumbered by the slightest inhibition and . . . as closely as possible akin to spoken thought" (227–28). Like the visionary William Blake, who influenced Ginsberg so strongly, the Surrealist artists sought a wonder, spontaneity, and subversion that they interpreted as "the end of adult self-control and obedience to conditioning" (Tytell 228). When he joins this quest via the scrupulous observation and recording of his own "vision haunted mind," Ginsberg enters the territory of "not-not not" liminality. There he energetically traces, uncovers, and recuperates the strips of living behavior that simultaneously conjoin and separate his (and our) socially determined identity roles, in search of a pathway from the bounded *societas* of unitary reason to the ecstatic *communitas* of magic, play, and uncensored paradox.

Burroughs, Montage, and Recutting the Reality Film

Burroughs's development of cut-up and fold-in techniques has strong affinities with the quest for threshold positioning of the authorial self. It can even be considered a sort of actualized analogy for the generation of liminoid insight through ritual manipulation of semiotic "behavior strip" material. "Present time leads to an understanding of knowing and open food in the language of life" (1987b, 100), he writes in *The Ticket That Exploded*, suggesting the importance of continually renewed presentness and simultaneity as defenses against the voracious "reality film" that wraps its hegemonic tentacles around every mind ensnared by *societas* and its ubiquitous agents. One method of achieving such presentness and simultaneity is to disrupt the linearity (and hence the temporality) of conventional communication.

Burroughs happened on the idea of cutting up texts when his friend and associate, painter Brion Gysin, impulsively sliced through a pile of newspapers with a small blade and made the resulting strips into a mosaic—not because of any ambition for a linguistic or semiotic breakthrough but simply because he felt it would be visually interesting. The reassembled text struck Gysin as hilarious when he read it, and he showed it to Burroughs as a curiosity. Burroughs disagreed with Gysin's readiness to write off the incident as a minor Surrealist gesture. Instead, as biographer Ted Morgan observes, he saw here a solution to his self-posed challenge of finding an escape route from nineteenth-century novelistic structure (321). The practice of folding texts back upon themselves followed later, as an extension of the cut-up method.

These devices have various precursors, such as Tristan Tzara's famous notion of composing a Dada poem by pulling disconnected words out of a hat; others cited by Morgan include the construction of journalistic pages, Marcel Duchamp's artful placement of four different texts within divisions of a square, and Von Neumann's economic principle of random action.[8] This pedigree notwithstanding, however, some of the period's most progressive writers had little patience with the idea when Burroughs introduced it with great enthusiasm in late 1959. Paul Bowles saw no point in alienating readers, sardonically suggesting that if an author's goal is to destroy sense, using a non-Latin alphabet would do the job more efficiently. Samuel Beckett was outraged by the thought of his texts being shuffled in the same hat with newspaper articles. Even some Beat figures had mixed or negative feelings. Corso enjoyed the cut-up as an activity but resented Gysin's call for a destructive attack on poetry and the word. Ginsberg remained loyal to linear development and felt Burroughs's regular prose was enough of a cut-up to begin with. His position was that the mind already cuts material up, so additional scissoring is gratuitous (Morgan 321, 324, 372).

The objection raised by Ginsberg is consistent with his vision of human consciousness as a phenomenon rooted in montage-like activity and therefore in a certain linearity or at least consecutiveness. Montage, he once observed in a discussion of William Carlos Williams's idiosyncratic arrangement of poetic lines,

> is logical—montage was at first considered to be illogical, and irrational, or surrealism was first considered to be irrational, until everybody realized that what really was irrational was a rearrangement of the actuality of mind consciousness into syntactical forms which didn't have anything to do with that was going on in the head! So that finally the practical, pragmatic, common-sense form of notation of thought, was the surrealistic one, because that's the way the mind works. (1983, 55)

That is to say, surrealistic form (conflated by Ginsberg with montage form) mirrors the real structures of mental activity and is therefore the most "practical" or "logical" template for artistic construction.

The argument that seemingly irrational or "romantic-expressionistic" arrangements of thought may in fact be the most "absolutely logical scientific notation" recalls Brakhage's insistence that the allegedly "abstract" elements in his films are not abstract at all but are materially accurate reconstructions (or at least approximations) of things seen in hypnagogic, hypnopompic, and other states of "closed-eye" visual perception. Burroughs had similar motives when he embraced the cut-up and fold-in, seeing these not as detours or disfigurations vis-à-vis productive thought, but rather as highly practical pathways to realms of consciousness not available through mental activities shaped by norm-ridden social conditioning.

Indeed, he concluded from his early experience with the cut-up procedure—going beyond Brakhage's romanticism to a mysticism more redolent of Ginsberg's thinking—that here was a source of extremely useful
announcements from a quasi-Jungian collective consciousness, circumventing temporality and therefore offering clues to future events.

Beneath their quibbling about aesthetic priorities, therefore, Burroughs and Ginsberg are not in serious disagreement about the relationship between montage-like literary practice and the accomplishment of
artistic tasks with humanly relevant, even downright utilitarian, goals.
("Bill actually thought that by mixing up medical articles they would locate a cure for cancer," biographer Morgan [324] reports.) Of course,
Burroughs had few regrets for the enormous amount of traditional sense-
making that was sliced away by his new techniques; and it is understandable why this distressed colleagues such as Bowles, who maintained a stake
in art as the conveyance and sharing of information. Burroughs's radicalism again finds an echo from Brakhage, though, who states that as an artist
he is "not at all involved in communication," since communication "is not
the point of art in the normal way we use it. . . . The arts traditionally exist
in mystery" (Higgins, Lopes, and Connick 60). Given the interest long
shown by Brakhage in escaping linguistic models, the source of this "mystery" may well reside in those aspects of art least connected to logocentricity; if this is so, the "mystery quotient" may increase precisely as the lin-
guistically rational "meaning quotient" is elided or evaded. Brakhage
seeks immersion in such mystery via strategies he has developed (as noted
above) for baffling the intellect and cultivating a "knowledge foreign to
language . . . and dependent upon perception in the original and deepest
sense," rooted in what he calls the optical mind (1963, n.p.). Although
words have been Burroughs's primary raw material, he has shown a keen
awareness of the filmic implications of his techniques and of their filmlike
ability to evoke sensory as well as informational logic; he remarks at one
point that cutting and rearranging a page "introduces a new dimension
into writing enabling the writer to turn images in cinematic variation.
Images shift sense under the scissors smell images to sound sight to sound
sound to kinesthetic" (1982, 36). It is therefore giving only part of the
story to observe, as Tytell does, that the cut-up form "perfectly captures
the disorder and confusion of madness" and that Burroughs "metaphysi-
cally refutes any distinctions between reality and fantasy" (117). Madness
and fantasy are aspects *of* reality. Hence, they do not lose significance or

signification as they spin into disorder and confusion; rather, they call for "realistic" representation as legitimately as do their "rational" counterparts in everyday "sane" experience. They receive this representation in Burroughs's word-montage sequences, just as hallucinations, dreams, and closed-eye visions do in Brakhage's hyperbolic films. Burroughs captures them with an accuracy worthy of the most "truthful" documentary cinema, moreover, albeit through wholly verbal discourse.

Burroughs's use of the cut-up and fold-in has been called a response to Kerouac's development of spontaneous prose. Burroughs has encouraged this idea by invoking spontaneity as an ideal of his own: "The best writing seems to be done almost by accident but writers until the cut-up method was made explicit. . . . had no way to produce the accident of spontaneity. You cannot *will* spontaneity. But you can introduce the unpredictable spontaneous factor with a pair of scissors" (1982, 35). Tytell states that the cut-up was intended as "a means through which [Burroughs] would objectively detach himself from romantic images, from tenderness, from personal associations and ties to his own words. It eliminated habitual reactions and conditioned reflexes, separated words from traditional referents, violated the normal syntax that influences rational behavior" (116). This is all true enough, but most important, the random, arbitrary, and mechanical aspects of the method provided a way for Burroughs to separate himself from *himself*—providing access to a quasi-Archimedean position outside self-generated consciousness, from which he could observe and manipulate the strips of his own thoughts and behaviors, as well as those that came to him from others via the printed (cuttable and foldable) page. The technique is thus an exfoliation of the infant-stage transitional behavior that leads toward play and artistic creation. Cutting-up and folding-in are nothing if not playlike activities, after all; and their linked processes of disjoining/conjoining are clear manifestations of the separation/denial-of-separation modalities associated with transition-phase thought and behavior. As definitively as Ginsberg during an act of performative improvisation or Kerouac in the throes of a writing-trance, Burroughs enters a state of liminoid in-betweenness when he slices or rewraps a printed page, transcribes the resulting verbal patterns, and (a key part of his practice that is often underrecognized by critics) subsumes these to the needs of his own fiction, either by modifying their content or surrounding them with material that he has written in a more conventional fashion. While pursuing their sophisticated "adult" goal of combating mental control and conditioning, Burroughs's methods retain an infantile refusal to acknowledge clear boundaries between "me-extensions and the not-me," and meanwhile connect with his child-like interest in products and properties of the body, especially functions and fluids of what Bakhtin calls the material bodily lower stratum. In both content and technique, Burroughs's work dramatically recalls Winnicott's statement that the playing child "manipulates external phenomena in the service of the dream and invests chosen external phenomena with dream meaning and feeling" (51). Its emphasis on disruption and discontinuity also recalls Turner's characterization of play as a reflexive interrupter.

The acts of not me-not not me creation that Burroughs accomplishes with his techniques are threshold phenomena in an additional sense, moreover, in that their raw materials are appropriated from the world of preexisting printed matter and manipulated into a state of *semirecognizability*, retaining a certain amount of "original identity" while being molded into a new shape dictated by Burroughs's disruptive intentions. It is also important to note that popular culture plays a prominent role in the material he typically chooses. Such material is seductive to Burroughs, who habitually betrays (through appropriation and imitation) an affection for science fiction, crime fiction, and their ilk. At the same time such works represent a sworn enemy of his, however, since they constitute an aggressively marketed form of the media-driven enslavement that enforces image addiction and nourishes commodity control.

Related to modernist practices including collage as well as montage, cut-ups challenge traditional notions of authorship while redefining traditional conceptions of beauty, artistry, and the boundaries between artwork and commodity. Burroughs's techniques go a crucial step further, moreover, by performing what Scott Bukatman calls "an incisive violence on the body of the text," producing not orderly concatenations of variegated materials but intuitively spliced sequences of disconnected signifiers that "exist in glittering isolation, outside temporality, outside history" (39–40).

Such surgical performances have their origins and outcomes in distinctly liminoid realms, transgressing boundaries of thought with truly postmodern abandon. The cut-up method may well be "the most appropriate technique for the marriage of opposites," as J. G. Ballard wrote (Bukatman 40–41), and Burroughs is among its most uninhibited pioneers.

Kerouac, Jazz, and Trance/Formation

Kerouac's development of a distinctive writing-ritual had one of its turning points when an evening of Lee Konitz's alto-saxophone playing suggested to him a new prose style marked by uninhibited phrasing and a quick, spontaneous flow of ideas.[9] This voice would be as fluid, mutable, and mercurial as the most improvisatory jazz and was therefore compatible with the verbal "sketching" technique that Kerouac was developing as a tool for "bop-trance composition." Both tropes used by Kerouac in conceptualizing his new paradigm for literary creation—jazz improvisation and spur-of-the-moment sketching—convey the specifically performative nature of the practice he wished to cultivate. Another key moment arrived when he became terminally annoyed with the need to change paper sheets in his typewriter (a problem that word processors have since rendered moot!) and began *On the Road* in early 1951 by taping sheets of drawing paper into a long roll, thus eliminating all interruption of his trancelike self-absorption as he pumped out rapid cascades of sentences.

The early novel *Visions of Cody*, an uncompromised bop-prosody exercise marked by effects of simultaneity and ambivalence, reflects even more radical engagement with liminal modes of self-observation and behavior-trip play. Under the sway of Kerouac's ambivalence, Weinreich has demonstrated, the foundations of conventional narrative—that which is linear, consecutive, and chronological—give way to an illusion that everything (birth, death, sense, perception, and so forth) is happening at once; and clear, meaningful sentences give way to recurring phrases, images, and patterns steeped in qualities of synaesthesia, synchronicity, and syncopation (61).

The third section of this novel, "The Frisco Tapes," reproduces conversations with Neal Cassady as transcribed by Kerouac from tape recordings made in his home. "The transcriptions stand as a series of mirrors turned toward one another, and the mind of Jack and Cody lies somewhere among them," Nicosia accurately suggests in his Kerouac biography, noting that the conversations wobble among multiple purposes and dimensions: Kerouac seeks information about Cassady for his novel, Cassady seeks material for his own literary work, both reenact earlier scenes and comment on passages already transcribed, the tape recorder produces ambiguous jump-cuts and ellipses, additional voices appear and disappear. And all this is followed by a section of the novel called "Imitation of the

Tape," in which Kerouac takes another giant discursive leap by parodying everything that has already occurred, both in and out of the book (372).

This is observation and manipulation of restored behavior with a vengeance. *Visions of Cody* is a novel in which the title character serves not only as a carefully drawn narrative figure and a thinly veiled real-life portrait of a friend but also as a doppelganger for the author, whose similarity to his protagonist allows him to indulge in lengthy dissections, examinations, and explorations of his own inner self. More reflexively yet, the novel finds its centerpiece in two acts of multilayered parody. The first parodic act (the Frisco tape) involves the literal recording, replaying, and transcribing of verbal material that is performative in its first-level manifestation—as festive conversation, initiated and "directed" by Kerouac—and doubly performative in its second-level and third-level appearances as (respectively) mechanically constructed audiotape and painstakingly transcribed writing for public dissemination on the printed page. The second parodic act (the "imitation" tape) multiplies the rambunctious in-betweenness of the foregoing threshold dialogue by blurring its relationship to "external reality" more profoundly still, using *mise-en-abîme* ambiguities to position both writer and reader in a potential space that represents neither author nor not-author, neither objectivity nor subjectivity, neither external "shared" reality nor internal "personal" reality. Under such circumstances, it seems particularly fitting that the second portion of the "Imitation of the Tape" is the satirical docufantasy entitled "Joan Rawshanks in the Fog," inspired by Kerouac's chance observation of Joan Crawford filming a movie scene.[10] Dealing with the filmmaking process, as discussed earlier, this virtuosic riff conflates the cinematic take and the mental memory-impression as routes to the self-distanciation that alone facilitates knowledge (however faulty, incomplete, and ultimately illusory) of the self and its surroundings.

Kerouac's jazz-trance composition method, which he continued to refine and redefine (if not to improve) in such later books as *The Subterraneans* and *Desolation Angels*, reflects his attempt not merely to enter the autotelic liminality-moment that a successful writing-performance provides, but to dwell within that moment—or take, or sense-memory, or flash of *satori*-like awareness—long enough to capture the "unspeakable visions" that he observes there and to render them as speakable as his synaesthetic jazz-movie-sketch-words will allow. It is no mere coincidence that the liminoid inflections of Kerouac's writing techniques are echoed by the subject matter of most of his important novels. These center on spiritually, psychologically, and/or physically decentered protagonists who seek out transformative spaces as sites for personal regeneration—in the undiscovered America of *On the Road*, the protean memoryscapes of *Visions of Cody*, the superreal Mexico of *Tristessa*, the hallucinatory mountains of *The Dharma Bums* and *Desolation Angels*, and so on—and explore these through rituals of travel that transpire simultaneously on mental and geographical levels. The voyages of these Beat heroes in space and time are Kerouac's voyages through psyche and spirit, tracing new points of passage across the borders, boundaries, and margins of conventional human rationality.

Hollywood and Its Discontents

> *She:* I wish I didn't have to make the scene with that plane tonight. I wish I never had to go back east. I wish, I wish, I wish . . .
> *He [overlapping]:* Hey, hey, play it cool, chick, now play it like cool. You've got to go. Everybody's gotta move. I mean, you can't stand still and wait for the next mushroom cloud, now, you dig?
> *She:* Crazy, but . . . as soon as I cut out you'll forget me.
> *He:* Oh, like, you're the most. But there's no tomorrow, not while the sky drools radiation gumdrops. I mean, you gotta live for kicks. Right here and now—that's all there is.
> —Beatnik in The Beat Generation, *directed by Charles Haas, 1959*

As self-designated safekeepers of consensus, classicism, and common sense, Hollywood and other manufacturers of mass-market culture sought to oppose the irascible urges of Beat-influenced artists—be these socially antagonistic, aesthetically experimental, spiritually transcendent, or just personally cantankerous—and to block any impulses toward liminality that might call into question their own tendencies toward monologism, homogeneity, and affirmation of the status quo. Hollywood movies dealing with such Beat-associated phenomena as jazz, drugs, the coffeehouse scene, avant-garde art and poetry, and relaxation of strictures on sex and racial "mixing" provide useful examples of how the motion-picture establishment mobilized during the '50s period (in accord with other social, cultural, and political forces) to contain and combat this multiform ideological foe.

In terms of content, these films generally try to defuse potential interest in Beat lifestyles by mocking, parodying, or misrepresenting them. Often the Beat subculture is attacked indirectly, with the bohemian "enemy" displaced to a location removed from most American moviegoers and referred to infrequently by name—or not named at all but invoked by vague references or euphemistic labels. One instance is the 1957 musical *Funny Face*, which moves its hero (Fred Astaire, creative commercial photographer) and heroine (Audrey Hepburn, potential fashion model) to Paris for their encounter with the "Empathicalists," a coterie of avant-garde enthusiasts compounded from clichéd Beat, bohemian, and Existentialist character types. Performance and art-making crop up reliably in films on Beat-related subjects but are generally treated in highly un-Beat-like ways, again showing Hollywood's wish to exploit popular awareness of Beat phenomena without appearing to emulate or endorse them. Music is invoked most often, reflecting the Beat interest in jazz and the suitability of jazz to spectacular public display; the range is sometimes extended to poetry recitation, painting and sculpting, or even the modeling and photo-snapping of *Funny Face*. In most cases, the performing or art-making is belittled by the movie in which it appears, and often it is presented as not much fun for anyone. Even when it is treated with some respect, as in certain jazz pictures that keep specifically Beat references to a minimum, its subjection to rigid classical-film structure ensures that it will appear as safely bottled entertainment—securely contained within a comfortingly familiar mode of simulation—rather than the playful, relativistic, autotelic, radically volatile creativity that the actual Beats embraced.

Much the same can be said of the style deployed in these Hollywood films. They rely on the monologic tendencies of classical cinema to reinforce the ideology of individualism (within consensus-approved boundaries, of course: no *eccentric* individuality allowed) and to define the self as a coherent, cohesive entity exercising free thought and action in an environment of social, political, and economic liberty.[11] In so addressing their audience, Hollywood movies take a stand against liminality, in-between personality states, and not me-not not me behavior—all of which are potentially destabilizing and therefore dangerous modalities of consciousness (and unconsciousness) that might indicate alternatives to official thought, escape routes from socioeconomic conformity, and pathways toward the precarious pleasures of creative spontaneity rather than the engulfing security of repetition and routine.

Modern Art as Murder

> *I will talk to you of art.*
> *For there is nothing else to*
>   *talk about,*
> *For there is nothing else.*
> Life is an obscure hobo bumming
>   a ride on the omnibus of art.
> . . . .
> The artist is, all others are
>   not.
> A canvas is a canyon or a
>   painting.
> A rock is a rock or a statue.
> A sound is a sound or it is
>   music.
> A preacher is a preacher or an
>   artist.
> Where are John, Joe, Jake, Jim,
>   Jerk?
> Dead. Dead. Dead. They were not
>   born.
> Before they were born they were
>   not born.
> Where are Leonardo, Rembrandt,
>   Ludwig?
> Alive. Alive. Alive. They were
>   born.
> Bring on the multitude, the
>   multitude of fishes.
> —Beat poet in A Bucket of Blood, *directed by Roger Corman, 1959*

Coffeehouses became an emblem of Beat activity during the '50s, and for good reason. A carnivalistic place devoted to casual contact among like-minded "nonconformists," the (Beat) coffeehouse distinguished itself from the (square) bar by deemphasizing alcohol, the establishment's drug of choice, while providing a place where illicit substances could be bought and traded, sexual liaisons could be initiated or pursued, and progressive forms of artistic expression such as jazz improvisation, free-verse recitation, and abstract-painting exhibition could flourish in a sympathetic atmosphere. Such places typically operated within the limits of the legal code, relegating drug use and other questionable business to covert (or semicovert) status. Still, the "beatnik" behaviors that they fostered ensured their reputation as sites of liminal activity—places not comfortably inside or altogether outside ordinary society, but somewhere on the behavioral and ideological margin, where acts discouraged as eccentric, radical, or simply weird in "normal" circumstances would be harbored and protected.

These havens of beatnik nonconformity became a handy reference point for Hollywood movies, which used them to signify social strangeness and unconventionality. It was not coffeehouses in themselves that aroused the deepest popular uneasiness, however, but the underlying notion that thoughts and behaviors unconfined by common sense might flourish within the physical boundaries (if not the spiritual boundaries) of the mainstream American community. Spurred more by the bizarre aura than the actual nature of the Beat sensibility, Beat-related movies tend to conflate wildly divergent (and wildly unrelated) cultural artifacts into hodgepodges labeled "Beat" with only the slimmest justification.

Roger Corman's sardonic melodrama *A Bucket of Blood*, released by American International Pictures in 1959, is one such film. It begins with a stereotypical beatnik—bearded, pretentious, self-consciously intellectual—reciting an improvised poem in a stereotypical coffeehouse. This instantly marks the movie's content as Beat-oriented and signals a Beat-unfriendly attitude to follow. As it happens, however, many of the film's sociological details are not particularly Beat at all. The resident musician at the coffeehouse is not a jazz player, for instance, but a folk singer with an acoustic guitar—indicating Corman's prescience as to the next big music craze among young listeners, but having little to do with the jazz-oriented Beat scene as described by '50s observers. (Folk music does seem quite at home on the sound track of Jonas Mekas's strongly Beat-related *Guns of the Trees*, but that film was released three years later in 1962, when folk music had begun to thrive.) Similarly, a typical beatnik breakfast in the film appears to consist of carefully munched California health food, quite different from the anything-goes, on-the-run meals (recall the commodified cornucopia in the *Visions of Cody* cafeteria scene) characteristically described in Beat literature. Sexual mores in the coffeehouse appear to mirror those of square society, moreover: A heavy woman coded as "unattractive" throws herself at the protagonist while a more convention-ally appealing woman remains prim and aloof from him despite her lack of other romantic attachments.

The film's mixture of hostility and condescension toward beatniks is best revealed in its attitude toward art. The coffeehouse—called the Yellow Door, as if all who gathered there were "yellow" dropouts too cow-ardly to face the real world—is decorated with ostentatiously modernist works never seen very closely by the camera. The plot centers on a young coffeehouse employee who wishes he could be an artist but is obviously too stupid for any activity more demanding than clearing tables. Alone in his room one night, he accidentally kills a cat, then covers it with clay and decides to display it as an artwork that he has "made." The most intellec-tual members of the coffeehouse clique immediately hail his sculpture as brilliant, assuming it to be a normal artwork made in a conventional man-ner. The protagonist next murders and sculpturizes a police officer who tries to arrest him for receiving (unsolicited) drugs from a Beat art enthu-siast; naturally, he receives another shower of praise for this clay-coated "creation." His secret is discovered after the subsequent killing and dis-playing of a nude model and then a local worker. Fleeing the police, he commits suicide in his room. "I suppose he would have called it 'Hang-ing Man,'" comments an art-loving beatnik upon seeing his strung-up corpse. "His greatest work."

With its art objects, art poetry, and art conversations, the film associ-ates the coffeehouse—and, metonymically, the whole Beat scene—with artistic achievements, aspirations, and pretensions. All the while, artis-tic discourse is seen as phony and ridiculous: Nobody can distinguish a real artwork from a clay-coated corpse, and the selling price of the pro-tagonist's "works" has more importance to some of the beatniks than the works themselves. "I thought you put money down," says the protagonist to a Beat admirer after the latter expresses enthusiasm over a $25,000 sale. "I do," the beatnik responds. "But twenty-five *thou*!" The film's view of art is consistently antagonistic, treating sculpture and painting as prod-ucts of individuals who are poorly socialized at best and destructively de-mented at worst.

It is "modern" or "abstract" art that comes in for the severest treat-ment, moreover, as if the works hanging in the coffeehouse were not only threatening but actually contagious in their perverse insistence on disrupt-ing "normal" beauty. The praise lavished on such works, and the resident poet's improvised verses—which he only recites once and then deliberately forgets, since "repetition is death"—are what inspire the protagonist to display his worked-over cat as an artwork, and it is never clear that he realizes the fraudulence of his activities. He keeps insisting he has "made" his works, never actually claiming to have sculpted them in a normal way; it is possible that he regards them as fully authentic art, and that he maintains secrecy about their origin not to protect his reputation as an artist but only to prevent people from finding out that he has murdered his "models." The film's message is as plain as it is simplistic: Contemporary art is weird and dangerous, and even "realistic" art made under its influence (like the protagonist's all-too-naturalistic works) is likely to be corrupt and subversive. The movie conveys this message in an ironic and deliberately tacky manner, but its satisfaction in flailing the eccentricities of the beatnik crowd is unmistakable.

Interestingly, similar things take place in an even tackier film, *Color Me Blood Red*, made six years later (1965) by Herschell G[ordon] Lewis, who wrote, directed, and photographed it. Here the artist is a painter, depicted as a (dangerously) liminoid character living in an isolated beach house. His contacts with other people come largely through his art, which the film associates with performance; his exhibitions are mounted in a gallery set up like a theater, with a stage at one end, on which he and a pretentious critic have arguments and discussions. Early in the story, the critic accuses him of being too commercial and, more specifically, of having an underdeveloped sense of color. When a girlfriend cuts her foot on one of his canvas frames, he uses her blood as paint for one of his works, and everyone is dazzled by its vivid hue, presumably achieved through creative use of ordinary paint. He continues with this technique, and after switching to his own blood for a while, he begins murdering local women to ensure a lasting supply. As in *A Bucket of Blood*, the protagonist creates his masterpiece when he meets his own death—mashing his bloody head into a canvas after being shot by the boyfriend of his latest potential victim. Also present during much of the story are a beatnik couple who speak in ostentatiously "hip" phrases and have a slightly more freewheeling sex life than most of the other characters.

Lewis's film is maddeningly coy when it comes to sex, building up to a couple of "skinflick" scenes that fail to happen. It is maddeningly gruesome when it comes to violence, though, peppering the action with grisly shots of corpses and enormous amounts (naturally) of blood. It is also grossly misogynistic in its near-exclusive use of women as prey for the painter and as objects of spectacular suffering for the movie's audience; in terms of visual emphasis, it could be argued that the entire film exists for the sake of one lengthy, sadistic shot depicting the second victim ooz-ing blood from intestines hanging out of her disembowelled torso. Lewis built his reputation on such nasty stuff, so it is not surprising to encounter it here. It is revealing to find such an art-hostile attitude festering within this filmmaking "artist," however, and to see it associated once again with a liminal scene that includes Beats among its inhabitants.

Beats and Headaches

> Cathy Crosby to star in "Beat Generation" by M.G.M., imagine a "beat"
> Crosby, revolting what?
> —Neal Cassady, letter, 1958

The Beat Generation was filmed for MGM by director Charles Haas in 1959 and later rereleased as *This Rebel Age*. It begins with the improbable spectacle of Louis Armstrong singing a song with flatly anti-Beat lyrics in a coffeehouse with a plainly Beat ambience. Armstrong was a powerful icon representing popular jazz during the '50s, when he himself was in his fifties and strongly associated with a wholesome, unthreatening variety of older-generation music; with or without his band, he appeared in at least twenty films between 1947 and 1963, including such establishment-oriented productions as Howard Hawks's *A Song Is Born* (the 1948 re-make of Hawks's *Ball of Fire*) and Anthony Mann's *The Glenn Miller Story* (1954). Since his brilliant but traditionalistic approach to jazz is quite different from the far-ranging experimentalism of bop, his presence in a film about such a supposedly cutting-edge phenomenon as the Beat Gen-eration—especially during the opening credits, when the atmosphere and subject of the picture are being introduced—suggests that the filmmakers are more concerned with reassuring and entertaining their audience than in pursuing an uncompromising study of their putative topic.

Sure enough, *The Beat Generation* turns out to have only a sidelong interest in the Beat Generation or anything connected with it; the narra-tive begins with Beat characters in a Beat setting but soon segues into standard cop-and-crook melodrama about a police officer's hunt for a rap-ist. The film's intermittent use of a Beat milieu—and its title, which sug-gests that Beats will be not *a* prime focus but *the* prime focus of the story—are not entirely gratuitous, however. Making the villain a beatnik, albeit one who glides in and out of Beat surroundings as easily as the movie itself does, is an efficient way of exploiting (and reinforcing) popular attraction/repulsion feelings toward Beat weirdness and dangerousness. The filmmakers do have a couple of socially significant topics on their minds, moreover, and connecting these with Beat-related sociology shows a certain slim logic.

The dialogue quoted at the beginning of this section is the first heard in the movie. It continues with this exchange of ripely stereotyped Beat phrases, attitudes, and ideas:

She: You know, in all the months I've known you, you've never even held my hand?

He: Oh, wow, like man, the love and marriage bit, now I put that down! That's for the rat-race, for the squares. Schopenhauer said, and I agree with him, *[reading:]* "Lovers are traitors who seek to perpetuate the whole want and drudgery of life, which would otherwise speedily reach an end." That *cat* Schopenhauer also said that this world, which is so real, with all its sunsets and Milky Ways, is nothing.

She: It's the only world we've got.

He [patronizingly]: Crazy.

She: Maybe we'll meet again some day, and you'll read your gone poetry and far-out philosophy—

He: Yeah, yeah.

She: —and maybe we'll have kicks to end all kicks.

He: Yeah.

This conversation ends when the young man, Stan, moves to another table for a talk with his father, who has come to tell Stan about his impending marriage to the young fiancée sitting next to him. Their dialogue reveals Stan's resentment of both his parents for their unstable love lives and marriages. (The stepmother-to-be isn't much better than the parents; apparently she "had eyes" for Stan before his rich father came on the scene.)

In the next part of the story, Stan knocks on the apartment door of a young woman presented as a normal, rather exuberant '50s type; when first seen, she is exercising with a hula hoop—that paradoxical liberator of hips, in an era when Elvis Presley's pelvic moves were considered fairly hot stuff—while listening to music and reading a magazine. Stan worms his way into the apartment with a claim of being there on business, hoping to repay money he borrowed from her husband. But once inside he turns the conversation first to jazz (still playing on the radio) and then implicitly to sex:

He: Hey. Hey, dig that jazz. I make that, very large.

She: It's like nothin' I ever heard.

He: Of course not, that's Roger Jones. He's the only cat who wails a bass without the strings. He doesn't want any catgut to get between him and the pure music of the virgin wood. One night Roger, he ripped off all the strings and he shouted, I'm music myself with nothin' between! That's far out, isn't it?

She [smiling]: I—I wouldn't know.

He: Well, that's the sound that really makes it. Icky bands are for moldy figs. May I sit down?

She: Please do. What's—what's a moldy fig?

He: Oh, wow, man, like—like the world is full of moldy figs. There's the squares who eat, sleep, go to work, vegetate—and while they vegetate, I swing. You understand?

She: I'm afraid I'm a little mixed up.

He: Oh, well, you'll learn to swing, ma'am, and when—

This exchange breaks off when Stan suddenly feigns a headache, takes out a tin of aspirin, and asks for a glass of water. When the surprised woman goes to fetch it, he puts on a pair of gloves and seizes her from behind, clearly initiating a rape. The film does not depict this rape, panning from the struggling woman and her attacker (who verbally encourages her to struggle and fight) to the aspirin tin lying on a table. The next shot finds him walking home, almost being hit by a passing car, and striking up a conversation with the driver: a police detective named Culloran, whose wife Stan then targets as his next victim. The rest of the film follows the exploits of Stan, known to the law as the Aspirin Kid, and the attempts of Culloran to track him down and apprehend him.

Two plot elements lend the story some psychological and sociological interest. One is that Stan's crimes are specifically connected with a pathological hatred of women and that Culloran is criticized by his friends and colleagues for having exactly the same trait, although in a less virulent form; no sooner does the Aspirin Kid rape a woman than Culloran (who was once married to a "tramp") subjects the victim to merciless interrogations and imputations of complicity. The other plot device of interest is that Culloran's wife becomes pregnant after being raped and cannot be certain whether she was impregnated by the Kid or her husband. This situation sets off a series of tentative decisions that add up to a catalogue of '50s responses to unintended pregnancy. The wife (a) decides to have an abortion, immediately vetoed by her husband on the ground that it would be illegal; (b) turns for help to a friend, who steers her to a Roman Catholic priest living conveniently across the street; (c) receives a lengthy antiabortion sermonette from the priest, in one of the film's most conspicuous set pieces; (d) decides to have the baby and give it up for adoption; and (e) gives birth to the baby and decides to keep it, whereupon Culloran returns to her (they have been separated due to his unease over her pregnancy and his obsession with finding the rapist) and the film concludes with a happy-family tableau in the wife's hospital room.

The climax of the story is a shoot-out and chase (much of it underwater!) that begins at a "Beat hootenanny" in a coffeehouse, initiated by Stan and demonstrating again the unrelated elements that Hollywood was capable of lumping under the "Beat" label. The word "hootenanny" is associated more with folk music than with Beat-style jazz, and the music heard within the scene has more guitar strumming than bongo thumping to it. As it plays, the Beats perform a childish dance that appears to be part conga line, part ring-around-the-rosey. The characters marked as Beat are equally disparate, including an Aspirin Kid look-alike (enlisted by the Kid as an accomplice to confuse the police) and a "Wrestling Beat" played by former prizefighter Maxie Rosenbloom, who engages Culloran in a grotesque physical struggle evidently meant to leaven the climax with comic relief. In all, the film's portrait of Beat life and leisure (if a distinction can be drawn between them) displays a conglomeration of shiftless "fringe" types whose carnivalistic gestures (from talking "jive" to squirting seltzer à la Clarabel the clown) are peculiar enough to produce a wan *frisson* in the mainstream audience but would probably be no fun to participate in or, for that matter, get very close to. The fact that this portrait is as factually false as it is attitudinally hostile appears to have been beside the point for the filmmakers.

The film shows glimmerings of intelligence as it acknowledges the reality of '50s misogyny, however, locating this bias within square culture and hip counterculture alike. It is explicitly suggested that the detective and rapist are mirror images of each other in their shared contempt for women; the only difference between them is that the Aspirin Kid expresses his hatred through psychotic action, and the cop makes his felt through suspicion and condescension toward the women in his life, especially the rape victims for whom he ought to feel at least a modicum of compassion. The detective's obsession with tracking down the Aspirin Kid is also seen as excessive (especially since it does not appear to be motivated by concern for the well-being of the female population) and even kinky. Some of Culloran's monomania might be attributed to rage over his wife's victimization by the criminal; but weighing against this interpretation is the fact that the most prominent result of his single-minded attention to his job is increased inattention and even apathy toward his wife—despite her pregnancy, her anxiety over the baby's paternity, and her agonizing uncertainty over the best course of action. Nor does he show any interest in the other women with whom his detective work puts him in contact, beyond their value as lures for the rapist, who may try to reestablish contact with former victims.

In sum, Culloran's relationship to women is clearly unhealthy, and the film calls attention to this fact in a clearly critical manner. What it does not do is make any kind of coherent observation on misogyny and the Beat Generation—remembering that the latter is supposedly the subject of the film—even though the real-life association between Beats and women had highly problematic aspects that certainly deserve commentary. This circumstance is most obvious and most troubling in some of Burroughs's work, as when he shows himself capable of writing an essay entitled "Women: A Biological Mistake?" that indicates (through much hedging and circumlocution) an affirmative answer to that not-so-rhetorical question.[12] (On the other hand, even so daunting a male chauvinist as Kerouac had flashes of enlightenment on the "woman question," as in *The Subterraneans,* when the heroine says of men that they "rush off and have big wars and consider women as prizes instead of human beings, well man I may be in the middle of all this shit but I certainly don't want any part of it." Her statement that men "are so crazy, they want the essence, the woman is the essence, there it is right in their hands but they rush off erecting big abstract constructions" [16] is also noteworthy, recalling feminist work by Luce Irigaray and others who associate patriarchal dominance with logocentricity and male subjection to language as Law.)

Use of the word "kid" takes on interesting resonances in the film, as well. The Aspirin Kid seems a rather jaunty nickname for the police to bestow on a criminal whom they themselves recognize as a particularly vicious and psychotic offender. At the same time, he may be the father of Mrs. Culloran's unborn "kid," whose questionable paternity generates one of the story's most poignant elements. Meanwhile, the film sporadically remembers its supposed interest in the Beat Generation, which is itself coded as a bunch of "kids" too immature to accomplish anything substantial in life or even to notice (or care about) the presence of a demented serial rapist in their midst; their "play" is shown at some length, but it is depicted as childish idiocy with no link to adult creativity or cultural productiveness. What all this ultimately signals is less a cogent statement about "kids" than an indication of diffuse uneasiness about questions of paternity, fatherhood, sexuality, marriage, maturity, and responsibility amid the dimly acknowledged (and even more dimly understood) sociocultural discontents of the late '50s. If the film can be said to take a stance toward this uneasiness, it is only insofar as liminality in these areas is disowned and disavowed as definitely as possible. The coffeehouse is exposed as a site of fatuity, danger, and hidden violence. The quasibeatnik Aspirin Kid is captured, still sputtering "Women are filth" but crying like Marlon Brando's character near the end of *The Wild One*. Culloran accepts the word "lunatic" as appropriate to his past woman-hating behavior and accepts his wife's newborn baby as his own, restoring the nuclear family to a dominant position in his life and in the movie. We may presume that he will never be troubled with Beats again, or with Beat-like tendencies within his own nature; and the spectator is encouraged to feel comforted on this score, as well.

Leaving aside the finale, the film's extreme conservatism is signalled most aggressively by the remarkable sequence wherein Mrs. Culloran pays her visit (not quite voluntarily) to the priest who advises her against an abortion. The cleric is presented in a conspicuously casual way, not berobed in his pulpit but wearing more or less casual clothing in the front yard of his home. Still, his manner is drenched in Hollywood's most self-consciously grovelling clichés regarding religion and its representatives; likewise, his words are freighted with *faux* friendliness and understanding as he pretends to allow Mrs. Culloran full freedom of action (she is not Catholic and therefore not a member of his official flock) while smoothly manipulating her (and possibly the film's audience) into the morally "correct" decision. (As with many religious figures in Hollywood movies, his holiness is so vast that it prevents him from using grammatical contractions—"can't" for "cannot" and so forth—when he speaks; this affectation gives his lines an amusingly stilted quality often encountered in such scenes.) This episode may reflect sincere religious belief on the filmmakers' part, or at least respect for the beliefs of some moviegoers. But whether or not this is the case, it provides a hefty measure of conventionally pious "redeeming social value" to balance narrative content that is fairly bold by late-'50s standards: incidents and dialogue involving rape, pregnancy, abortion—a word that is never actually used—and verbal formulations (e.g., "I might be carrying a rapist's child") that would have met strong censorial pressures in Hollywood just a short time earlier. Such were the prices paid for the American film industry's growing expressive freedom as the postwar period proceeded; and such was the sort of "spicy" material and equivocating treatment that Hollywood found appropriate to blend with vaguely defined Beat Generation signifiers in its attempt to hold onto adult audiences while tapping into a burgeoning "youth market" that was still being discovered as the '50s came to an end.

Blacks, Whites, and Blues

While the makers of such films as *A Bucket of Blood* and *The Beat Generation* treat Beat-related phenomena with a mixture of hostility and timidity, others attempt to capitalize on Beat issues and behaviors—associated with social marginality, spontaneous creativity, avant-garde artistic leanings, and other traits conjuring up visions of on-the-edge liminality— without limiting their audience by invoking the Beat label itself. Many '50s-era movies about jazz may be read as excursions into Beat-like territory, with or without actual Beats along for the trip. Films with the word "blues" in their titles often fall into this category.

Pete Kelly's Blues, directed by Jack Webb in 1955, signals a Beat-like sensibility in its very first moments by lavishly romanticizing the heritage of African-American life and music. The precredit sequence shows (at great length) the truly liminal phenomenon of a black funeral in the South, at the end of which a black cornetist loses his horn. The story's white hero (Pete Kelly, played by Webb) then acquires this instrument in a freight-car dice game, which injects the film with still more signifiers— rootlessness, "on the road" traveling, faith in chance and happenstance— connected to Beat interests. When we subsequently meet Kelly in his mature life as a musician at a '20s speakeasy, we learn that he has a strong affection not only for jazz in general but also for this horn in particular; when a mischievous woman (Janet Leigh) tries to let someone else play it at a party, for instance, he douses her in a convenient pool of water and stalks indignantly away. The movie thus adds (a) the black provenance of the cornet to (b) the depth of Kelly's feelings for the cornet, leading to

(c) the possibility that the cornet will inspire in Kelly a similar attachment to all black music and musicians. Hollywood was not ready for such an attachment in 1955, however. Kelly loves African-American music, but he has not hired one African-American musician for his totally white band; and when the story finds time for Ella Fitzgerald to have a turn in the musical spotlight, her band is totally black. Respect for black music is thus duly shown, but only with color lines drawn as firmly around the narrative as around American social relations at large. The actual purpose of the cornet is not to serve as a sociocultural transitional object linking the worlds of white and black music—which are seen to be quite distinct, except in genealogical terms—but rather to function as Kelly's personal transitional object, to which he shows the sort of unexamined devotion that a baby might bestow on a blanket or other infantile plaything. If he treated this object in a truly adult way, thinking about its cultural history and drawing conclusions that could deepen his artistry, both his story and his music might gain resonant new dimensions. The fact that this development doesn't occur shows the film's lack of even superficial seriousness with regard to its ostensible subjects of music, creativity, and the interrelations of these with "human nature."

Looking at the film on its own light-entertainment terms, the idea behind it—with its tale of a musician (Webb) mixed up with a wealthy lover (Leigh) and mobsters in the Prohibition era—is apparently to give audiences the vicarious thrill of feeling caught up in the liminal (and Beat-like) excitements of jazz, intoxication, and danger, but at the comfortable distance of approximately three decades after the narrative takes place. Additional distancing comes from the stiffness and stylization of Webb's directing, which counterbalances any impulse to liveliness and spontaneity that the film might have indulged. (Stiffness and stylization were two of Webb's trademarks, as the '50s television series *Dragnet* demonstrated week after week.) To be fair, it must be acknowledged that the film's musical numbers (by Fitzgerald and Peggy Lee as well as the Kelly character's combo) are depicted in long takes that allow the performances to develop their own rhythm, pacing, and spur-of-the-moment momentum. Dialogue scenes are often filmed the same way, however, and these are burdened with such stilted, wooden acting that there is little sense of watching "real" behavior. It is likely that the film's long takes do not represent a stylistic choice aimed at lending authenticity to the musical numbers, but rather the reluctance of early CinemaScope filmmakers to cut within scenes unless necessary for narrative purposes. Bearing this out, there is no concern for jazz-joint realism in the movie's sound engineering. When the boozy chanteuse of the story (Lee) sings a ballad in an intimate nightclub, her voice is heard with crystal clarity while the instruments playing directly behind her are relegated to the sonic background with a thoroughness and precision that would be impossible in a "real-life" setting. All semblance of jazz-world (or Beat-like) spontaneity is rendered safely ineffectual by the calibrated technology of the Hollywood mixing room.

The Systematic Derangement of Rimbaud

When he called for a "systematic derangement of the senses," poet Arthur Rimbaud generated an intellectual wave that would ultimately reach figures as diverse as the core Beat writers and Sylvester Stallone of *Rambo* fame. Among the far-flung recipients of Rimbaud's influence was Paul Newman, who stars in the 1961 film *Paris Blues* as an American jazz trombonist with the extraordinary name of Ram Bowen.

Compared with a slightly earlier jazz-film like *Pete Kelly's Blues,* this romantic drama (directed by Martin Ritt, who is often associated with "social consciousness" and "problem" pictures) shows relative sophistication on both artistic and sociocultural levels. Newman and Sidney Poitier play American musicians (trombone and saxophone, respectively) based in Paris, where they meet a couple of American tourists (Joanne Woodward and Diahann Carroll) in town for a two-week vacation. Newman makes Carroll's acquaintance first and is obviously attracted to her despite (or because of) their racial difference. He pays little attention to her companion until the white tourist aggressively pursues him, whereupon the white characters become lovers and Poitier moves into his "logical" position as the black woman's boyfriend. The film thus reinforces the ideological notion of homogeneous racial pairing, yet conveys the fragility of this norm by hinting that the couples could have formed differently if those involved had followed their spontaneous "instincts" rather than allowing ingrained habits to steer them into a more "proper" track.

Sexual behavior is also treated in a comparatively mature way, with no hedging about the fact that Newman and Woodward start having sex almost as soon as they get together. The film's ability to be this frank may have been abetted by its casting, since its most obvious lovers are played by an actor and actress known to their audience as a married couple off the screen; note also that the story is set not in the United States but in Paris, familiar to American moviegoers as a "libidinous" locale. Moreover, its sympathetic depiction of close black-white relations was surely supported by the screenplay's care to make the white couple the real protagonists of the story, relegating the black couple to secondary status. (The "mixing up of the races" decried by a belligerent character in *Too Late Blues*, released in the same year, was no casual matter for many American spectators.) Still, the film does look at sexuality and black-white friendship with unusual directness for its period. And this is connected to a reasonably intelligent depiction of a Beat-like milieu where spontaneous creativity is fostered and even encouraged. Nobody in the film is really a Beat, but Newman and Poitier use Beat-type words and phrases like "chick" and "dig it," and Newman's attitude toward women is charged with a Beat-like refusal of long-term commitment in favor of "kicks while they last." Perhaps fearing that such quasi-Beat signifiers would lead audiences to infer that more unsavory Beat goings-on are happening offscreen, the film brings a particularly dangerous possibility—drug use—into the open and deals with it in a suitably conservative way. One secondary character, a flamenco guitarist, is addicted to cocaine. Newman strives to pull him away from his "habit," receiving unexpected support when they encounter a former flamenco star reduced by narcotics to poverty and dementia. So great is the curse of substance abuse, however, that Newman's colleague backslides and even tries to inveigle Newman into getting high with him, precipitating a final break between them. This subplot leaves no doubt regarding the film's disapproval of liminoid behaviors less benignly recreational than consensual sex and racially mixed friendship.

Back on the romantic front, both love affairs get a bit rocky, and the Newman-Woodward pair fall into particular peril because of the contrast between her small-town American practicality and his Beat-style penchant for off-the-cuff living. Interestingly, however, the film uses both relationships as vehicles for exploring larger issues. In the case of the white couple, Newman's character is not satisfied with being a "mere" jazz musician with a gift for improvising. Rather, he wants to be a "real" composer who writes his music down for orchestras to play. (This longing is no ephemeral fantasy of the *Paris Blues* screenplay but reflects the yearnings—and inferiority feelings—of numerous actual jazz musicians; they include the brilliant Charlie Parker, whose astonishing gifts did not prevent him from envying classical composers and engaging in experiments—e.g., the *Bird With Strings* recordings—combining American-style jazz with European-style classicism.) A climactic moment occurs when Newman has a long-awaited appointment with an impresario, who informs him that he is not yet "ready" for serious composition, although he might be successful if he pursues formal study in counterpoint, harmony, and so forth. This incident leads him to accept Woodward's plea and agree to return to the United States with her, but at the last moment he decides to stay in Paris and see how much farther he can take his musical ambitions. This decision accords with the development of his character throughout the movie and consolidates his status as a sincere artist whose Beat-like tendencies are understandable and even defensible, if also painful to others with more "solid" personalities.

Carroll also wants Poitier to join her in the United States, and their argument has a specifically racial dimension. He tells her forthrightly that he likes Paris better than the United States because the French regard him not as a "Negro musician" but simply as a "musician." (His sense of freedom from racial oppression in Paris is so strong that he feels no hint of resentment when a little boy addresses him and Carroll as "Monsieur Noir" and "Madame Noir," hearing this as a neutral designation of physical appearance.) By contrast, Carroll feels that "home" can only be where one's roots and family are located. The two of them must therefore be Americans, she argues—optimistically adding that black and white people are working hard in the United States to make things better for everyone, which means he is not solving "the race question" by living abroad but *could* help solve it if he stayed "home" and joined this effort. At one point she emphatically tells him there is "no place on this planet" that is not miserable for some race, color, or sex; her reference to gender inequality (in 1961, well before the blossoming of the modern feminist movement) adds to the apparent intelligence of her character and the movie in which she appears.

Paris Blues has little to do with Rimbaud, derangement, or extremes of liminality, despite the prominence of homonymous Ram Bowen in its cast of characters; nor does it deal with fully fledged Beat characters, despite its use of verbal, visual, and musical cues that foreground Beat-related interests. Unlike many films that do treat purportedly Beat subjects, however, it foregoes signs of overt paranoia or hostility via-à-vis Beat material, avoiding the usual Hollywood need for wholesale denial and rejection thereof.

And it does feature a large amount of genuine jazz. Duke Ellington composed the score; and while his career was associated mainly with big

bands rather than the small combos favored by bop players, he had a consistent ability to mold and orchestrate the sound of his large group with a
subtlety and precision normally found only in the more intimate context
of small-group interplay. The music is often allowed to pump away during
dialogue scenes, moreover, lending pulse and atmosphere to the drama
and indirectly echoing the voice-and-music polyphony of Kerouac's recordings with such jazz instrumentalists as Al Cohn, Zoot Sims, and (surprisingly) Steve Allen. Louis Armstrong, that near-ubiquitous jazz symbol
of the postwar era, makes another of his film appearances in *Paris Blues*,
as a minor character called Wild Man Moore; leave the "e" off his last
name, and you have a stark reflection of the prevailing white attitude toward assertive black people in Western society and Hollywood movies.
Moore's only major scene is a battle-of-the-bands jam session that occurs
when he and his group invade the club where Newman and Poitier play.
Still, his presence may almost be said to preside over the narrative—just as
the (romanticized) spirit of African-American life presides over aspects of
the Beat project—since his image is often glimpsed in photographs and
posters even when he himself is nowhere around. He embodies a profound
spontaneity, creativity, and marginality of which the Newman and Poitier
characters represent only dim echoes. *Paris Blues* would be a deeper and
richer film if it paid more attention to him, or ditched his comparatively
dull colleagues and focused on him entirely. Still, by acknowledging his
importance at all, however vaguely, the movie achieves a higher level of
intelligence and insight than most jazz or Beat dramas of its time.

Inside the Beatcave

Beat Girl, a British film thoroughly in the mold of contemporaneous Hollywood pictures—and duly released in the United States, as *Wild
for Kicks*—was directed by Edmond T. Greville for the English production arm of MGM in 1962. Dealing with London teenagers who think of
themselves as Beats, it carries Beat-film music beyond the folky sounds of
The Beat Generation and *A Bucket of Blood*, but manages to skip over bebop and zoom straight into rock-and-roll. True, there is a scene where the
heroine's stepmother establishes her *bona fides* as a "cool chick" by praising West Coast jazz and Dave Brubeck; but the latter is hardly the most
swinging pianist she might have chosen, and the teens' acceptance of
her credentials makes one wonder how Beat they really are.[13] In any case,

rock-and-roll (with electric guitars, etc.) seems to be their natural element, which points the film ahead to the swinging-England scene of the later '60s rather than back to the Beat-bopping '40s and '50s.[14]

The story focuses on a schoolgirl named Jennifer who lives with her father, an architect, and her recently acquired stepmother, a twenty-four-year-old Frenchwoman who wants desperately to build a good home with her new family. The father turns out to be well meaning but ineffectual, spending too little time "understanding" his daughter because of his obsession with designing a futuristic city that will keep wind, rain, and noise out of its inhabitants' lives. (A logical progression from the Levittowns of '50s America, this design is presented as social engineering at its most advanced and most intimidating; the filmmakers don't seem quite sure whether they fear or admire it.) The stepmother turns out to be a former prostitute and "exotic dancer" whose life changed when Jennifer's dad fell in love with her. After a long succession of fights, feuds, quarrels, and arguments, the family comes tentatively together when Jennifer witnesses the murder of a dance-hall proprietor by one of his strippers, a former colleague of the stepmother. This occurrence apparently brings home to Jennifer the fragility of human nature and the arduousness of the road that her stepmother has trod.

The film's portrayal of Beatness conflates generic adolescent anomie (postwar variety) with alleged Beat nihilism and despair over the future. The dialogue distances itself from sympathy with Beats near the beginning, when a schoolmate calls Jennifer a "crazy one" and "part of that beatnik crowd," describing the latter as "a gimmick from America. Hopeless and soapless!" A later scene, between Jennifer and her father, pitches the same portrait of Beat world-weariness as the first scene in *The Beat Generation*, again linking hepcat pessimism with the pointlessness of life in the nuclear age:

He: Where do you get your kicks from? Sitting around in cafés listening to gramophone records? Jiving in underground cellars and caves?

She: You are a real square, aren't you?

He: This language, these words—what does it mean?

She [excited]: It means *us*, something that's ours. We didn't get it from our parents. We can express ourselves, and they don't know what we're talking about! It makes us *different*.

He: Why do you need to feel so different?

She: It's all we've got. Next week, voom—up goes the world in smoke, and what's the score? Zero. So now, while it's *now* we live it up. Do everything. Feel everything. Strictly for kicks!

He: You'll find there's more to life than—kicks, as you call it.

She: Oh please, cut out the message. People like you build cities, but you don't begin to understand the first thing about us who'll have to live in them.

He: You'd better go to bed now, Jennifer.

The movie is not altogether hostile to Beat attitudes, however, and shows some interest in excusing them, if not exactly sharing them. When it moves outside the troubled family's home, the narrative sets up a fairly direct contrast between two liminal spaces with different histories and functions: the Off Beat, a coffeehouse where the teenagers hang out, and Les Girls, a strip joint (possibly named after George Cukor's punningly titled 1957 musical) where the stepmother's secret is revealed and the climactic murder occurs. Each is seen as a disreputable and transgressive place, but the Off Beat never erupts into any violence more dangerous than a fistfight. (A couple of life-risking "chicken" sessions, obviously inspired by *Rebel Without a Cause*, take place outdoors; and nobody gets hurt.) While evenings at the Off Beat seem fairly joyless and pointless, the film allows the Beat teens to argue that their homes are even more joyless and pointless, populated with boring parents who make no effort to communicate with (much less fathom and appreciate) their alienated offspring. The youngsters' anomic habit of lounging around the Off Beat's cavelike basement is traced not only to fears of the nuclear future but also to memories of the disrupted past; the cellar is likened to the World War II air-raid shelters and bombed-out neighborhoods in which the Beat characters spent a miserable part of their childhoods. "I tell you, man, this is a home from home for me," says one habitué of the cave, who recalls living like a "scared rat underground" during the war and later improvises a bit of "rat-race rock" on his guitar, linking the literal rats of decimated London to the well-known metaphor for postwar discontent. (Describing the bombing of his childhood home, another Beat uses the same word—"voom"—that Jennifer used to evoke nuclear annihilation, quoted above.) Meanwhile, tremendous scorn is heaped on a Beat caught bringing liquor (disguised as cough medicine) onto the premises. This incident reminds the teens of their decadent parents, especially the fathers, who come off like so many Colonel Blimps to their disaffected children. Indeed, the booze is denigrated for being age-inappropriate in both directions at once: Alcohol is called "for squares," meaning for dull grownups, and also "kid stuff."

By contrast, liquor flows at Les Girls, where strippers gyrate and the unsavory manager is played by Christopher Lee, already established with young audiences as a monster specialist in Hammer horror films such as *The Curse of Frankenstein* (1957) and *The Horror of Dracula* (1958). He waxes seductive toward Jennifer when she visits his club to investigate her stepmother's past, and the film assumes him to be utterly unsuitable for her even though its most important subplot (involving the stepmother) hinges on the notion that people can reverse their bad tendencies if they fall in love with someone who is basically a good influence. In sum, the brand of liminality represented by Les Girls is clearly unacceptable in comparison with that of the Off Beat, perhaps because the Beat joint allows for spontaneous and participatory moments—youngsters dance and even make their own music at times—while the older folks at Les Girls just sit and gawk at the strippers. The message appears to be that Beats are aimless, apathetic, and immature, but so are the squares who construct and run societies like this one, and at least the Beats have excuses for feeling the way they do. In any case, life will never be easy for the Beats, according to this movie that ends with a murder, a family united more by trauma than affection, and a Beat throwing his smashed-up guitar in a garbage can while muttering the screenplay's last words, "Only squares know where to go."

Music and Addiction

The discourse of addiction that plays a supporting role in such films as *Paris Blues* and *A Bucket of Blood* is foregrounded in *The Man With the Golden Arm*, directed in 1955 by Otto Preminger. The film is based on a novel by Nelson Algren, whose "walk on the wild side" interests have led some literary historians to associate him loosely with the Beats.[15]

Frank Sinatra plays the aptly named Frankie Machine, a working-class New Yorker who has just kicked a heroin habit with medical help at a Federal prison clinic. His new ambition is to use the musical skills he learned in prison and become a jazz drummer. In a pointedly ironic aspect of the plot, it is the police who cause his return to addiction. Aware that he must not revert to his old ways of living, Frankie strives to obtain an audition with a jazz band. When an old friend (actually a sort of village idiot played by Arnold Stang with mousy insouciance) shoplifts a suit for him, he is promptly arrested for wearing it; he misses the audition, and in order to leave jail, he must cooperate with a gambler who wants him back in his old job as a dealer for illegal card games. Thoroughly enmeshed in the "old ways" he had hoped to avoid, he is easy prey for the heroin dealer (Darren McGavin) who stalks him from the moment of his arrival home. More pressure comes from his wife (Eleanor Parker), whom he married out of sympathy after car-crash injuries disabled her; although she can now walk again, she keeps this a secret from Frankie, who forgoes romance with an attractive neighbor (Kim Novak) because of loyalty to his spouse. The film builds to a climax, interweaving elements of play, artistic aspiration, and addiction as Frankie is forced to deal a marathon poker game so he can obtain the heroin that will steady his hands and allow him to pass a new drumming audition. Another climax shows him re-renouncing heroin through "cold turkey" withdrawal.

The milieu of *The Man With the Golden Arm* is not Beat and unconventional but blue-collar and drab, using character names with clearly marked ethnicity (the bar owner, the card-game proprietor, etc.) to signify individual backgrounds and also the immigrant-based social economy of the neighborhood; this device allows the film to allude to underprivilege, discrimination, and other sociocultural ills without plunging into (or even acknowledging) racial problems per se. The limiting (and in some ways liminal) confines of the neighborhood are emphasized by two strategies. One is the use of studio sets conveying a claustrophobic atmosphere, heightened by careful juxtapositions of specific places, such as the location of the pusher's first-floor apartment directly across the street from the bar where much of the action unfolds. The other is the deployment of strikingly long takes (many involving expressive camera movements) that deliberately physicalize the space of the story, establishing the on-screen neighborhood not as a setting constructed by editing processes but rather as a preexisting locale through which the characters/camera/audience must continually find their way. Against this setting, the rhythms and voicings of Elmer Bernstein's score—and more straightforward jazz when Frankie shows up for his audition with what turns out to be a band featuring drummer Shelly Manne—suggest freedom *from* the urban jungle and immersion *in* that jungle's energy and physicality.

Frankie's heroin dependency can be seen as a bad residue of transitional-object behavior, since addiction is one of the phenomena that may result when a transitional object is given up by the developing psyche;

fetishism is another (Winnicott 9). Although narcotics addiction cannot be equated with fetishism, both have roots in infantile object-relation experience, and this fact provides a useful basis for interpreting behaviors like dependency and reliance on talismans. Frankie's quest in *The Man With the Golden Arm* may be viewed as an attempt to replace his pathological reliance on heroin with a more benign relationship to the drumsticks that symbolize his new aspirations.

Alter Ego

Attachment to a talisman is more forceful in some films about horn players, perhaps because a brass or woodwind instrument—which demands direct contact with lips and breath—has an unmediated connection with oral and respiratory functions that the drums of *The Man With the Golden Arm* and *The Gene Krupa Story* do not. *Young Man With a Horn*, directed by Michael Curtiz and released in 1950, is quite explicit about the trumpet as a fetish or at least a talisman. Its hero, played by Kirk Douglas and loosely based on jazz musician Bix Beiderbecke, carries his horn everywhere he goes and comments on the physical intimacy he has with it, noting that it's like a part of himself. (The music of a trumpet, he points out, does not have to travel as far as the music of other instruments.) One of his lovers, an aspiring psychoanalyst played by Lauren Bacall, describes the horn as his "alter ego," defining the term by explaining, "It simply means your other self." The horn is not just his other self, moreover, but also a substitute for a missing parent: When he remarks that his mother died when he was a child—an event included in the film's introductory scenes—the psychiatrist-in-training observes that he has successfully found something to replace her. (Given the pat simplicity of this one-to-one symbolism, Bacall's character might better be described as a pop-psychologist-in-training.) As if to reinforce the necessity of talismanic objects for "creative" characters, the film also presents a jazz pianist, played by Hoagy Carmichael, who is equally dependent on nearly continual retention of a treasured object; since the piano is obviously not suitable for such minute-to-minute companionship, he uses cigarettes as a substitute, so tenaciously that "Smoke" has become his nickname.

The ultimate ambition of the Beiderbecke character is to play a note that has never been heard before; this quasimystical dream recalls the Beat ambition to improvise linguistic feats unlike any reachable through standard writing practices. He receives his early coaching from an African-American trumpeter whose name—Art Hazzard, connoting both aesthetics and chance or spontaneity—is as unabashedly symbolic as that of Wild Man Moore in *Paris Blues*, if somewhat different in its implications. As in *Pete Kelly's Blues*, among other films, the mantle of jazz greatness is seen to pass from a black to a white figure. But in *Young Man With a Horn*, the physical and psychological decline of Art Hazzard is followed by the similar decline of the movie's protagonist, who ends the story as a miserably addicted alcoholic—loss of his trumpet has led to a compensatory drinking habit—lying delirious in a treatment-center bed and hallucinating that an ambulance siren is a trumpet hitting the never-heard note of his dreams. The film is accurate in suggesting that Beiderbecke died an early and alcohol-related death; and it could be called prescient with regard to at least one Beat figure, since its hero vaguely resembles Kerouac, who would expire under vaguely similar circumstances about twenty years after its release.

Despite the validity of its cautionary climax, however, the film lacks the courage to follow through on its awareness of talismanic psychodynamics and the pathology of addiction. No sooner does the protagonist undergo his musical hallucination than Smoke appears, ending his narration with the announcement that our hero recovered from his troubles and lived to become a greater artist (as well as a finer human being) than ever. Rarely has Hollywood's convention of the "tacked-on happy ending" been more shamelessly employed or transparently artificial. As a product of mainstream ideology, *Young Man With a Horn* is eager to warn us of the dangers lurking in spontaneous (jazz/Beat/hipster) living; as a product of commercial cinema, it is equally eager to rescue us from leaving the theater with those dangers too vividly in mind.

Looking? Who's Looking?

> *Buzz:* So I say, who needs New York? Only the buildings got roots there—and they don't go too deep. Sure, we're looking. Todd says if we keep moving we'll find a place to plant roots and stick. With me it's fine—just—moving.
> *Old laborer:* You don't make sense, boy.
> *Buzz:* Well, maybe. But you know. You dig.
>
> —Route 66

163

The publication of *On the Road* by Viking Press in 1957 was followed by a good deal of critical controversy, and also by a good deal of interest in the motion-picture rights to Kerouac's spontaneous-prose odyssey.[16] Warner Bros. offered $110,000 for them, and according to a letter from Kerouac to Cassady, the studio wanted Kerouac to play the Sal Paradise role; but Kerouac's literary agent, Sterling Lord, received word that Paramount and Marlon Brando were also interested and decided to demand $40,000 more.[17] Word later arrived that Brando considered the novel too "loose" for Hollywood treatment, whereupon Kerouac vainly tried to revive the actor's interest with a letter describing how he would adapt it to the screen. While he was at it, he took the opportunity to mention his ideas for bringing all the film and theater of America "up to par with her Divine Poets" (Nicosia 564), as he colorfully (and self-congratulatorily?) phrased it.

Although nothing came of this letter, Hollywood renewed its enthusiasm for Beat matters in general and *On the Road* in particular when Kerouac submitted *The Dharma Bums* for publication. Jerry Wald of Twentieth Century-Fox contacted Kerouac about an *On the Road* screenplay consultation, and Brando (back on the scene) asked Lord not to sell the film rights until he could submit a bid. Wald was apparently serious about adapting *On the Road*, but he wanted to echo *The Wild One*—which had earned much attention for Brando and others—by making a movie more brutal than Kerouac's novel; he particularly wanted the Dean Moriarty character (a surrogate for Cassady) to die in an automobile crash at the end, which would allow the movie to capitalize on the real-life death of actor James Dean, who coincidentally shared Cassady's birthday.

Kerouac was distressed with some journalists and intellectuals who insisted on linking Beat attitudes with hostility and even violence. (Hollywood filmmakers made this link too, of course, in such movies as *The Beat Generation* and *A Bucket of Blood.*) Norman Podhoretz, for example, had asserted that the Beat ethos "shades off into violence and criminality, main-line drug addiction and madness." He also claimed that Kerouac's books contain a "suppressed cry" of "Kill the intellectuals who can talk coherently, kill the people who can sit still for five minutes at a time, kill those incomprehensible characters who are capable of getting seriously involved with a woman, a job, a cause" (346, 355). Striking similar notes, Art Cohn had written in the San Francisco *Chronicle* of "the new religion, the Jehovah of the Beaten handed down from his Mount: Thou shalt kill for the sake of killing. Thou shalt defile all flesh, including your own . . . " (C. Cassady 291). Protesting that not "killing" but rather "peace" and "tenderness" were his priorities, Kerouac declared that he would allow no film containing "cruelty" to be made from any of his books. This statement prefigured his later objection to suggested violence in the film version of *The Subterraneans,* when Jack/George Peppard defends Mardou/Leslie Caron with a beer bottle in his hand;[18] and it anticipated his unhappiness with the moment in *Pull My Daisy* when the Larry Rivers character points a revolver-like finger at Gregory Corso's head and says, "Pow," introducing a note of childish violence that "played into the hands of literary snobs," as Kerouac later complained.[19]

Wald subsequently shifted his attention from *On the Road* to a request for an original screenplay on a new subject. A few months into 1958, the film rights to *The Subterraneans* went to MGM for $15,000, and Kerouac agreed to sell *On the Road* to the small Tri-Way Productions for $10,000 more, far less than his agent had dreamed of not long before. Kerouac received only ten percent of this modest sum before the production company—having commissioned a screenplay from Gene Du Pont and enlisted Mort Sahl, Cliff Robertson, and Joyce Jamison to play Dean, Sal, and Marylou, respectively—went defunct. With the novel still unfilmed, Robert Frank and Alfred Leslie decided they would like to complete their already started film trilogy (discussed above) with an *On the Road* adaptation; but Leslie felt that so much on-location filming would be impracticable, the rights would probably have been out of their price range anyway, and Kerouac was apparently reluctant to put the property into the hands of such inexperienced filmmakers (Allan 1988, 190). By the end of the '50s, it appeared *On the Road* might never arrive on the theatrical screen.

Television producers were also interested in the novel's possibilities, though. Kerouac appears to have been wary about parting with the rights on their terms, but CBS sidestepped any such problem by enlisting veteran TV writer Stirling Silliphant to concoct *Route 66,* in which the 1949 Hudson of Dean and Sal became the 1960 Chevrolet Corvette of Buzz and Todd, who roamed the American roadways on a weekly basis in search of "a place where we really fit—a kind of a niche for ourselves, you know?" as Buzz puts it in a mid-series episode.[20] Buzz is the more Beat-like of the two, coming from an underprivileged background that helps account for his dissatisfaction with ordinary, stationary life: He grew up in the St. Francis Home for Foundlings in New York City's notorious Hell's Kitchen neighborhood, and upon graduating from that institution took a job on the East River, where he happened to work for Todd's father. Todd had the advantage not only of said father but also of a prep-school and Yale University education; but the father died just after giving him his treasured 'Vette Stingray, and this inspired in Todd a wanderlust as profound as Buzz's own.

Setting the tone for the program, which ran successfully from 1960 to 1964, the first installment ("Black November") brings Buzz and Todd to the town of Garth, Mississippi, which turns out (in the manner of John Sturges's melodrama *Bad Day at Black Rock*, among other films) to be collectively hiding a nasty secret: that during the World War II years, when the town housed a prison camp, the resident patriarch (Mr. Garth) gratuitously killed a German prisoner and also a local minister who tried to shield the victim. This incident took place in the shadow of a huge "wolf tree," beneath which the bodies are still buried. The symbolism of this sinister tree—chopped down at the end of the episode, allowing rays of hope to shine anew—suggests that rural America is no more "naturally" innocent or virtuous than the urban scene; hence the inability of Buzz and Todd, like Kerouac before them, to find a nice little place in either country or city and simply settle down. Asked by an automobile mechanic what he is looking for, Buzz sums up a facile version of Beat restlessness: "Looking? Who's looking? Like I say, you live it the way you feel it. When it moves, you go with it. Todd says I got unrest. So what's wrong with unrest? It's as good as anything. Besides, we're all stuck with it. You got it. Sure. I see it in your hammer. I been looking ever since I can remember." The last sentence suggests a prelogical, almost metaphysical dimension to Buzz's quest, which was evidently prompted by events, emotions, or ideas so early in his history that he cannot recall a period antedating them. In any case, he and Todd certainly do move around a lot, sometimes within a single episode—such as "Good Night, Sweet Blues," in which an elderly jazz singer played by Ethel Waters asks them to reassemble her old combo for a final session before she dies, and the heroes (Buzz is identified as a "jazz buff") obligingly visit Pittsburgh, Kansas City, Chicago, and New York before their weekly hour is up.

It is a little-noted fact that Kerouac himself had no fondness for driving, the myths fostered by *On the Road* notwithstanding. In keeping with his rejection of violence in Beat-related material, he was even less fond of the violence—mild though it was by later standards—in *Route 66*, which he felt was obviously influenced by his books and public persona. (It did not escape notice that George Maharis bore a distinct resemblance to Kerouac and may have received his starring role for this reason.) Determined to act on his outrage, Kerouac recruited two lawyers to sue the producers for plagiarism; but both advised him that there was "insufficient evidence" (McNally 272).

As discussed earlier, Kerouac loved film not only as a pastime and diversion but also as a meaningful popular art; this is attested by his frequent references to such figures as W. C. Fields and Joan Crawford, which point to deeply personal meanings, as when Fields is likened to his father or Crawford is mythologized as a symbol of American dreams and longings. He also bought into the mystique of Hollywood fame and glamour, as his excited reference to a possible *On the Road* acting job for Cassady indicates. At the same time, however, Kerouac saw the frequent crudity, constant commercialism, and built-in repetitiveness of Hollywood film as all-too-typical ingredients of the mainstream culture that Beat thinking wanted to reform, supersede, or flatly reject; and his reaction to *Route 66* is best understood in this light. The important "Joan Rawshanks in the Fog" section in *Visions of Cody* gains much of its effectiveness from Kerouac's ability to spin out verbal refractions of specifically cinematic qualities; yet despite its vigorous deployment of these filmlike devices, the piece's wry and rueful undertones leave little doubt that Kerouac sees the film industry as a manipulative, phony, even degenerate parody of the youthful idealism and enthusiasm that energize Kerouac/Duluoz as he chronicles the spectacle of Hollywood behind the scenes.[21] It is no wonder that the weekly rituals of *Route 66* failed to flatter him with their rote recyclings of his earlier work. More specifically, the novel that inspired *Route 66* is anchored in Kerouac's quest not merely for a more pleasing or pleasant America but for a heightened state of spiritual energy and enlightenment. The compulsive traveling of Dean and Sal is more psychically than physically significant, since the book represents an early stage in Kerouac's own movement from expansive worldliness to introspective withdrawal.[22] As a peripatetic entertainment devoted to glancing social encounters, speedily resolved adventures, and superficial human relationships, *Route 66* stands in relation to *On the Road* as commercially driven exploitation of the worst sort, substituting easy pleasures of the world for the challenging pleasures of the soul toward which Kerouac's voyagers instinctively gravitate.

Work!??!

> And so now they have beatnik routines on TV. . . . Beat comes out, actually,
> of old American whoopee and it will only change a few dresses and pants
> and make chairs useless in the living room. . . .
> —Jack Kerouac, "The Origins of the Beat Generation," 1959

Route 66 was not CBS's first foray into the Beat world. *The Many Loves of Dobie Gillis*, featuring beatnik Maynard G. Krebs as the eponymous protagonist's best friend, had debuted in 1959 and continued its run through the 1963 season. Maynard wore a goatee, a floppy sweatshirt, and sneakers wherever he went. His favorite word was "like," used as an all-purpose seasoning for all syntactical occasions. His least favorite activity was work, and his yelp of plaintive echolalia— *"WORK!??!"*—erupted whenever this syllable was uttered in his presence. (Amusingly, he seemed equally panicked whether someone was suggesting that *he* work or was using the word in an altogether different context, such as "Things will work out.")

Maynard was an invention of the program's writers, not a carry-over from the Max Shulman story collections (*The Many Loves of Dobie Gillis, I Was a Teenage Dwarf*) on which the show was based. He resulted from CBS's correct assessment that the indolence, aimlessness, and insouciance attributed to Beats by mainstream opinion would be perceived as humorous and appealing (if not laudable or enviable) if embodied by a suitably sweet character. Analysis of his name reveals some of the thinking that went into his manufacture. Most of the *Dobie Gillis* characters—Thalia Menninger, Zelda Gilroy, Chatsworth Osborne Jr., Dobie himself—combine ordinary last names with uncommon first names evidently meant to seem vaguely silly in their failure to conform with '50s norms. Maynard goes a step further. His somewhat unusual first name (always pronounced with a flat American "erd" rather than a high-toned British "ard") is followed by an incongruously formal middle initial (signifying a slightly absurd pretentiousness shared by Herbert T. Gillis, the protagonist's self-important father) and a last name whose brevity (after the preceding three syllables, concluding with the open-ended "G" sound) and arbitrary plurality (more than one Kreb?) has the effect of a belchlike punch line after a mock-dignified buildup.[23]

As played by Bob Denver, a former English teacher and future *Gilligan's Island* regular, Maynard reflects the assertiveness of his tripartite name only insofar as he marches to a drummer slightly different from that heard by his middle-middle-class friends. He insists on his ultracasual clothing and knows his own mind in matters of taste: loves jazz, hates WORK!??!, is wary of "chicks." But otherwise he behaves no more or less bizarrely than the other characters in what is, after all, a TV comedy. Most important, he is not a Beat but a beatnik, indistinguishable from the bourgeoisie in all but a few superficial mannerisms. The late '50s were years when the *New York Times* could see fit to print an assertion that establishment types were "not criticizing [Beat] clothing and beards or their way of life, except when it becomes immoral" (quoted in McNally 271), and as Kerouac biographer Dennis McNally notes, the Maynard character was a perfect pop-culture construction in such an atmosphere: a childlike (one might better say puppylike) eccentric whose honesty, loyalty, and morality were plain to see (271–72). As an imaginary playmate for viewers, he was as lovable as anyone on television; as a specimen of the Beat Generation, he was a caricature whom right-thinking Americans could laugh into inconsequentiality every single week.

*E*nter Cassavetes

> *Johnny Staccato is a private detective. He works at it because it pays well and he likes to spend money. But for sheer pleasure he's a jazz pianist— highly regarded by other musicians but not interested in actually working as a musician. Being a young man who can devise ways to get what he wants from life, however, Staccato makes it a practice to combine his two pastimes at a place called* Waldo's: *a jazz hangout on MacDougal Street in Greenwich Village where he gets his calls, keeps appointments with clients, and spends his spare time playing piano with the swinging groups that work there.*
>
> —liner notes, Staccato sound-track album

Another television haven for jazz and Beat-like gestures was *Staccato*, starring John Cassavetes, produced in 1959–60 by Revue Productions in association with the NBC network. More emphatically than *Route 66* and less comically than *Dobie Gillis*, this program defines liminality by representing it not as a state of removal *from* mainstream norms (à la Buzz and Todd, and minimally by Maynard) but rather as an appropriation of border positions *within* the social given. That is, the protagonist lives, works, and plays within the boundaries of normal urban society; yet he is positioned as a maverick with vaguely Beat tendencies (bound up with jazz, creativity, the Village subculture) through his ability to straddle a variety of discursive areas that have somewhat contradictory implications: detective work/music playing, physical toughness/artistic sensitivity, financial success/bohemian surroundings, and so forth.

The show is more interested in Staccato's crime-busting activities than his musical proclivities. The series premiere ("The Naked Truth," with Staccato protecting a would-be singer from violent enemies) devotes a fair amount of time to jazz at Waldo's; yet a later episode (such as "The Mask of Jason," with a *noir*-ishly lighted Mary Tyler Moore fleeing Bert Remsen as her burn-victim ex-husband) might show virtually no jazz-playing at all.[24] Elmer Bernstein's jazz-inflected score is frequently on hand, though, to remind the audience of the program's basic premise. Noting that *Staccato* marks Bernstein's "first background score for the medium of television," the sound-track album identified his *Man With the Golden Arm* music as the inspiration for "modern jazz backgrounds" in other movies and TV shows. Bernstein himself resisted calling *The Man With the Golden Arm* a jazz score, although he acknowledged using "jazz elements" to create its distinctive moods.[25] Still, it had plenty of jazz-happy imitators, and jazz became popular on TV series during this period; besides Bernstein's return to the territory in *Staccato*, instances include Blake Edwards's stylish *Gunn*, with Craig Stevens playing detective Peter Gunn to Henry Mancini's pop-jazz themes, and *M Squad*, with Lee Marvin as a hard-boiled police officer whose pugnacious activities are often accompanied by jauntily tinkling themes.[26] Titles of individual numbers played on *Staccato* range from "Greenwich Village Rumble" and "MacDougal Street Special" to "The Jazz at Waldo's" and "Like Having Fun." This program's obsession with Greenwich Village place-names illustrates the tenacity of the mythic Beat-Village connection despite the preference of the early Beats for less gentrified locales such as Times Square and environs, not to mention their strong presence in San Francisco, a continent away.

Back to the Blues

> Barroom thug: You know, I wouldn't trust my wife around these musicians. I hear they give parties that go on all day and all night—a lot of drinkin', takin' dope, mixin' up of the races, bad things like that. . . .
>
> . . . . .

Immigrant bar owner: I know all you see at your parties—a lot of cheap dames and beards.
   Young jazz musician: What's the matter with beards? All the old Greeks used to wear them, didn't they?
   Bar owner: Yeah, but they were not finger-popping daddies, kiddo!
   . . . . .
   Another musician: Why don't you come to the party tonight, Nick?
   Bar owner: Oh, I'm too old for beatniks. . . . The philosophy of this country is not like the philosophy of my country. Over there you find a woman, you love that woman. Right? And you don't need no party, you don't need no dames. One woman. . . .
         —Too Late Blues, *directed by John Cassavetes, 1961*

The most historically noteworthy aspect of *Staccato* is the fact that Cassavetes plays the protagonist, marking one of his early associations with dramatic material carrying Beat or Beat-like connotations.[27] Cassavetes followed up his personal and professional interest in jazz and hipsters with the 1960 experimental drama *Shadows*, which strays far from the classical-style parameters of *Staccato* and will be discussed presently; he then pursued this interest with the 1961 jazz feature *Too Late Blues*. This film points in some directions that Cassavetes' career would later take, but maintains an aura of Hollywood correctness that links it more closely with *Staccato* than with *Shadows*[28] or such mature Cassavetes works as *Minnie and Moskowitz* and *Husbands*, which it slightly resembles in some ways. Cassavetes produced and directed *Too Late Blues* for Paramount from a screenplay he wrote with Richard Cass. The music, composed by David Raksin, is played by a group including drummer Shelly Manne—who was also heard (and seen) in *The Man With the Golden Arm*—as well as bassist Red Mitchell, pianist Jimmy Rowles, saxophonist Benny Carter, trumpeter Van Rasey, and trombonist Milt Bernhart.

In his first dramatic role, pop singer Bobby Darin stars as a pianist named John "Ghost" Wakefield, who heads a small-time jazz band that plays more for love than money at this stage of its career. The group has a nasty-seeming agent—although he may be seen as bluntly honest rather than simply offensive for the fun of it—whose unpleasant manner causes acute distress for a would-be singer (named Jess Polanski, played by Stella Stevens) in whom Ghost becomes romantically interested. She responds to Ghost in a directly physical manner that surprises and shocks him. Rejecting her sexual advances in favor of a more "meaningful" relationship, he asks where she got the idea that sexuality is the most effective way to reach out to another person; she answers with the infelicitously scripted query, "Where would I stand without my body?" Ghost asks her to think about such matters more deeply, and she declares that she doesn't think, because she could not predict what would follow from this activity. She adds that the best policy in life is to do what seems best at any given moment. In her continually (if unreflectively) improvised style of living, she is closer to Beat attitudes and practices than is the jazz-riffing Ghost; she also anticipates many later Cassavetes characters in this regard—especially women, often played by Gena Rowlands—although *Too Late Blues* makes an imperfect introduction to the Cassavetes *oeuvre* because of compromises required by the studio for which it was produced.

Ghost pursues his interest in Jess, bringing her into a horseplay-filled baseball game and then an emotionally complicated saloon scene, where a drinking bout with the eccentric Greek proprietor leads to a brawl sparked by the obnoxious agent. Ghost fails to fight in this brawl, even when he is roughed up by a conspicuously mean person. This failure to fight does not bother Jess, who says she still loves him, but he appears to be ashamed of his passivity. Another band member takes her home, and she reverts to her aggressive sexuality. Shortly later, at a long-sought recording session, Ghost refuses to play his favorite blues number, apparently because Jess—now the band's vocalist—is not there to sing it. Ghost asserts his ownership of the number, on the grounds that he wrote, scored, and suffered over it; he then breaks up with the band, taking a stance of this-gig-isn't-good-enough-for-my-great-tune. He asks the agent to make him famous, and the agent fixes him up with a rich old woman (called the Princess) as a gigolo. She gets him a sell-out job as pianist in a club where nobody pays attention to the music. A year later he finds Jess working as a prostitute in a bar; she almost commits suicide after seeing Ghost, but proclaims her love when he comes to her rescue. He takes her to a club where the rest of the old band is playing, and after telling him to leave, the band members play an up-tempo number that induces Jess to croon her old blues, whereupon they join in with her.

Despite the marginal status of *Too Late Blues* as an *auteur* production, it anticipates later Cassavetes films in some ways. Moments that prefigure subsequent movies include Jess's attempted suicide (*A Woman Under the Influence*, 1974), backstage glimpses in a nightclub (*The Killing of a Chinese Bookie*, 1976), the horseplay at the bar and baseball game (*Husbands*, 1970), and the bar owner's sudden rage in the opening scene (*Minnie and*

Moskowitz, 1971). The film's restless, close-in camera style was also to become a Cassavetes trademark; the same goes for its choreographed blocking of groups (particularly males) and its overlapping dialogue (or, more accurately, muddled collections of verbiage mixed into an impressionistic aural blend). Still, there is more of Hollywood's conventional shot/countershot construction here than in most films directed by Cassavetes, and the story development is also relatively conventional, with a substantial investment in linear cause-and-effect psychology.

These qualities notwithstanding, the film does reflect Cassavetes' fascination with marginal people and Beat-related ideas. Looking first at the movie's attitude toward African-American life—of particular importance in a story dealing with jazz—the credit sequence is revealing. It begins with shots of black children listening raptly to a jazz performance; then it becomes clear that Ghost's (white) band is playing for the pupils in a school. The implication is that jazz, originated by blacks, has now been taken over by whites, who present themselves as "experts" to blacks! Cassavetes seems to acknowledge this interpretation of the sequence (and the irony embedded within it) when he has a black child run away with the saxophone player's horn, whereupon the musician chases the youngster to retrieve and reclaim it.

Addictive behavior also plays an important role in the film; drinking is a major activity, as it often is in Cassavetes' work. Ghost concocts a whimsical drink for himself, Jess, and the bartender, and it turns out to be excellent despite its unlikely (and potent) ingredients; a drinking contest—full of fun and conviviality at first—sparks the story's major fight scene; and so forth. Drinking often seems an actualized metaphor for spontaneity and improvised living, key elements of the movie's quasi-Beat concerns. Certainly the use of addictive substances, and the transitional-object dependency in which it is anchored, has more positive connotations here than in such films as *The Man With the Golden Arm* and *Young Man With a Horn*, not to mention such an ultrasquare addiction film of the period as *A Hatful of Rain* (a 1957 melodrama about drug addiction, directed by Fred Zinnemann from Michael V. Gazzo's screenplay).

Broadly considered, *Too Late Blues* combines a fundamentally conventional approach with undissimulated (and sometimes quite interesting) vagaries of personality and motivation. Still, the latter appear to grow less from Cassavetes' vision of human complexity and mercuriality (as in later films) than from conflict and compromise resulting from his uneasy relationship with Paramount Pictures and its classical-style imperatives.

173

Along with the conceptually bold *A Child Is Waiting*, which concluded the studio-based phase of Cassavetes' filmmaking career, *Too Late Blues* constitutes a mildly productive digression in his movement from the audacious *Shadows* to the mature explorations of intricate existential states that would follow in later years. It also shows less involvement with Beat-like values than *Shadows*, whose divergences from Hollywood convention—in production, performance, and style—provide appropriate material for this study's segue from Hollywood and network products to radically avant-garde works produced outside commercial settings.

Spontaneous Bop Filmmaking

> *The film you have just seen was an improvisation.*
> —*last credit line*, Shadows

> *First,* Shadows *is not part of the Beat da-da-da.*
> —*Parker Tyler,* "For Shadows, *Against* Pull My Daisy"

Beat or Dada or both or neither, *Shadows* marks a clear departure from film-industrial norms, beginning with its source of financing. An opening credit identifies it as "Presented by Jean Shepherd's Night People," and this statement is accurate. Shepherd hosted a mildly eccentric '50s-era radio program incorporating music, conversations, and rambling monologues about his childhood, army days, and other personal subjects.[29] Visiting the show in 1957 to promote Martin Ritt's drama *Edge of the City*, in which he played an army deserter opposite Sidney Poitier's waterfront laborer, Cassavetes found himself disparaging the film, claiming he could direct a better one and asserting that he would make "a movie about *people*" if everyone listening would send in a small contribution. This statement may have reflected impulsive bravado rather than calculated maneuvering by a young artist who later admitted that "never in his wildest dreams did he actually expect anyone to send a nickel, and had no idea what to do with the money once he got it" (29, 32), as Cassavetes scholar Ray Carney reports. But be this as it may, about $2,000 in small contributions arrived for Cassavetes at the station within the next few days. He gathered a group of performers, rented a 16-mm camera and the necessary lights, and began work on an unconventional drama that would not be completed until nearly three years and two versions later. The first version was improvised in 1957 under Cassavetes' guidance; the second was shot in 1959 from a Cassavetes screenplay, and contains only limited material from the previous edition.[30]

Appropriately, given its unorthodox genesis and artisanal mode of production, *Shadows* reveals affinities with the Beat world before the opening credits are over—by showing one of the main characters threading his way through a youthful, music-filled party with a cigarette jammed in his mouth, dark glasses perched over his eyes, and a set of bongo drums (a peculiar touch, since we later learn he is a jazz trumpeter) clutched in his hand. He is played by Ben Carruthers and also named Ben Carruthers, since the characters are all named after the performers who portray them. Once arrived at the party, he slouches in a corner with a look of beaten-down alienation on his face; he looks more comfortable moments later, in the first shots of the narrative proper, striding down a city street in a similar uniform but with dissimilar energy and verve.

Liminality is a constant for the major characters in *Shadows*; the very title of the film signals an in-betweenness partaking definitively of neither light nor darkness. The central figures of the story—Ben and his siblings, Hugh and Lelia—are members of an African-American family, but only Hugh (played by Hugh Hurd) is obviously "black" in appearance. Besides positing this ambiguity on a narrative level, Cassavetes embeds it within the performances by casting the roles of Ben and Lelia with an actor and actress (Carruthers and Lelia Goldoni) whose physical appearances might be read as either "white" or "black" depending on the racial overtones of the context in which they are seen. These characters go through various experiences: Ben carouses with friends, picks up women, gets beaten up; Hugh looks for singing gigs, dickers with his agent, has a bad experience onstage; Lelia banters with one male friend, sleeps with another who then rejects her for racial reasons, and takes out her resulting anger on a third; and so on. The incidents amount less to a linear narrative than to a string of existential trials, continually testing the abilities of characters *and* performers to generate and sustain coherent moment-to-moment personae. (The answer to a problem posed by David E. James—"often it is difficult to know whether Ben Carruthers's parody of the James Dean hipster is a function of the actor or the role" [1988, 88]—is easily answered: both.) The film insists that not just behavior but *personality* is a function of self-invention and self-definition, needing constant renewal to avoid a desuetude that equals psychological stasis and spiritual death. This stress on presentness is what links Cassavetes' cinematic ethos most closely with

the Beat valorization of spontaneity and the aesthetically grounded quest
for an eternal now.

Arguing that Cassavetes introduces a gap between the ongoing self
and its momentary expressions, Carney gives the major Cassavetes movies
a unique position on the spectrum of narrative films. At one end of this
spectrum are commonplace, instantly decodable movies wherein characters have behavioral "surfaces" and emotional "depths" that clearly reveal
one another; impulses are readily transformed into expressions that can be
seen or heard. Farther along the spectrum are more sophisticated films
that speak *for* their characters via conventions of mise-en-scène, music,
and so forth; these movies can present relatively complex characterizations, but they still ensure that "essences" and "appearances" are firmly
connected and efficiently conveyed to the spectator. Cassavetes' works fall
into a third category wherein representation is more provisional, socially
and cinematically, and (unstated but implicit in Carney's argument) the
familiar metaphor of surface/depth is supplanted by a more productive
concept of expressive *displacement.* Cassavetes takes for granted that consciousness cannot be coherently translated into either personal behavior or
filmic convention, because blockages and slippages arise at every turn.[31]
The gap separating intention and performance allows room for games and
role-playing behaviors that are generally smothered in other sorts of films.
Such activities are clearly conducive to autotelic moments, and the flourishing of these in Cassavetes' work, where ordinary time and performance
time often commingle with boisterous energy, propels identity into a state
of "not me-not not me" multiplicity that is rarely encountered so forcefully and insistently in cinema.[32]

Truth, Essence, Race

Film Culture honored *Shadows* with the first Independent Film Award
in 1959, for showing an "improvisation, spontaneity, and free inspiration that are almost entirely lost in most films from an excess of professionalism" and for exuding "an immediacy that the cinema of today vitally
needs if it is to be a living and contemporary art" (Sitney 1970, 423–
24).[33] To the extreme displeasure of *Film Culture* proprietor Jonas Mekas,
however, Cassavetes' penchant for improvisation and free inspiration led
him to reshape *Shadows* in radical ways after the supposed completion
of the film. It emerged in a new edition that ran about twenty-five minutes longer while retaining less than half the footage used in the original

hour-long version. "My realization that I was betrayed by the second version of *Shadows* was the last stone" (Hoberman 101), Mekas wrote in his journal in late 1959; and when he praised the film in 1962 for having an "immediacy of the dramaless, beginningless, and endless episode," as well as a freedom from "literary and theatrical ideas" (Sitney 1970, 91–92), it was the early 1958 version to which he referred.

Mekas is not the only critic to find *Shadows* less than satisfactory in its revised (and for Cassavetes official) form. James finds in it such laudable qualities as maturity, economy, immediacy, and "a humanist translation of social issues into psychodrama that reinvigorates the codes of the acted, narrative, realist fiction film" (1988, 88). Yet in these very factors James finds the roots of limitation, compromise, and dissimulation. "The restriction of improvisation and profilmic play to the simulation of dramatic characters in an essentially orthodox plot and unified diegesis . . . does not investigate alternatives to the conventions of the industrial feature and its received social functions, but only re-legitimizes them," he writes. The film thus clashes with "the ideology of the subculture it explores and from which it derives its interest, and also with its own partial appropriation of the beat priorities, the aesthetic elaboration of the real-life experiences of its participants" (1988, 89–90).

A careful examination of *Shadows* casts doubt on aspects of this criticism, however. While characterization, plot development, and diegetic unity are indeed commonly associated with industrial filmmaking, these parameters may be attacked as reified or reactionary *per se* only if one thoroughly essentializes them. To illustrate this idea with a few diversified examples, Jean-Luc Godard's *Le gai savoir* has simulated characters, Chantal Akerman's *Jeanne Dielman, 23 quai de Commerce, 1080 Bruxelles* has what might sound on paper like an orthodox psychological-thriller plot, and Michael Snow's *Wavelength* has a conspicuously unified diegesis; yet none of these drastically unusual works can credibly be accused of relegitimizing industrial-film conventions and their received social functions. Rather than deploring the restriction of improvisation and play to those parameters in *Shadows*, therefore, one might more profitably note how multivalent are the characterizations, how interstitial is the plot structure, and how multiform is the diegesis of the film, by comparison with the overwhelming majority of narrative features produced in the United States during decades of virtually unquestioned classical-style hegemony. Seen in this context, *Shadows* emerges as precisely an investigation (if not a full-scale implementation) of alternatives to industrial conventions and the social functions associated with them. (The latter point is incidentally supported by the reception of the film, which never gained a firm foothold on the theatrical circuit.)

As indicated above, James posits "the aesthetic elaboration of the real-life experiences of its participants" as a Beat-related *telos* within the film. Through this, he continues, the film means "to empower [the performers'] fictional interaction with the added energy and credibility of the quasi-therapeutic working through of real-life relationships." He then goes on, however, to cite the casting of a white actress (Goldoni) in a black role (Lelia) as a "prevarication" that demolishes the "pseudo-existentialist, documentarist pretensions" of the film while reenacting the "pandemic exploitation" of black women. Again, this criticism needs examination. It is reasonable to label the aesthetic exploration of biographical and autobiographical material as a Beat priority, given the predilection of all the core Beat writers for such activity.[34] The racial fragmentation of *Shadows*, however, is best understood not as a betrayal of the film's "vaunted authenticity" but as a sign that its authenticity is to be found in quite another area—or two areas, rather, which point to the real fundamental interests of the movie: (a) a radical questioning of the presumption that filmic discourse is a reliable coupler of semiotic "truth" and ontological "essence" and (b) a further questioning of the very existence ascribed to such "truth" and "essence" by epistemological consensus and aesthetic/cinematic convention within the sociocultural mainstream. Like a number of other qualities placed into question by the film—for example, the musical talents of Ben and Hugh, neither of whom demonstrate any such gifts[35] within the diegesis—Lelia's racial identity is indeterminately inscribed on the levels of social behavior, psychological motivation, and cinematic representation. In short, her continual shifts and slides make it hard for us to decide just "what" and "who" she is, and we suspect she is not quite certain, either. If her identity is to have any sort of real epistemological existence—if it is to be knowable in any meaningful sense, by those inhabiting the film or those watching the film—it must be sought within the intuitive, ambivalent area of "intermediate" or "potential" awareness, which acquires personal and cultural vitality only through the dialogic interaction between "self" and "other" in which all consciousness is necessarily rooted. It is here that normative supposition (e.g., the assumption of Lelia's lover that blackness and whiteness are self-evident) collides with autotelic performance (e.g., Lelia's insistence on continually redefining her personality) to produce a counternormative discourse with paradoxical implications that Cassavetes, in a bold Winnicottian spirit, chooses to embrace rather than resolve. This discourse suggests that racial identity is not a bounded enclosure that delimits possibility, but rather a threshold traversed by multivalent, interpenetrative energies that introduce more psychological and behavioral prospects than they foreclose. Like the men with whom she shares the story, Lelia is not enough of an artist, shaman, con operator, or spiritual acrobat to sustain the synchronic satisfactions of her "not me-not not me" performances for very long. But very much like Cassavetes, who presides over the film with the nervous intensity of the sidewalk hipster he portrays in a cameo appearance, she has the instinctive courage to forge her own character in a liminal space where rationality flirts incorrigibly with its opposite and the strictures of *societas* show encouraging signs of weakness when challenged by the unspeakable visions of a sufficiently eccentric individual. (The liminality of her self-defined position is exemplified by the fact that she does not actively "pass" for white; this distinction is one of the things that separate her from superficially similar characters in such postwar films as Sirk's *Imitation of Life* and Elia Kazan's *Pinky*.) She is a flawed heroine, but she is a heroine nonetheless, and to equate the black/white performance of Lelia/Goldoni as character/actress with the cynical casting of Leslie Caron as Mardou Fox in MGM's version of *The Subterraneans*, as James does, is to misread the film's significance.

Also dubious is James's charge that *Shadows* falls into "contradiction with the ideology of the subculture it explores and from which it derives its interest." The appropriation of Beat behaviors and hipster mannerisms by characters in *Shadows* is a measure of the degree to which those characters (as part of Cassavetes' design) fall short of the film's investment in self-invention and self-revision. The frequency of this falling-short is a strong indication that Cassavetes is not seeking consonance with "the ideology of the [Beat] subculture" but rather is criticizing that subculture's superficially observable norms, paradigms, and formulations as unnecessary limits (at best) and soul-killing entrapments (at worst) for those who elect to assume them. Cassavetes here takes an implicitly Bakhtinian stance, valorizing a dialogic model of processive instability over the monologic tendency toward normative stasis in human interaction; and he takes a complementary Lacanian stance, seeing cultural paradigms of all kinds (including subculture and counterculture variations) as inherently stifling systematizations (compare Lacan's theory of the entry into language) to which the subject cannot pledge allegiance without a perilous loss of psychological flexibility and spiritual freedom.[36]

Cassavetes' own statements accord with these notions. "All my life I've fought against clarity—all those stupid definitive answers," he has said. "Phooey on a formula life, on slick solutions. It's never easy. I think it's only in the movies that it's easy. And I don't think people want their lives to be easy. It's a United States sickness. In the end it only makes things more difficult" (quoted in Kouvaros and Zwierzynski 26).[37]

Heading Underground

I lighted a candle, cut a little into my finger, dripped blood, and wrote "The Blood of the Poet" on a little calling card, with ink, then the big word "BLOOD" over it, and hung that up on the wall as reminder of my new calling. "Blood" writ in blood.
—Jack Kerouac, Vanity of Duluoz

I mean poetry poetry, poetic poetry with a capital P, a polite belch on top of the blood-red depths, the depths repressed into poematics, the poematics of the blood bath of reality.
—Antonin Artaud, "Coleridge the Traitor"[1]

We don't want false, polished, slick films—we prefer them rough, unpolished, but alive; we don't want rosy films—we want them the color of blood.
—First Statement of the New American Cinema Group, 1961

Blasting the Mainstream

■ In autumn of 1960, twenty-three independent filmmakers—summoned by Jonas Mekas and Lewis Allen, a stage and film producer—met at the Producers Theater in Manhattan and voted into existence The Group, a "free open organization of the New American cinema."[2] This meeting was not the first in which independent filmmakers looked for increased communication and commonality. Maya Deren led such a group as early as 1953, hoping to accomplish various practical tasks (facilitating crew and equipment acquisition, obtaining bulk discounts on goods and services, producing a catalogue of members' works, etc.) and seeking to "bring together, for mutual action and protection, the hitherto isolated film art-

ists, [and] to act as a liaison center between the film artist and his public" (quoted in Rabinovitz 80).[3] Five other filmmakers—Shirley Clarke,
Willard Van Dyke, Richard Leacock, Albert Maysles, and Donn Pennebaker—founded the cooperative Filmmakers Inc. in 1958, attracting
others (Frederick Wiseman, Charlotte Zwerin, etc.) in the early '60s and
generating enough activity for Clarke to claim that "a lot of the American
New Wave film movement and the development of cinéma vérité took
place with all of us interacting with each other" (Rabinovitz 110).

The Group began its activities with particular energy and enthusiasm,
however, and made a strong impression on the psychology of the avant-
garde scene. Among those participating were Mekas's brother Adolfas
Mekas, then preparing his *Hallelujah the Hills*; Clarke, director of *The
Connection* and other innovative films; Lionel Rogosin, director of *On the
Bowery* and *Come Back, Africa*, powerful and innovative films on alcoholic
street life and racial repression, respectively; Robert Frank and Alfred
Leslie, codirectors of *Pull My Daisy*; Ben Carruthers and Argus Speare
Juilliard, who appeared in *Shadows* and Jonas Mekas's feature *Guns of
the Trees*; Gregory Markopoulos, whose completed avant-garde films in-
cluded the trilogy of *Psyche*, *Lysis*, and *Charmides*; Bert Stern, director of
Jazz on a Summer's Day; Edward Bland, the African-American director
of *The Cry of Jazz*; Sheldon Rochlin, still preparing his debut film; Peter
Bogdanovich, doing the same; producer Walter Gutman; film distributor
Émile de Antonio; theater manager Daniel Talbot; attorney Jack Perlman;
and others. In their "First Statement" they cited as kindred spirits the
Free Cinema in England, the *Nouvelle Vague* in France, the "young movements" in Poland, the Soviet Union, and Italy, and none other than Cassavetes, a non-Grouper but clearly a "new generation" compatriot.

The statement went on to blast mainstream cinema (defined, or rather
undefined, in bracingly broad terms) for being "morally corrupt, aesthetically obsolete, thematically superficial, temperamentally boring," and
prone to a "slickness" that functions as "a perversion covering the falsity
of their themes, their lack of sensitivity, their lack of style." After this
warmup, the statement asserted its concern with "Man" and "what is happening to Man" and rejected "classical principles" in art and life. Then
followed a nine-point declaration of aims and purposes. Producers, distributors, and investors would be barred from interfering with "personal expression" until a work was ready for projection; censorship would
not be tolerated; financial investment in film would be rethought with an
eye to establishing a "free" industry; successful production of profitable

low-budget films (made for \$25,000 to \$200,000) would validate the "ethical and aesthetic beliefs" of their makers; filmmakers would not re-organize the distribution/exhibition system but would "blow the whole thing up" and restart it from scratch; a cooperative distribution network would be established; the East Coast would acquire a film festival to show-case "New Cinema" from around the world; unions would be exhorted to use "more reasonable methods" when dealing with low-budget produc-tions; and film profits would be set aside to guarantee the completion costs and laboratory fees of other filmmakers. The statement concluded by as-serting The Group's difference from "organizations such as United Art-ists"; its determination to make films rather than money; its solidarity with overseas colleagues in advocating "the New Man" as well as "the New Cinema"; and its desire for "art . . . but not at the expense of life."

Members of the original Group took diverse artistic roads in the months and years after the appearance of this declaration, with its ener-getic mixture of the clear-sighted, the fuzzy-minded, the proudly idealis-tic, and the unabashedly practical. Rogosin and Stern never equalled the widespread impact of their early work; Markopoulos despaired of Ameri-can cinema ever recognizing his genius and sought a more hospitable en-vironment overseas; de Antonio became a brilliant director of politically charged documentaries; Talbot made mainstream support of non-Holly-wood cinema into a lifelong calling; Bogdanovich went Hollywood with a vengeance; and so on.[4] Of the material goals listed in the statement, only a new distribution system was soon realized, when the Film-Makers' Co-operative was launched in early 1962. In sum, The Group's activities did not set American cinema on a new and corrected course, nor did the or-ganization clear an uninterrupted pathway for its members to pursue their inspirations wherever and however these might lead. But to argue thus is not to denigrate The Group or its aspirations. Some of its participants proceeded to create works of lasting and extraordinary merit, bolstered in part by the collectivity's moral and material support. The very marginality of the organization generated a sense of liminal specialness and even pu-rity within some members, moreover, which provided a spur to continued radicalism in thought, theory, and accomplishment.[5]

In any case, the most lasting result of the Group's existence was its ratification of Jonas Mekas's emerging status as a self-designated young patriarch for the "new generation" of cinematic revolutionaries. And many of Mekas's values—his contempt for commercialism, his visionary enthusiasm, his linkage of aesthetic and ethical goals—were steeped in the

Beat sensibility, itself heavily influenced by the Romantic tradition that he much admired.[6] The activities of neither Mekas as an individual nor The Group as an organization can be said to have culminated a pattern of pre-1960 history, or defined an essence of circa-1960 practice, or designated a *telos* for post-1960 developments. Still, together they encouraged a Romantically inclined emphasis on self-generated intuitiveness, emotionalism, symbolism, and mythopoeia, all of which played a large role in connecting what was starting to be known as "underground" film with values linked to the Beat scene.[7]

*L*ousy Squares, Lousy Hipsters

> Besides, there is still a great deal of conventional propaganda pouring out of the underground. Shirley Clarke's concern with Negroes in The Connection *and* The Cool World *may be politically advanced, but hardly formally fancy.*
>
> —Andrew Sarris, "The Independent Cinema"

It is not difficult to trace a fundamentally Romantic self-image in films by major avant-gardists of the '40s, '50s, and '60s, manifested in Stan Brakhage psychodramas, Kenneth Anger magick shows, Gregory Markopoulos myth-movies, and many other works. It also marks such a Beat-inflected documentary as Mekas's diary film *Lost, Lost, Lost* (1949–75), wherein the filmmaker/narrator frequently invokes his status as privileged observer ("I was there. I saw it all. I recorded it all.") and includes seemingly casual shots (of the Mekas brothers themselves, for instance) showing signs of self-conscious posing for the camera, complete with pastoral backgrounds and eye-expressions redolent of inward gazes into soul-depths accessible only to the artistically blessed. Other filmmakers took it upon themselves to question romanticized notions of the artist, however, and also to interrogate scientist notions of the artist as an objective recording presence. (Romanticized and scientist conceptions of cinema often exist separately from each other but have coincided at times, as in *Lost, Lost, Lost.*) One such filmmaker was Shirley Clarke, whose Beat-related drama *The Connection* moves forcefully in this direction.

Most of Clarke's work shows strong interest in jazz, spontaneity, and artistic collaboration. These concerns showed up early in her career. Her first films took much of their inspiration and imagery from dancing, choreography, and music appropriate to those pursuits. One of her first major undertakings was the production of film loops for the United States Pavilion of the 1958 World's Fair in Brussels, under the supervision of Willard Van Dyke, who sought a "new film form based on imagery which allows . . . a continual flow of ideas on one general theme" (Rabinovitz 100). The words "continual flow" may not automatically suggest improvisation and jazz, but Clarke turned promptly in this direction, joining her colleague Pennebaker in an effort to "make jokes of everything because we had been told there would be no sound, and the one thing we couldn't do was jazz. So I made them all jazz." The favored means for this was montage that privileged theme-and-variation motifs and valued formal properties over figurative ones (Rabinovitz 100). Clarke's gravitation toward jazzlike forms continued in such films as *Bridges-Go-Round* (1958, made from rejected loop footage) and *The Connection* (1961). The latter joins her jazz interests with important new elements: an actively critical stance toward the claimed "objectivity" of *cinéma vérité* and a desire to explore and explode the related (and Romantic) myths of (a) cinematic transparency and (b) authorial privilege of both the "dispassionate documentarist" and "soulful cinépoet" varieties.

The Connection spends all of its 105 minutes with a group of heroin addicts waiting (à la the heroes of Samuel Beckett's modernist classic *Waiting for Godot*) for the title character, a dealer who will supply their narcotic "fix." The narrative takes one unexpected detour when the "connection" arrives with an elderly "sister" from the Salvation Army by his side. She has no idea what sort of iniquitous den she has entered; we eventually learn that her presence on the street helped the drug dealer evade capture by the police a short while earlier. (It is interesting that both *The Connection* and *Pull My Daisy* have a visit by a churchly *naif* as a narrative centerpiece, providing an opportunity for each film to play insider hipness against outsider squareness in very obvious ways.)

The Connection is a highly collaborative film—directed by Clarke; written by Jack Gelber from his heatedly discussed Off-Broadway play of 1959; featuring on-screen music performances by the Freddie Redd Quartet; and starring members of the Living Theatre, whose original stage production was directed by Judith Malina and designed by Julian Beck, the founders of that radically innovative troupe.[8] Perhaps the most impressive sign of the movie's opposition to both conventional "auteur" cinema and independent "poetic" cinema is its insistence within the story on film's collaborative nature and on the impossibility of an author creating either "documentary" or "original" expression without dialogic interactivity.

The movie is presented as a documentary shot in a drug addict's apartment; this message is conveyed explicitly through a printed on-screen statement that substitutes for opening credits and implicitly through a number of deliberately conspicuous editing and camera-work choices. The picture was supposedly filmed by a director named Jim Dunn and subsequently edited (after Dunn's unexpected departure) by J. J. Burden, who was the camera operator during the shoot. At first, the pseudodocumentary looks like an ordinary direct-cinema production, following the action with a roving (often handheld) camera and failing to disguise gaps in the footage, anomalies in the editing, glimpses of the filmmaking apparatus, and the like. Clarke's film-about-film reveals its deeper concerns when the diegetic "director" comes into the camera's range, complaining about the dullness of his "material" and exhorting his "characters" to be more visually and dramatically interesting. He is eventually goaded by some of the junkies—who accuse him of voyeurism, ignorance, and arrogance—into learning about their lives by sharing their narcotics. The apparent pointlessness of his resulting (hip) intoxication then joins with the manifest pointlessness of his established (square) identity to disillusion him entirely—already a failure as an objective documentarist, he is now a failure as a soulful film-poet, too—and this presumably leads to his off-screen exit from New York, as indicated in the film's opening statement. The point made by Clarke and her collaborators is plain: Artist and subject are inextricably linked within the power/knowledge networks that define them and articulate their concerns.

Reception of *The Connection* at the time of its initial release has been traced along three axes: as a Beat movie, as an example of New American Cinema, and as a transgressive outrage that sparked aggressive censorship and court battles.[9] These categories are not mutually exclusive, of course, since the film's status as oppositional "New American Cinema" is closely related to its treatment of countercultural subject/narrative/characters,[10] and all of this helps account for the antagonism aroused by the work in some places, much of it centered on legal action over its use of the word "shit" as a slang term for heroin. Lauren Rabinovitz casts aspersions on the film's countercultural credentials by connecting it with the Living Theatre, which allegedly made a practice of claiming loyalty to marginalized and oppressed groups while carefully positioning itself outside such groups (drug addicts, blacks, etc.) at the same time.[11] According to this argument, filmmaker Clarke simply plugged into a "site for a we/they opposition" constituted by the theater troupe and the play, "within which the Beat Generation's disaffection with white, bourgeois cultural norms was able to assume expression while remaining contained within white, bourgeois culture (including Broadway and off-Broadway theatrical productions)." To present oneself as a beatnik or hipster on such terms "was to be anti-status quo and anti-square . . . while not actually being so marginalized as to be without political or economic power . . . " (Rabinovitz 117–18). The trouble with this reasoning is similar to a weakness of James's case against *Shadows* as noted above, to wit, the value of the film lies more in the degree of independence and oppositionality that it *does* attain than in the degree to which it falls short of a critically suggested *post facto* standard. It is more productive to weigh *The Connection* as play and film against other instances of white, bourgeois culture—such as actual Broadway and Off-Broadway shows of the period—than against an undefined ideal that would presumably consist of hyperauthentic productions by members of marginalized and oppressed groups who somehow manage to assemble dramatic spectacles while remaining unassociated with mainstream social, economic, or political effectuality. The latter phenomenon has occasionally existed (the mature works of Jack Smith are an example) and is certainly to be prized when it is encountered; yet its rarity disqualifies it as a critically realistic norm serving to invalidate all works of less phenomenal accomplishment. This fact is especially true given the useful role played by *The Connection* (in both the Living Theatre's staging and Clarke's filming) as a highly visible and ultimately successful challenger of very real constraints against freedom of expression: *de facto* rejection of "unpleasant" subject matter by "respectable" theater audiences, and *de jure* prosecution aimed at purveyors of "obscenity" in film.

As both play and movie, *The Connection* represents a multilayered liminality. Clarke supports this notion in her 1961 comment that "it is about this group of people who . . . are frankly escaping. But their way of escape is through a kind of revolt, they revolt against the standard. . . . The people they call beats . . . are responding against conformity. And what if it is the lunatic fringe?" (Rabinovitz 118). The film underscores the liminal status of its junkie characters by restricting its visual range to the apartment in which they wait for their drugs; the apartment itself is filled with signifiers of physical and spiritual marginality.

A characteristic moment will serve to illustrate this point. The significantly named Leach, proprietor of the apartment and grudging host to his companions, is complaining that the fix he just received has not gotten him high. Cowboy, the connection, is telling him to relax and enjoy whatever intoxication his increasingly high drug tolerance *does* allow. Other men are lounging around and passing the time with random activities. The camera roams about the room observing details: disregarded newspapers piled on a wooden stairway; a sign reading, "Heaven or Hell— Which Road do You take?" next to a disconnected electrical wire; a cold iron stove; more unheeded newspapers; an open magazine displaying nude photographs of women; wrinkled and ignored paperback books; a filled-up ashtray perched precariously on a windowsill; a bucket marked "FIRE" on a high pedestal against a wall; a bare lightbulb hanging from a cord; a badly cracked windowpane; another sign reading, "We Mail . . . *Anywhere*"; a skull-shaped candle next to a small clock; a small framed photograph of Charlie Parker playing his sax; a strange wall-drawing with disembodied hands, straight and curved lines, and what might be Hebrew lettering; and sundry other objects.

As haphazardly gathered as they appear to be, these artifacts are richly expressive of life on the borderline of conventional society. Some betray a wish to engage with the mainstream in some way—newspapers, books, the "We Mail . . . *Anywhere*" sign with its suggestion of open-ended possibilities. Others suggest the liminality of a prison (the forlorn girlie magazines) or a slum (the cracked window, the naked lightbulb). Others are ambivalent, such as the "FIRE" bucket (connoting both danger and safety) and the filled-up ashtray tilted on the windowsill (filth contained but still visible and threatening to spill out). Most dramatic and revealing is the first of the two signs: "Heaven or Hell—Which Road do You take?" It inscribes the entire location as a "road" rather than a destination; at the same time, the stasis of the men cluttering the place reconfirms that this "road" must be transcendental (Heaven or Hell?) rather than material in nature, connecting not physical positions but socially, psychologically, perhaps spiritually determined states. Some denizens of the *Connection* pad are clearly unstable and probably untalented (Ernie, Sam), but others are creative enough to show artistic (the four jazz musicians) or intellectual (Solly) awareness and ability. In their quest for a transformative space that offers some promise of freedom from a deadeningly bounded and rationalistic culture, all have converged in the kind of liminal space that is not so much constituted by boundaries as hovering *on* the boundaries demarcating geographically, socially, and spiritually marginal territories. These strung-out beatniks are "on the road" in more than one important sense.

Clarke's film accompanies the existential liminality of its characters with a cinematic liminality of its own, reflexively exploring the margins between fiction and documentary style. Fiction is inscribed in Gelber's script and the film's mimetic performances. Documentary style is inscribed in such signifiers as obviously handheld camera work and editing discontinuities. Reflexivity is inscribed in those filmic signifiers and also in the narrative interaction between "director" and "characters." The movie is all fiction, of course; but its desire to appear otherwise is a key element in its embrace of liminality as a necessary aspect of oppositional cinema. (This part of Clarke's artistic trajectory would be extended in such subsequent films as *The Cool World* and *Portrait of Jason*, which move farther into "real life" than *The Connection* does.)

If fundamental components of the liminal/liminoid state include investments in play, ritual, self-observation, and restored behavior, as suggested above, then *The Connection* stands as a sophisticated incursion into precisely this domain. It links the playfulness of cinematic reflexivity and the self-observation of filmmaking procedures with attention to the repetitive rituals of (a) filmmaking itself and (b) characters who are at once marginalized from mainstream society (they are chronically poor and unemployed) and hopelessly dependent on the rites of capitalistic exchange (through the purchase and consumption of drugs) that drive this society. All this contributes to the film's value as a study of restored-behavior aesthetics. On one level, Clarke manipulates "strips" of reflexive narrative material that have clear connections with her own activities as shaper of the film itself. On another level, she exploits liminal/liminoid space as a territory for the exploration of tabooed subjects and transitional phenomena with social possibilities that are both positive (ludic and pararational expression) and negative (retention of comforting objects/behaviors in addictive/fetishistic forms). *The Connection* thus emerges as an extended threshold narrative in which ordinary/narrative time and performance/reflexive time intertwine to form an imperfect but imposingly complex (and dauntingly idiosyncratic) exercise in synchronic in-betweenness. This characteristic marks the film as both Beat in its sensibility and "underground" in its intentions.

It is also an eloquent microcosmic study of '50s sociological conditions. Its on-screen filmmaker (who bears a physical resemblance to Mike Nichols, a self-styled "hip" comedian at this time) is a painful parody of the period's cinema intellectuals, peppering his on-set instructions with pretentious art-movie references. A bona-fide hula hoop is dragged into the action, identified by Solly with "the Roman symbol for death" and used by Sam as a transitional object (he tosses it away with a spin that causes it to roll right back to him) that signifies his ambivalence toward dangerously marginal living; later, Leach's near death from an overdose is partly filmed through it. In addition, a key segment of the dialogue sums up the status of the addicts as simultaneous opponents, outcasts, and slaves of bourgeois capitalism in a consensus-driven society. This conversation transpires just after the idle talk has turned momentarily to sports, prompting Leach to remind his associates rather primly that "baseball ain't hip." The roaming camera passes over the (diegetic) filmmakers' tape recorder as the talk continues, suggesting the discussion's significance vis-à-vis the group that Leach has just addressed as "you square daytime bastards":

Cowboy: What's wrong with the daytime scene of being square? Man, I got nothing against 'em. They got lousy squares, and they got lousy hipsters. Personally, I couldn't make a daytime work scene. I like my hours the way they are, but that don't make me no better, man. No.
Leach: You know what I'd do if I had a daytime job, Cowboy?
Cowboy: What would you do, man?
Leach: I'd work about—about six months, just to establish credit, you dig? And then I'd go out and get me every type of charge card that there is. Food, liquor, travel. You know, man? I could—I could fly all over this world, baby, and what could they do? Throw me in debtor's prison or something? No, man. Like—like, we're living in the United States of America, baby. And we're free here.
Cowboy: Oh, Leach, what movies you been seeing, huh?
Leach: It's possible, man, it's possible.
Cowboy: It sounds like a lotta work, man, an awful lotta work.

Shortly after this exchange, Cowboy becomes unprecedentedly playful and sings a couple of lines from the Irving Berlin song "White Christmas," remarking that "we're living in a white society" and asking if anyone has "ever seen black snow." This question perks up Sam, who hears the word "snow" and asks if they are "gonna get high again." And so ends the possibility that verbal discourse in this unconventional but unquestionably '50s-style household might turn to meaningful interrogation of its miserably unsatisfactory status quo. To ring a change on Cowboy's phrase, these men are lousy squares *and* lousy hipsters at the same time. That ultraliminal condition is their attainment and their tragedy.

*C*ommunion Versus Communication

> [R]eduction of the link between art and society to a purely negative function, which from the artist's point of view is alienation, is a new historical fact of incalculable importance and profound meaning. When critics and observers of avant-garde art praise or blame it for refusing even to serve, let alone express, contemporary society, they fail to take into account the fact that the avant-garde is not only the direct expression of a negative cultural relation, but is also the expression of the human and social condition that created this schism in the cultural order.
>
> —Renato Poggioli, The Theory of the Avant-Garde

Stan Brakhage would have qualms about Renato Poggioli's statement. "There has been a large case made that most of my work and public life have been literally in protest against the Hollywood binding experience. . . . That may be so," he has said. But then he adds, "I've never consciously worked to do that. . . . Perhaps there's a subconscious aspect of Luther in me . . . but I never hammered any dicta to the door in protest" (Higgins, Lopes, and Connick 60).[12] In the Bakhtinian spirit of positive negation discussed in Part One of this study, Brakhage has during his career (a) refused to emulate the suturing, interpellating products churned out by the commercial film industry, instead striving to eliminate all narrative and theatrical "clutch" from his works, and (b) left open the possibility of respecting the commercial film industry's better products ("I've always cared for the movies") as long as they are not mistaken for true art. The arts, he asserts, have always

> been involved in inspiring people, quite distinct from influencing them. To inspire, one must create a milieu where each person is respected as a unique individual, and yes, each audience as a culture of the combinations of individuals, *as distinct from a herd.* When I go to the movies I wish to be *herded.* . . . I'm really hungry for a tribal dance gathering which is what the movies are for me. And yes, I want to be communicated with. But in art appreciation, it is so much different, even opposite from the ordinary

dance or religious gathering. The word "religion" itself comes from *religare*, "to bind back," and the art impulse is always to inspire uniquenesses which we can then share with each other. (Higgins, Lopes, and Connick 60)

In this statement, Brakhage does not acknowledge that the carnivalesque "tribal dance" can be at once a site of gregarious collectivity *and* creative individuality. (He also bypasses important differences between Hollywood movies and tribal-dance experiences, such as their differing approaches to the relationship between performance and spectacle.) In a broad sense, however, he shows a discriminating respect for what carnival theory calls the positive pole of popular-festive energy, coupled with an awareness of the distinction between liminal and liminoid experience; in this instance "the movies" represent a recurring set of (liminal) social excursions into the ludic and carnivalistic, and "art appreciation" represents a more private, idiosyncratic, and inspirational phenomenon—in short, a liminoid communion (not communication) with the mystery that for Brakhage is at the core of artistic life.

These attitudes have much of the Beat spirit about them. Such avatars of the Beat sensibility as Kerouac and Ginsberg maintained a lively interest in the world of popular-festive culture but tended to keep a critical and ironic distance from it in their work, placing more faith in the perceived uniquenesses of their own hearts and minds than in the words and spectacles spun by servants of *societas* and its agendas; like Brakhage, they measured the success of their art more by the numinousness of its expression than by the numerousness of its audience.

This is not to say that either Brakhage or the core Beats were shy about singing the virtues of their work to the world at large, or hesitant to dream of being embraced by an Establishment belatedly recognizing the excellence of their endeavors and the purity of their cause. Still, the comparatively small size of the Beat movement was a predictable result of its preference for self-absorbed intensity over other-directed propriety, and the same can be said *(mutatis mutandis)* for the avant-garde filmmaking community. The public image of the Beats reached its high point in 1959, thanks partly to the blend of celebrity and notoriety that was accumulated with a sort of purposeful inadvertence by Kerouac and his peers. At this time, *Life* could show a crowded Coffee Gallery in its "Only Rebellion Around" spread, and veterans of the first "Howl" reading could recall the substantial troupe of San Franciscans who had gathered on that momentum-building occasion. Yet there is nothing in Beat history to compare with the Woodstock phenomenon that cemented the importance of the Hippie movement as a convergence of *mass* culture and *counter*culture with epoch-making implications. As a Romantically inclined group with an investment in inwardness—geared to introspection, intuition, and inner transformation sparked by private contemplation or interactions among small circles of like-minded souls—the Beats leaned instinctively away from the tribal dances of liminal experience, preferring to explore the unspeakable visions of the individual within their own liminoid terrain. Here they encountered paradoxes there was no need to resolve, boundlessness there was no need to fathom, and marginality there was no need to define, recuperate, or justify. Brakhage and some other film experimentalists delved into similar territory during the years of Beat ascendancy, seeking the flash of *satori* and the glow of synchronic ecstasy in works that wandered far from mainstream priorities. In much of this activity, spontaneity was a key value.

Wild Form

All of the core Beat writers took a complex view of spontaneity that has often been oversimplified by critics and readers who fail to look beyond the popular legend of a Kerouac or Ginsberg spinning out torrents of prose or poetry without a hitch, a revision, or even a backward glance. Beat fellow traveler John Clellon Holmes articulates this legend when he describes his vision of Kerouac at the typewriter, "staring into the blankness of the space in front of him, careful not to *will* anything, and simply recording the 'movie' unreeling in his mind. . . . Somehow an open circuit of feeling had been established between his awareness and his object of the moment, and the result was as startling as being trapped in another man's eyes" (Donaldson 590). This description accepts and reproduces Kerouac's own assertion in a 1952 letter to Holmes that he was beginning to discover "something beyond the novel and beyond the arbitrary confines of the story . . . into realms of revealed Picture . . . *wild form*, man, wild form. Wild form's the only form holds what I have to say—my mind is exploding to say something about every image and every memory . . . I have an irrational lust to set down everything I know . . . " (Donaldson 589). This is clearly the same Kerouac self-depicted in his late novel *Desolation Angels* as spending a whole afternoon "writing poems high on benny in the parlor" and then arguing with a character representing poet Randall Jarrell, who uncaps a bottle of Jack Daniels and says to Jack Kerouac/Jack Duluoz,

> "How can you get any refined or well gestated thoughts into a spontaneous flow as you call it? It can all end up gibberish." And that was no Harvard lie. But I said:
> "If it's gibberish, it's gibberish. There's a certain amount of control going on like a man telling a story in a bar without interruptions or even one pause."
> "Well it'll probably become a popular gimmick but I prefer to look upon my poetry as a craft."
> "Craft *is* craft."
> "Yes? Meaning?"
> "Meaning crafty. How can you confess your crafty soul in craft?"

Hereupon the Gregory Corso character takes sides against Duluoz and accuses him of being "full of theories like an old college perfesser, you think you know everything." Duluoz seizes the last word by yelling after his departing friends, "If I had a Poetry University you know what would be written over the entrance arch? . . . Here Learn That Learning Is Ignorance! Gentlemen dont burn my ears! Poetry is lamb dust! I prophesy it! I'll lead schools in exile! I dont Care!" (280–81).[13]

As always, Kerouac/Duluoz is quick to defend his ideal of spontaneous prose—or "free prose," as he thought of it early in his career, or "wild form," as he called it in his Holmes letter. But there are some revealing formulations in the *Desolation Angels* passage just quoted. First, he admits there is a possibility that mere gibberish will be produced. Second, he suggests that this possibility is reduced, or its results tempered, by the fact that a certain amount of control is being exercised. The spontaneous, improvisatory, perhaps bennied-up writer is not a raving verbiage-machine hurling out every word that comes to mind. Rather, he resembles a man telling a barroom story—that is, a self-aware narrator with a consciously construed tale; a knowledge of his audience and the context of their coming together; and a desire to share experience by verbal means for the satisfaction of all who care to participate. It appears the old perfesser has theories after all, reluctant though he may be to acknowledge them as such.

Spontaneity was not an all-consuming gimmick nor an excuse for indiscriminate spewing, then. It was a carefully considered means for accomplishing such clear-cut goals as recording a greater amount of thought ("set down everything I know") and tapping deeper levels of thought ("confess your crafty soul") than conventional techniques allow. There was also an element of social commentary and even protest in Kerouac's embrace of spontaneous prose. If he echoed the unprecedented speed of the contemporary world in the rapidity of his method and the celerity of his subject matter, he also parodied the consumer-goods overproduction of the '50s in the sheer torrent of his language and used spur-of-the-moment excesses in an attempt to "avoid the restrictions of society without depriving himself of its pleasures" (145–47), as literature critic James T. Jones suggests.[14]

Kerouac's implicit parody of machine-age productivity in such works as *Visions of Cody* and *On the Road* finds another expression in his *Book of Dreams*, a record of dream images and visions that he recorded by "looking at the pictures that were fading slowly like in a movie fadeout into the recesses of my subconscious mind," and writing these down "nonstop so that the subconscious could speak for itself in its own form, that is, uninterruptedly flowing & rippling" (1961a, 4). This interest in dreams and semiautomatic writing ("I wrote these dreems with eerie sleeping cap head . . . I hardly knew what I was doing let alone writing") has obvious connections with the Surrealist movement, which is itself linked to the very socioeconomic forces it ostensibly wants to elude; post-Beat filmmaker Raúl Ruiz has wittily observed this irony by noting his suspicion that the Surrealists "wanted to keep you busy even while you were asleep. It's a capitalistic problem. They wanted you to use your own dreams to make machines that can produce work, that can produce money or objects. It's an obsession with the production of culture" (Spigland 80).[15]

Like the Surrealists, the core Beat writers act on a conviction that absolutely anything can be turned to account in artistic production. Yet since spontaneity and all-inclusiveness are not ultimate goals in themselves, the Beats build a certain amount of leeway for revision into their methodology, albeit in forms that are far from obvious and may well be considered rather crafty, especially (and ironically) in Kerouac's case. This semicovert revision-work is one of the areas in which Beat practice reflects the performative dynamics of restored behavior, whereby an artist—seeking to explore issues of consciousness, identity, and culture by evading or transcending the "normal" roles of social, transindividual life—treats living behavior (here represented by spontaneously improvised writing) in the same manner as a film director treats photographed material (here, manipulation of that writing through subsequent processes of shaping, selection, and recombination).

One view of Kerouac's *oeuvre* holds that his obsessive return to certain core material—the autobiographical themes and events that shape the Duluoz Legend novels—itself constitutes a kind of revision, as the writer repeatedly revisits similar or even identical material and takes the opportunity to review and reshape this material in every new encounter (Weinreich 120).[16] Another view, with a psychoanalytical slant, suggests that Kerouac rebelled against constraints and confinements that had frustrated him as a child by propelling his adult self into a willed spontaneity that had to be learned and practiced; this hypothesis gives literal truth to Holmes's account of Kerouac directly "following the movie in his head," suggesting that Kerouac's gift for recollection (Memory Babe was a childhood nickname) allowed him to compose (and perhaps revise) in his mind before sitting down at the typewriter, and then to treat the one-time-only "spontaneous" typing process as itself an opportunity for final revision (Jones 150–51).[17]

The latter argument can lead to romanticizing Kerouac's "magical gift" of spontaneity, however. This situation occurs when Jones asserts, "There is a sense in which all creation—all thought, indeed—involves complete disjunction. The true work of art must break with the past, with convention, with the habitual, with the anticipated" (152). One might respond with Winnicott's psychoanalytic observation that "in any cultural field *it is not possible to be original except on a basis of tradition.* . . . The interplay between originality and the acceptance of tradition as the basis for inventiveness seems to me to be just one more example, and a very exciting one, of the interplay between separateness and union" (99).[18] Disjunction in art, that is to say, is rarely as complete as Jones claims. He is most helpful when he portrays Kerouac's spontaneity not as a magical gift or a severance of convention but as a tool developed by Kerouac for fulfilling his (Buddhist) desire to evade or transcend the ego. Kerouac approached this goal by combating the illusion of ego as a continuously existing entity, seeing the "I" of his writing and his life as a spontaneous and ephemeral creation. In any case, it is certainly true that Kerouac acquired and developed his spontaneity just as a jazz musician acquires and develops the principles of improvisation; and he practiced it in a knowing and self-aware manner that allowed room for what critics call revision and Cassady called "prevision" (Jones 151–52), inserting this into the temporal and epistemological gaps between mental conception and physical execution on one hand, and between different reworkings of congruent material (in different works over the course of his career) on the other.

Ginsberg and Burroughs also found ways to pursue spontaneous writing while assuring that their final products would be something other than heedless outpourings of unfettered verbiage. Ginsberg's refinement of "auto poesy" was steeped in the notion of spontaneous composition. Yet a characteristic description of the technique by Ginsberg shows that inspiration coexisted with deliberation: Writing about his "Wichita Vortex Sutra," he states that it was "composed directly on tape by voice, and then transcribed to page: page arrangement notates the thought-stops, breath-stops, runs of inspiration, changes of mind, startings and stoppings of car" (Schumacher 478). Even the justly celebrated "Howl," a famously spontaneous work that marked a breakthrough for Ginsberg precisely because its run-on composition allowed him to evade inhibition and self-censorship, went through much reworking after the initial stages of its development. Immediately realizing that the new work was far from perfect or complete, the poet started right away to reshape it. He then sent the early pages of his "first draft scribblenotes" to Kerouac, who was such a strict spontaneity cop that he pounced on the manuscript's typographical strikeovers as evidence of revision and demanded to see Ginsberg's original "lingual spontaneity" or nothing! Work on "Howl" continued for some time, and Ginsberg tested the "Moloch" section at public readings, subsequently adapting its structure to the print medium by rearranging lines, reciting them aloud to assess rhythm and sound, and altering phrase lengths; this went on through more than twenty drafts (Schumacher 203–4, 217). It was not until 1971 that Ginsberg had the courage to improvise poetry in public, which he first did at a benefit for a Tibetan Buddhist meditation center. He later called this experience "really awkward and unfinished, but it was so profound . . . and so liberating when I realized I didn't have to worry if I lost a poem anymore, because I was the poet, I could just make it up" (Miles 1989, 442).

Burroughs developed his cut-up and fold-in methods between the composition of *Naked Lunch* and *Nova Express* as a way of introducing an element of spontaneity and unpredictability into his work; he also hoped these devices would narrow the gap that he perceived between writing, which deals with abstractions, and visual art, which has long benefited from montage/collage techniques applied to palpable materials. He has resisted the idea that these methods should be toyed with indiscriminately, however. For one thing, he finds genuine meaning embedded within the

properly fragmented text: "I would say that my most interesting experience with the earlier [cut-up] techniques was the realization that when
you make cut-ups you do not get simply random juxtapositions of words,
that they do mean something, and often that these meanings refer to some
future event." For another, he treats the mix or montage of printed elements as a channel to follow rather than a monument to be preserved: "I
may take a page, cut it up, and get a whole new idea for straight narrative,
and not use any of the cut-up material at all, or I may use a sentence or
two out of the actual cut-up." He adds that it is "not unconscious at all,
it's a very definite operation. . . . It's quite conscious, there's nothing of
automatic writing or unconscious procedure involved here." As an example he cites his screenplay *The Last Words of Dutch Schultz*, calling this
"perfectly straight writing. Nonetheless I cut up every page and suddenly
got a lot of new ideas that were then incorporated into the structure of
the narrative. This is a perfectly straight film treatment, quite intelligible
to the average reader, in no sense experimental writing" (Odier 28–30).
Many passages of such Burroughs works as *The Soft Machine* and *The
Ticket That Exploded* fall definitively into the category of experimental
writing, of course, thanks largely to cut-up procedures. Such procedures
are susceptible to processes of revision and manipulation, however, just
as—to employ terminology applied to dream work by psychoanalytic theory—the "primary" previsions of a Kerouac fantasy or a Ginsberg verse
improvisation are subject to "secondary" revision and structuration. Wild
form is not as wild as it appears.

*S*peed

It is no accident that theorists have used filmmaking as a metaphor
for restored-behavior activity, since the act of revision—shaping, reworking, transmitting, and transforming material taken from living action—is
inherent in nearly all filmmaking practice. Filmmakers revise when they
retake shots (as Kerouac indicated in his "Joan Rawshanks in the Fog"
fantasia), either repeating them in near-identical forms or changing them
with variations in camera setup or mise-en-scène; and they revise when
they articulate filmed material through editing. Avant-garde filmmakers,
often seeking autotelic expressivity not anchored in linear narrative, have
taken a particularly keen interest in cinema's capacity for allowing "secondary" editing of "primary" footage. The postwar period saw a new flow-
ering of montage innovation in such movies as Maya Deren's dance-films,

Kenneth Anger's baroque hallucinations, Bruce Conner's found-footage cinépoems, and Brakhage's propulsion of film aesthetics into terrain even more profoundly refigured. The content of Anger's work echoes interests of the Beat writers at times, from the exploration of liminal locations and liminoid mental states (e.g., *Eaux d'artifice*, 1953; *Inauguration of the Pleasure Dome*, 1954/66) to the confrontation of such tabooed subjects as homosexuality and drug use (e.g., *Fireworks*, 1947; *Scorpio Rising*, 1962–64). It is Brakhage and Conner whose styles most strongly bring Beat priorities to mind, however, via the intricately meshed shooting/editing strategies of the former and the recuperative, polyphonic montage (discussed earlier in this study) of the latter. Both charge their work with Beat-like density, energy, and speed, using montage as an important means (although not the exclusive means, as will be shown) of accomplishing their aesthetic goals.

Brakhage's conception of montage, and of the sequential relation between shooting and editing, has undergone many changes over the years. By his own account, he started working in film "as primarily shaped by the influence of stage drama." But he soon found poetry and painting more "growth-engendering sources of inspiration," and discovered music to be a wellspring of insight for both his "photographic aesthetic" and "actual editing orders" (Sitney 1987, 134–35). In keeping with this trajectory, his early work of the '50s bears clear traces of theatrical mise-en-scène and narrativity (e.g., *Desistfilm*, 1954), which yield to tropes and techniques that can loosely be called more "painterly" and radically "poetic" (e.g., *Wonder Ring*, 1955; *Anticipation of the Night*, 1958) as his career makes its first important strides. His montage became more expansively free-associative as his long major phase began (with *Anticipation of the Night*), but until the start of his *Songs* cycle (1964–69) he apparently gave photographing and editing more or less equal weight.[19] His shift to 8-mm in the thirty *Songs* led him to replace many of his elaborate editing practices with more extensive in-camera editing and, one gathers, to place more trust in his ability to wrest final-form footage from the activity of shooting itself. In many cases, he came to see editing as closer to *selection* than to *creation*, and he justified his statement that *The Text of Light* (1974) was sequentially "arranged" and "composed" rather than invasively "edited" by citing "an energy in the amount of shooting which editing again can leak out for you" (D. James 1988, 48).[20] Here one sees a parallel with Kerouac's celebration of primary composition over secondary revision, borne out by Brakhage's comment, also regarding *The Text of Light*, that "[w]hat's interesting to me is the energy of immediacy. . . . Editing is always an afterthought." In a similar vein, he has stated that the earlier *eyes* (1970) was "mostly assembled, rather than edited, [and] is thus the surest track I could make of what it was given to me to see" (*Film-Makers' Cooperative Catalog No. 7*, 48).[21] It may be said that Brakhage follows "the movie in his eyes" just as closely as Kerouac follows "the movie in his head."

One must be cautious of generalizing about an artist as prolific and in some ways mercurial as Brakhage, and much of his later work manifests a distinct return to montage as a key creative element. He spent "exactly one year" editing two days' worth of photography for *The Governor* (1977), for example, and such late-'80s works as *I . . . Dreaming* and *Marilyn's Window* represent finely balanced combinations of the editing and shooting processes. Many other instances could be cited, including such non-figurative works as the *Arabic Numerals* series (1980–81) and the *Egyptian Series* (1983), in which it can be difficult at times to determine where photography leaves off and montage begins. Even his most intensively shooting-oriented periods have shown an awareness of montage's value for producing both uninhibited emotive power and the sense of intuitive order that transforms expressive intensity into coherent art. If it has been more necessary for Brakhage than for Kerouac to emphasize the importance of secondary revision at certain points in his career, it is partly because Brakhage's primary material often appears to be more abstruse and difficult to "decode" than Kerouac's; that is, Brakhage immediately transforms the real-world referents of his works into expressive artifacts, most notably through highly gestural camera movements, while the bulk of Kerouac's work reflects an attempt to evoke people, places, and events in terms that sustain a high degree of real-world recognizability despite their often radical divergence from literary conventions.

Be this as it may, Brakhage has long conceived of filmmaking as a deeply Romantic activity, rooted in the artist's capacity for reimagining the world and thereby reencompassing and reinventing it. To state the matter in different terms, he has produced a vast *oeuvre* devoted to capturing on film a gesturally inflected record of the visible world that represents himself in a "not me-not not me" position reflecting (a) his own perceptions and (b) the mediation of those perceptions by cinematic inscription. One result of his Romanticism has been a general tendency to privilege the shooting process because of its profound involvement with the biophysiological acts of seeing and moving, just as Ginsberg has increasingly sought to align thought with physiology through chanting, singing, and the poetic use of vocal timbres and rhythms. "Respond Dance," the title Brakhage gives to a published group of excerpts from letters, could be a name for his own practice of using the camera as a spontaneously choreographed extension of his own perceptual processes.[22]

Even when editing plays an essential role in Brakhage's mature work, cuts are often embedded almost imperceptibly in the flow of images. Annette Michelson notes this in *Anticipation of the Night*, where an image-sequence may be "fused by a camera movement sustained over cuts" or by "movement or direction either repeated or sustained through the cut." In this way editing joins camera movement and light as agents for "[d]issolving the distance and resolving the disjunction Eisenstein had adopted as the necessary conditions for cinema's cognitive function" and thereby "positing the sense of a continuous present, of a filmic time which devours memory and expectation in the presentation of presentness" (1973, 37). In the resulting films, Michelson observes in a later article, one finds the aspiration "to a pure presence in which the limits separating perception and eidetic imagery dissolve in the light of vision as Revelation, uncorrupted by the Fall that is called the Renaissance, as perpetuated in the very construction of the camera lens" (1991, 61). Montage is a useful although not indispensable tool in this struggle of theory and praxis to move away from what Brakhage has called "a weary awareness of too much materialization in mere or more mirroring" and toward "a more than reflective source of illumination" (1963, n.p.). The effort to conjure up a continuous present, through artworks devoted to presenting presentness, accords with the Beat endeavor to privilege the immanence of the moment over the flux and flow of temporality as conventionally conceived. "Everything is in the same moment," writes Kerouac in the "121st Chorus" of *Mexico City Blues*; he adds later that "It's all happening / It won't end / It'll be good," and he concludes, "Forward to the Sea, / and the Sea Comes back to you / and there's no escaping . . . " (121).

Conner's montage stands (very roughly) within the broad liminal territory between that of Brakhage, with his fusion of camera-dance and editing, and that of Tony Conrad (in his flicker-film phase) or Austrian filmmaker Peter Kubelka, with their philosophy of frame-by-frame construction. Like all of them, Conner favors density and rapidity, if less consistently than the others do. While the intuitive quality of his editing leans toward Brakhage, however, his insistence on the creative primacy of montage over photography leans heavily toward Kubelka's end of the scale, and away from the Beat preference for primary creativity over secondary reworking. In any event, Conner's montage is anchored in a relationship to the camera that is vastly different from Brakhage's physicalized shooting and Kubelka's treatment of photography as a gathering of frames for editing purposes. Conner has not used or even possessed a camera during much of his career, and has created most of his finest works from found footage—a resource that Brakhage has usually avoided[23] and that Kubelka and Conrad implicitly ironized when they composed films (respectively, *Arnulf Rainer*, 1958–60, and *The Flicker*, 1966, etc.) entirely from blank leader.

Conner maintains a strong connection to the Beat aesthetic, however, in that his approach to this footage (which comes largely from old movies) is not only polyphonic, quotational, and intertextual but also spontaneous, instinctive, and improvisatory. He has said that applying for financial grants is a perennial problem for him because he ordinarily has no idea what form a film will take until he has actually made it; he also acknowledges that he has edited some works "until they just went away," that is, until the process of paring away "unnecessary" material proceeded so far that nothing "necessary" turned out to remain (Sterritt, personal interview, 1982).

The latter remark suggests the image of a sculptor working with a block of stone, and Conner has indeed had a considerable career as a sculptor; he has also been a graphic artist and a designer/performer of light shows. He made his first movie, *A Movie*, from found footage in 1958, considering this endeavor to be an outgrowth of his work as a collagist. Although this film grows moody and dark during its twelve-minute running time, it begins rambunctiously and amusingly, borrowing from the Marx Brothers comedy *Duck Soup* the notion of chaining together heterogeneous responses to a single narrative-film situation, namely, a chase that turns into a surreal stampede. The idea of intuitive montage may be considered the most productive root of Conner's films, helping to explain everything from his disdain for overliteral linkage cuts to his avoidance of color film, which varies in tone more than black-and-white film and therefore creates distractions when used in found-footage assemblages. Conner's most profound difference from Brakhage, and from many of his peers in avant-garde cinema, is his desire to manipulate strips of film/

behavior that have been generated entirely by others (directors, cinema-tographers, performers, etc.) before his arrival on the scene; he acts as what Bakhtin would identify as an orchestrater of preexisting discursive mate-rial. This characteristic places him not only in the liminoid territory be-tween the "multiple me's" of his own socially constructed identity but also on the threshold between "self-expression" and the calculated appro-priation of preexisting cultural artifacts. In this trait, and in his wish to fracture the stuff of existing movies so as to expose their mechanisms and destroy their manipulative capacities, he is closer to Burroughs than any other filmmaker except those (most notably Anthony Balch) who have themselves collaborated with Burroughs.

Another factor linking Conner with the Beat sensibility is the impor-tance of music in his *oeuvre*, not only as an establisher of mood but also as a fundamental organizing principle. He regularly employs music tracks, from the Ottorino Respighi tone poem in *A Movie* to the Ray Charles pop song in *Cosmic Ray* (1962), the Miles Davis exotica in *White Rose* (1967), the new-wave pulse by David Byrne and Brian Eno in *America Is Waiting* (1981), and originally composed music in such films as *Crossroads* (1976) and *Take the 5:10 to Dreamland* (1976). In some cases, the selection and timing of music are (respectively) his starting point and steady reference point for the montage process, as in *Valse Triste* (1977), one of his greatest works, where an insistent three-quarter rhythm on the music track rein-forces editing that (obliquely echoing a Brakhage practice noted above) often carries movement across cuts to a number of disparate shots. This film's companion piece, *Take the 5:10 to Dreamland*, employs original mu-sic (by Patrick Gleeson) as part of a contrasting attempt to evoke a state between waking and sleeping (very different from Brakhage's hypnagogic representations) by means of comparatively static sequences—and to do this "without making a totally boring film" (quoted in MacDonald 249), as Conner has said.[24]

An additional factor in Conner's montage is his aforementioned ten-dency to privilege speed and density in many (although by no means all) of his most substantial works. He recognizes this tendency with much irony, acknowledging that while he despises television advertising, it has "affected the way that people make movies," and that he himself "might be guilty of that tendency in ads to get as much information as possible into a short period of time." Still, he does not "necessarily intend that you see everything that's going on. . . . Sometimes it's just the rush of images that's important" (MacDonald 251, 246). At other times, moreover, he uses a contrasting montage strategy—repetition and reiteration—to create powerful dynamics of structure and meaning. This strategy may operate in a slow mode, as in *Crossroads*, or in a more rapid mode, as in *Report* (1963–67). In the first half of this film, footage of John F. Kennedy's assassination is edited into iterative bursts of overlapping imagery that work a forceful variation on the "visual stutter" (1973, 35) identified by Michelson in Eisenstein's work; this effect both multiplies the hideousness of the event and transforms it into a monotonous, mechanically reproduced artifact that anticipates the advertising and media-marketing themes on which the film's second half focuses. Along with such works as *America Is Waiting* and *Mongoloid*, with their ferocious (and very Burroughs-like) attacks on media promotion of conformity and violence, *Report* is one of Conner's most emphatic exercises in the darkly carnivalistic practices of interruption (disarming, nullifying) and inversion (exposing, parodying) of conventional—and conventionally deadening—cinematic discourse.

*F*lower Thief and Atom Man

> This is a wild mad rough cut like no Hollywood director would dare show the public for fear of having his ideas stolen. We defy anyone to cop our style.
> —Ron Rice, program note, The Queen of Sheba Meets the Atom Man

> [The Queen of Sheba Meets the Atom Man] is a protest which is violent, childish, and sincere—a protest against an industrial world based on the cycle of production and consumption.
> —Alberto Moravia, L'Espresso (Rome)

> Jesus was a beatnik.
> —Title of book held by bearded man in Senseless

Ron Rice, who completed only a handful of films before his death at the age of twenty-nine, chose a different but equally intuitive route toward exploding the approved varieties of filmic expression and establishing his own purposefully challenging alternative. Neither his shooting style nor his montage is as kinetic as Brakhage's, and he shows none of the interest in found-footage construction that typifies Conner's work. Rice belongs instead to what may be called the Wandering Beat school of avant-garde filmmaking, focusing on distinctive outsiders as they meander through the postwar environment and undergo experiences that are as sad, silly, and strange as the protagonists themselves.

Rice's identification with the Beats was forthright, as the posthumous Rice papers published by Mekas in 1965 make clear. In a comment on "Being BEAT and CREATION," he writes that Beatness means "the absence of ambition directed towards obtaining money. Practically all the people spend their days in the active pursuit of Money. Those few who ignore this trend are given a special grace, the freedom of the mind which enables them to Create and receive the Joy." In the next passage he adds that "the idea of 'Beat' has been shit on enough by those who are financially secure due to recognition obtained from the electromagnetic mind fields of great swingers," suggesting (with a hint of Burroughs-like paranoia regarding technology and mental energy) that Beat enterprises face opposition from beneficiaries of sociocultural power structures. The echo of Burroughs is also strong when Rice attacks the "New Realism" in painting as a "plague," warning that the "brain peddles the same shit as all public communications push" and that the "sinister, powermad conspiracy of mind control through ART, will close the last door of the individual. Business minds have already installed money meters on public shithalls. Next the Galleries, then the eye itself." Rice remains fundamentally optimistic, however. "Ginsberg, Burroughs creating a new form," he writes with an uncharacteristically direct reference to specific Beat figures. "Rejected at first. Now it is impossible for those who do not wish to attempt to comprehend the message to turn back the clock. The works of the New writers are there and will take their place in the stream of Mankind's Culture." The same goes for the New American Cinema, which is "just the first crack in the ice." High among the priorities of genuine art, meanwhile, must be a Kerouac-like emphasis on spontaneity. "Why bother to analyze anything," he asks in a letter to the *Village Voice*, signed Mr. Da Zen Dada, his sometime pseudonym. "See where analysis has brought the human race, the world is on the brink of destruction . . . " (R. Rice 113–14, 119).

Rice implicitly agrees with Kerouac's insistence that the heart of Beatness is beatitude. Friends and associates of Rice make this point explicit. Writing in 1968 about *The Queen of Sheba Meets the Atom Man*, an anarchic epic that Rice began in 1963 and never completed, Mekas declared,

> I have no doubt that psychoanalysts [and] various other kinds of analysts will have a field day with this work. It will take the most despaired (shocked?) ones among us, and the most beatified ones—those who are either at the end of the rope or those who are at the very beginning of it—to see, experience & understand this movie directly, immediately, & nakedly, and be liberated for a more subtle & intense life.[25] (121)

In a sermon devoted to Rice's first completed film, *The Flower Thief* (1960), the Reverend Al Carmines wrote in 1962 that the Beat movement "is not so much a prophetic thrust into a super-sophisticated future as it is a reminder of an ellusive [*sic*] and uncompatable [*sic*] past. It finally is conservative in the most natural and ultimate sense. It is a call to remember and to see that the most intimate of daily doings and objects that surround us, and that we use unconsciously are profound and plenteous in meaning, richness and joy." Later he calls the Beat endeavor "an attempt to strip off the layers of accumulated impersonality—brittle cultivation that winds itself around us as mindlessly and unconsciously as a shell around a snail. Layers that keeps [*sic*] us just right—just proper temperature—for a just proper life." Eventually he speaks of the Beats and the Christian saints together, identifying their message to "our self-assured and confidant [*sic*] age" as, "Watch out—You may be on holy ground" (R. Rice 124–25).[26] Ginsberg and especially Kerouac would have been delighted with this association of Beatness, spiritual conservatism, an almost pantheistic sense of holy plenitude, and recognition of the power that resides within the actual, the ordinary, the quotidian.

The Flower Thief reflects all these qualities by plunging into an utterly liminoid territory that stands with the most pararational domains carved out by the Beat poets and fictioneers. Its unnamed hero, played by Taylor Mead, is a child-man roaming the streets and sidewalks of San Francisco, where he encounters a series of friends, foes, and authority figures; ultimately, after a highly stylized narrative climax wherein he is executed by firing squad for urinating in public—only to spring heedlessly back into the movie for its last scenes—he finds a lover for a fleeting beach-front romance. The film is positioned as a Beat statement, with jazz on the sound track along with verbal references to the United States as a sick society and to nonconforming citizens as troubled members of a troubled world. At the same time, it prefigures some aspects of the Hippie movement, doing so with surprising precision, considering how early the film was made. The hero's childlike nature and fondness for flowers make him an almost-literal "flower child," and there is a reference to LSD, a hallucinogenic drug that would not become notorious to Americans at large until further into the '60s era.

The movie is also a subtly reflexive work, since its hero is constructed partly on a film-historical model. "In the old Hollywood days movie studios would keep a man on the set who, when all other sources of ideas failed (writers, directors), was called upon to 'cook up' something for filming," Rice has written, calling *The Flower Thief* a memorial to "all dead wild men who died unnoticed in the field of stunt" (annotation in *Film-Makers' Cooperative Catalogue*, 406). Although little is specifically made of this reflexive element, the Beat behaviors of the Flower Thief are as marginal to conventional urban life as the Wild Man's presence was to the "normal" routine of the Hollywood studio system. The Flower Thief also spends a fair amount of time in Beat-like liminal locations, such as a jazz joint (the trumpeter there appears to be bop pioneer Dizzy Gillespie, although little but his puffed-out cheeks and exotic hat is visible on-screen) and an abandoned building where a bit of male-female recreation spurred Carmines to rhapsodize that "[a]ll the subtly [*sic*] of Hollywoods demi-gods and goddesses seems mechanical and tawdry against the sight of that slight man and rather hefty woman laughing, and playing, and running in the debris."

In a bold and Beat-like maneuver, Rice and Mead take the Flower Thief's resemblance to a child beyond metaphor and into actuality. He comes into close contact with schoolchildren in the first scenes of the film, and shortly afterward he places a small flower on the forehead of a baby in a perambulator—in a gesture that is part ludic self-expression, part secular-sacramental rite. He looks and acts like a radically "immature" individual throughout the movie, moving with a shambling gait and loose gesticulations, and even losing his pants at one point, just as his lower bodily stratum is aimed directly toward the camera. He acquires an obvious transitional object, moreover: a large teddy bear that becomes his constant companion. Here the notion of play becomes inextricably linked with his personality, as he treats the stuffed animal with whimsical affection; he even has an elliptical sex scene with it, underscoring the transitional object as a site of highly charged libido. (After a man and woman emerge from a locker where they have presumably had sex, the Flower Thief hops into it with his toy, which he is cheerfully hugging when spoilsports yank the door open.)

The film also connects play with its notion of ideal culture. The movie itself is a reflexive example of such culture, since it intersects with ludic activities on all of its levels; that is, the film is not only *about* play, it *is* play. Both its geographical setting (the North Beach area of San Francisco) and its psychological tone (virtually everything is focalized through the Flower Thief's perceptions) are implicitly set up as in-between or intermediate territories, bearing the potential for nonconventional (Beat-like) activity and hence serving as symbolic origin-sites for new forms of (individual) play and (social) culture. Since the story begins with the Flower Thief rambling through the urban environment and concludes with a love/sex encounter in an intimate seashore setting, its progression may be charted as a movement from city, boundaries, and *societas* to nature, boundlessness, and *communitas*; not coincidentally, the last portion of the film contains many specifically carnivalesque images, from the game arcade where the Flower Thief meets his lover to shots of fireworks and a carousel (which is doubly carnivalized by being run backward and shown at pixillated speed) that symbolize the hero's momentarily ecstatic state. (In a vivid example of carnivalesque inversion, the Flower Thief himself is seen arbitrarily upside down in one shot, conveying a sense of his hyperbolic *jouissance* near the end of the film.)

Limiting interpretation of the film to a schematic trajectory of *communitas* to *societas*, however, would diminish its richness as pararational expression. In a willing acceptance of paradox, Rice posits the city as both (a) confining concrete jungle and (b) liberating site for anarchic play by what Kerouac would call the irrepressible fellaheen; simultaneously he posits the film as (a) intelligible cinematic narrative and (b) disjunctive autotelic spectacle. The camera's unwavering, always celebratory fascination with Mead's semi-improvised performance reveals Rice's appropriation of the actor as a surrogate who renders visible his own social attitudes and personal impulses. These then serve as behavior strips that Rice manipulates into uninhibited cinematic self-observation.

For all its idiosyncrasies of form and content, *The Flower Thief* shares important qualities with another Beat-related film of the early '60s. *Lemon Hearts*, made by Vernon Zimmerman in 1960–61, again features Mead as the quintessential outsider, this time wandering through a painting exhibition that triggers a series of flashbacks and cutaways. These have a strongly carnivalesque quality, as Mead parodies social and cultural conventions ranging from marriage rituals to haute-bourgeois tennis playing. Here there is an edge of hostility to Mead's performance and personality, however—especially when he literally spits at society while mimicking a sort of Beat pope—that does not appear in *The Flower Thief*; this difference points toward the cutting satire of Hollywood hypocrisy that surges through Zimmerman's next film, *To L.A. . . . With Lust* (1961). The structure of *Lemon Hearts* recalls not only *The Flower Thief* (which Zimmerman helped Rice produce) but also *Pull My Daisy*, where a moment of silence during the Bishop's visit generates a string of free-associative scenes, much as the art-gallery tour in *Lemon Hearts* does. Also like *Pull My Daisy*, the Zimmerman film has a Beat-poetic sound track, consisting of Mead's own poetry. "My mother is dead, my father is living dead, my brother is a lawyer and all that jazz, jazz, jazz," he recites at one point, amusingly indicating that the progression from "dead" to "living dead" to "lawyer" constitutes an ascending scale of sociocultural horrors. Taking a wide range of positions ranging from antiauthoritarianism to outright anarchism, Mead's verbal self in *Lemon Hearts* is as pungently expressive as his gestic self. "Woman is in a diddley-bop position in America," he states, sounding like a protofeminist years before the modern women's movement had gathered its full steam. "Big Stupid is watching."

Rice followed *The Flower Thief* with the equally Beat film *Senseless* (1962), a nonnarrative meditation on Western sociopolitical norms that finds these not merely illogical but wickedly destructive. Sentimentally dedicated "To Jack Kennedy," it uses a bullfight in Acapulco as one of its key tropes; at one point it intercuts the public torture of the besieged bull with scenes of a disabled man being tormented (kept from his wheelchair, prodded with a cane, etc.) by an anonymous assailant on an urban street. (The image of a legless man under attack and the film's largely Mexican setting recall Luis Buñuel's savage *Los Olvidados*, released a decade earlier; both films are eloquent attacks on social viciousness.) Another striking cut juxtaposes a jumbled mess of movie film with two densely composed shots of wires strung on telephone poles. Suggesting both the complexity and fragility of modern communications, this moment blends social critique with autocritique of Rice's own favored medium.

The ironically titled *Senseless*[27] was followed by *Chumlum* (1964), pointing in new directions for Rice with its powerful colors, its sophisticated use of multiple superimposition, and its rejection not only of narrative but also of the sociocritical "sense" that *Senseless* and *The Flower Thief* possessed. By the time of this film, Rice seems less a socially disaffected Beat than an aggressively psychedelic Hippie; the primary key to the minimal "meaning" of *Chumlum* is provided when star Jack Smith aims a hashish pipe at the camera. Drug use was frequent in the Beat community, but it was the Hippies who raised it from a facilitator of liminoid insight to a veritable *telos* unto itself; and drug abuse was evidently a contributing cause to Rice's early death from bronchial pneumonia (Renan 178). In keeping with the Beat spirit, however, it appears to have aided his creation of three major completed films as well as an uncompleted epic— *The Queen of Sheba Meets the Atom Man*, bringing together an African-American earth mother and a white man whose "name" summons up the nuclear-age society that Rice was so eager to carnivalize—and a small amount of exquisitely wrought footage from a Mexican project that suggests fresh aesthetic terrain for Rice's interest in color and superimposition.

Baillie, Meyer, Jacobs

Among other avant-garde filmmakers who shared and explored aspects of the Beat spirit during the '50s and early '60s, Bruce Baillie was one of the most widely respected. Two early works, *On Sundays* (1960–61) and *Have You Thought of Talking to the Director* (1962), blend formal properties of traditional documentary (in the former) and traditional narrative (in the latter) with strong impulses toward spontaneity (in both), achieving poetic and at times visionary effectiveness. More substantial works that followed these, such as *To Parsifal* (1963) and *Quixote* (1964–65), have subtle affinities with Kerouac's novels in at least two areas: their fascination with the concept of the hero—one thinks of Kerouac's transformation of Neal Cassady into a hero with a dozen faces, to vary Joseph Campbell's phrase—and their journeying across both physical (geographic) and psychic (liminoid) landscapes. The impassioned *Mass for the Dakota Sioux* (1963–64) conjures up Kerouac's sensibility with its references to Roman Catholicism in its title, structure, and music, and with its romanticized regard for the American past.

Interests redolent of the Beats, and especially of Kerouac's fiction, also course through the jazz-inflected kineticism of *Yellow Horse* (1965), the dreamlike exoticism of *Tung* (1966), the microcosmic circularity of *All My Life* (1966), the mystical minimalism of *Still Life* (1966), the urban poeticism of *Castro Street* (1966), and the idyllic physicality of the Mexican tone poem *Valentin de las Sierras* (1967). Baillie's most ambitious work, *Quick Billy* (1967–70), is structurally influenced by the *Bardo Thodol* or *Tibetan Book of the Dead* and also, in the last of its four sections, by the Hollywood western; its final on-screen title says, "ever westward eternal rider," a phrase Kerouac might have metaphorically appended to the end of more than one book and, indeed, to his career (and life) as a whole. Summarizing his career in 1971, Baillie stated, "I have to say finally what I *am* interested in, like Socrates: peace . . . rest . . . nothing" (Sitney 1979, 169). Once again, Kerouac's spirit echoes through the void.

Andrew Meyer never achieved Baillie's prominence in avant-garde circles, and his accomplishments have been regrettably overlooked since his untimely death from AIDS in the early '80s. His films share interests and concerns with Baillie's early work, however, and have much of the Beat spirit about them.

Meyer began his career in 1964 with the remarkable *Shades and Drumbeats*, a moody cinematic visit with a self-marginalized commune on the Lower East Side of Manhattan; a Beat sense of streetwise liminality runs through it, beginning with its title. It has an energy and drive similar to that of Warren Sonbert's mid-'60s *Amphetamine* and reflects a similar openness to the most intense varieties of experience. Markopoulos captured its Beat-like spirit in a 1964 lecture, when he said it is "incensed with the values which man forgets, caught in the sedge flats which he calls his streets" (quoted in *Film-Makers' Cooperative Catalogue*, 371).[28]

The discovery of overlooked value in the actual and ordinary is indeed one of Meyer's priorities, as his Warhol-influenced fable *Match Girl* bears out. His most extraordinary work is *An Early Clue to the New Direction*, a twenty-eight-minute narrative filmed in 1966; it features Joy Bang as a young woman in search of a romantic companion, René Ricard as the object of her affection, and Prescott Townsend as the Ricard character's aging lover. With a title borrowed from the Beatles comedy *A Hard Day's Night* (1964) and a compassionately affirmative approach to sexuality across boundaries of age, gender, and convention, the film moves between fantasy and reality with ease and assurance. Meyer's *oeuvre* also includes *Annunciation* (1964), a string of New Testament scenes re-created during a New England autumn; *1 x 1* (1965), a brief coming-of-age story; and the ambitious *Sky Pirate* (1969), a feature-length drama about a young man whose social and personal discontents lead him to hijack an airplane.

Ken Jacobs felt a strong personal identification with the Beat Generation during the '50s and '60s, and his urban romanticism is plainly visible in such works as *Window* (1964), *Air Shaft* (1967), *Soft Rain* (1968), and *The Sky Socialist* (1964–65, revised 1986).

His most emphatically Beat-like films are his early collaborations with Jack Smith, however. Both are dated 1959–63, and both are concerned with exploring and exploiting spontaneity as an undervalued cinematic quality. "Material was cut in as it came out of the camera," Jacobs writes of *Little Stabs at Happiness*, "embarrassing moments intact. . . . I was interested in immediacy, a sense of ease, and an art where suffering was acknowledged but not trivialized with dramatics. Whimsy was our achievement, as well as breaking out of step" (annotation in *Film-Makers' Cooperative Catalogue*, 268). Also central to this film's method and effect is its eclectic sound track. Incorporating elements as diverse as popular music of the '20s and Jacobs's spoken commentary on his broken friendships with people depicted on-screen, it serves variously as enhancement, counterpoint, and contradiction vis-à-vis the images it accompanies.

The more extravagant *Blonde Cobra* was crafted by Jacobs from footage of Smith shot by Bob Fleischner, whose original intention was to make a pair of light-comedy monster movies. (The title *Blonde Cobra* takes a key word from each of the comedies' planned titles.) The film was given to Jacobs after Fleischner and Smith decided to terminate their project, and Jacobs treated it not as a set of fragments from an incomplete story but rather as raw material for an entirely new work; in its finished form it has a collage-like quality (recalling structural devices of Ginsberg and Burroughs) marked by discontinuous editing and long, imageless moments when Smith's verbal performance carries the film by itself. The method used by Jacobs in recording Smith's voice recalls the way Frank and Leslie recorded Kerouac for *Pull My Daisy*, made the same year when *Blonde Cobra* was started. "I played him selections from my 78 collection," Jacobs reports, "music from the '20s and '30s, sometimes only the beginning of a record and if he liked it would restart the record and immediately record. I don't think there was a second take of anything" (annotation in *Film-Makers' Cooperative Catalogue*, 268). This situation does not exactly echo that of *Pull My Daisy*, since Kerouac listened to new music through earphones as he watched the film footage and improvised his voice-over; also, Kerouac recorded three different takes, with material from all three spliced into the final version of the movie. Jacobs and Smith worked from impulses similar to those of Kerouac and his collaborators, however, and the results of their labor have at least as strong a Beat inflection as the more widely known Frank-Leslie film. This fact is reflected in Jacobs's description of *Blonde Cobra* as "a look in on an exploding life, on a man of imagination suffering pre-fashionable lower East Side deprivation and consumed with American 1950's, 40's, 30's disgust" (annotation in *Film-Makers' Cooperative Catalogue,* 269).

The film's spontaneous nature is reinforced by the requirement that a "live radio, loud and clear" be switched on (tuned to a station carrying talk rather than music) at two points during every projection of the film. This device also contributes to the status of *Blonde Cobra* as a purposefully liminal work. On one level, it occupies a borderline position between narrative and nonnarrative; staking out this deliberately ambivalent stance, Jacobs writes that it is "an erratic narrative—no, not really a narrative, it's only stretched out in time for convenience of delivery." On another level, its employment of a nondiegetic (indeed, nonfilmic) radio places it on the boundaries between cinema and multimedia art, between the fixity of film and the immediacy of live broadcasting, between the "purity" of a single work and the "contamination" of intrusion from an outside source. In form and content, *Blonde Cobra* is as radically "in between" conventional positions as the socially alienated artists who created it.

Into the Reality Studio

> This idea of choosing the right host is itself an important aspect of the quality of a viral entity.
> —Douglas R. Hofstadter, "On Viral Sentences and Self-Replicating Structures"

> Nobody is permitted to leave the biologic theater....
> —Williams S. Burroughs, Nova Express

Literary works created with Burroughs's cut-up method appear as ordinary blocks of prose until reading reveals an expansive network of *faux* continuity, discontinuity, and paracontinuity that explodes chronotopic linearity and combats what Burroughs sees as the viral infectiousness of language. Both the cut-up and the fold-in have clear parallels with cinematic montage, which similarly involves the elision and recombination of semiotic material; the effects in Burroughs's writing have been duly likened to effects of cinema, by critics and by Burroughs himself. Cinematic variants of the cut-up method have been used successfully in avant-garde film, moreover, particularly in films of Antony Balch that are constructed according to cut-up principles. These are all fairly short works, although Balch formed a company called Friendly Films in 1971 for the purpose of making a *Naked Lunch* feature from a screenplay by Brion Gysin; this project was aborted when Mick Jagger decided not to take a starring role because of antipathy to Balch as director of the movie (Morgan 453).

The most widely known of Balch's films, *Towers Open Fire* (1963), subjects a science-fiction narrative (with a voice-over written and spoken by Burroughs) to cut-up manipulations that destroy its linear structure and render it at once more impressionistic and more paranoid than it would likely have been otherwise. Certain of Burroughs's other trademark ingredients are also present, including the destruction of a villainous "Board" of Nova Mob-type executives who disappear from the movie in abrupt cuts that might have been inspired by the early cinema of René Clair or even Georges Méliès.

Balch's film *The Cut-Ups* (1963) contains less narrative and more cyclical repetition; and its repetitive material is imbued with a more musical or "poetic" atmosphere. In this work, four shot-sequences are segmented and recombined according to arbitrary metric considerations. (Balch hired a film editor to cut the original sequences into one-foot strips and splice them together in a recurring 1-2-3-4 order; he felt no need to do the splicing himself, since he conceived it as a mechanical rather than an artistic task [Skerl and Lydenberg 173].) The film makes a certain "sense" in visual terms: It includes a segment with a "rolling" theme, for instance, in which a painter wields a paint roller while someone else rolls up a large canvas and another person unrolls the underpants worn by a young man. Still, its visible "characters," like those of *Towers Open Fire*, seem less fully realized than the invisibly constructed figures of Burroughs's prose fiction.

More effective than the visual configurations of these films are their verbal elements, especially the sound track of *The Cut-Ups*, which comprises four tape-recorded phrases that have been cut up and respliced into a layered collage of sense-drained speech: "Yes. Hello. / Look at this picture. / Does It Seem To Be Persisting? / Good. Thank you." Combining the film-reflexive meaning (however limited) of its semantic content with the musicality of what amounts to a round or canon structure, this phrase-sequence gains much of its aesthetic resonance from the cut-up process.

Linkage between cinema and Burroughs's compositional system may be traced beyond similarities of method, moreover, to issues of longstanding importance in film theory. Here it is necessary to recall the connection between Burroughs's rationale for the cut-up aesthetic and his view of pararationality as a defense against the cosmic conspiracy that he metaphorically depicts in his literary mythos.

Most of his major fictions from the Beat Generation period deal in one way or another with a power struggle between the Nova Mob, an invasive gang of intergalactic control freaks, and the Nova Police, sworn enemies of the mob and its program of destructive manipulation. The crafty *modus operandi* of the Nova Mob is to gain dominion over human beings by molding words and images into false realities that foster conflict, confusion, and chaos in earthly affairs. The mob's activities bring to life the most malignant implications of Burroughs's hypothesis that language constitutes a semiotic web imposing on people an insidious complex of limiting assumptions and coercive systematizations. As a semiotic phenomenon with language-like functions, film is another controlling instrument—specifically, a "reality studio" that flings a stream of influence and interpellation at submissive individuals. Therefore it warrants as much vigilance and opposition as do other manifestations of the Nova Mob con game.

The figure who most vividly represents the Nova Mob's rigid control of language/image realities is Mr. Bradley Mr. Martin, the gang's boss. He carries a doubly dual name: Mr. Bradly Mr. Martin is his usual moniker, but he is also known as Mr. and Mrs. D on some occasions. These multiple names suggest the proliferation and fecundity praised in Bakhtin's view of carnivalism; yet Bradley Martin is emphatically the opposite, described by Burroughs as "The God of Arbitrary Power and Restraint, Of Prison and Pressure." While as "a God of conflict in two parts," as Burroughs calls him (Stephenson 62), he is not compatible with the teeming multidimensionality of dialogics, he may be seen as a darkly dialectical figure, in keeping with Bakhtin's view of dialectics as wan and desiccated, representing the dry bones rather than the living heart of dialogism. At times he also functions as the Ugly Spirit, another negative parody of liberating Bakhtinian grotesquerie.[29]

Above all, the cosmic impresario Mr. Bradley Mr. Martin is "just an old showman," as he repeatedly calls himself—directing the "Reality Film" in which ordinary people are the unwitting and helpless performers, and writing the "Board Books" that generate the Reality Film's narrative. Operating as his surrogates, proxies, and deputies are all the "official" persons, organizations, networks, and systems that claim for themselves the power to define, preside over, and impose on others the "reality" that best suits the mob's appalling goals, including the ultimate aim of inducing an explosive Nova State, for which the mob will be the sadistically exultant audience. In the Nova Mob's use of seemingly innocuous delegates and agents, readers of Louis Althusser may recognize a science-fictionalized echo of his contention that entrenched authorities and establishments reproduce themselves and their messages by hailing or "interpellating" individuals through what he terms "Ideological State Apparatuses"—mass media, educational institutions, political parties, religious organizations, and the like. These interpellations present the human subject with a psychodynamically compelling effect of monocentric unity. (This idea has been explored by film theorists via the "mirror stage" phenomenon in Jacques Lacan's theory of subject formation, which holds that the inherently divided psyche gains an illusion of oneness through seeing its literal or figurative reflection in the world outside itself.) Through this unity-effect, the interpellating ISAs—definitely including classical Hollywood film, whose unity-effects are famously effective—seduce the decentered, nonunitary self with the illusion of monadic coherence. Further illusions may attach themselves to this process for their own sustenance and propagation.

Burroughs's weapon against such interpellation is a radical montage that celebrates discontinuity, non sequitur, and irrelevance. He advises that "the use of irrelevant response will be found effective in breaking obsessional association tracks." This ploy is extremely useful, since "all association tracks are obsessional" (1987b, 213). Asserting that "what we see is determined to a large extent by what we hear" (1987b, 205),[30] he admonishes us to bypass all sensory input, to interrogate all semiotic reasoning, and to recognize that "whatever you may be you are not an 'animal', you are not a 'body', because these are verbal labels" (1970, 57).[31] The cut-up method allows the construction of alternative "verbal bodies" whose grotesquerie (literally unheard-of) serves to dialogize and carnivalize the language structures that are continually attempting to seduce and coerce us. Burroughs bases his anti-Nova Mob counterattack on the conviction that disorder and disorientation are double-edged swords, capable of being turned back on the mob even as that unsavory gang prepares to enjoy the

Nova State that will bring its conquest of humanity to a climax. The trick is to confuse the minions of Mr. Bradley Mr. Martin just as thoroughly as they succeed in confusing us, and even more important, to sever our addiction to the illusory brainstorms that they foist upon us, thereby inoculating ourselves against the language/image virus that flourishes under their regime. Only thus will we be able to understand the exhortation of Uranian Willy the Heavy Metal Kid, also known as Willy the Rat, who "wised up the marks" in *The Soft Machine*:

> This is war to extermination—Fight cell by cell through bodies and mind screens of the earth—Souls rotten from the Orgasm Drug—Flesh shuddering from the ovens—Prisoners of the earth, come out . . . Wise up all the marks everywhere Show them the rigged wheel—Storm the Reality Studio and retake the universe . . . Photo falling—Word falling—Use partisans of all nations— Target Orgasm Ray Installations . . . Take Studio—Take Board Books—Take Death Dwarfs—Towers, open fire. . . . (155–56)

It is for these reasons that Burroughs inscribes on the cut/folded page a cut/folded verbal body that defies monologic order in all its forms and guises. Cutting and folding are not acts of destruction but of creation, exorcizing what Beat-associated poet Gary Snyder has called "the negative and demonic potentials of the unconscious" (Stephenson 72).

Key elements of Burroughs's mythos have been profitably examined in connection with Gnosis, a religious philosophy that developed before A.D. 200 in the Middle East and some Roman communities. Gnosis sees the visible world as "a kingdom of evil and of darkness" (58, 60), in historian Kurt Rudolph's words, held in slavery by a malevolent creator and a gathering of auxiliary troops, all of whom must be unequivocally condemned by the enlightened.[32] Redemption is to be found in mystically acquired knowledge, which bestows upon the knower a divinely inspired understanding that not only transcends but drives out and replaces the circular, self-deluding dynamics of mere faith. Burroughs is not the only Beat figure to generate ideas compatible with Gnostic philosophy. Kerouac discovered Gnostic texts during his Columbia University days, appreciating their heretical (and carnivalesque) tendency to reverse the terms of traditional myths and allegories, as well as their insistence on rejecting the physical world in favor of spiritually revealed awareness (Tytell 188–89).

Ginsberg's poem "Howl" has been seen as an engagement with problems and challenges of transcendence, which have antecedents in Gnosticism as well as other religious and philosophical traditions (Stephenson 51).

The parallel between Burroughs's mythos and the Gnostic world view is located by Gregory Stephenson in their shared inscription of "the material world as illusory, the body as the primary impediment to true being and identity, and escape from the body and the world of the senses as humankind's paramount concern" (59–60). As this conception plays itself out in Burroughs's fiction, the malevolent powers or Archons of Gnosticism, led by the blind god Sammael, become such Nova Mob avatars as Green Tony, the Blue Dinosaur, and Iron Claws; all are grotesque yet profoundly anticarnivalistic figures devoted to the confinement of human consciousness in traps of ego-bound physicality. Just as Gnosis aims at a transcendental (and profoundly liminoid) knowledge rather than mere intellectual learning or theoretical analysis, so Burroughs aligns himself with the Nova Police and their goal of "the liberation of consciousness from matter," in Stephenson's words, never forgetting the highly Bakhtinian goal of this liberation, "the restoration of multitudinousness" (Stephenson 62).

Creation of meaning is the necessary battleground for this attempt, since according to Burroughs, what originally scared humanity into time, body, and shit was (as discussed earlier) nothing other than "the word" of the "Alien Enemy" who holds humanity prisoner under the open skies (Burroughs and Ginsberg 1963, 65; Burroughs 1980, 12). Burroughs's conflation of language, excrement, and confinement within biological norms—and his hope that understanding of this deadly combination will lead to an eruption of apocalyptic purgation—is concisely summarized by critic Cary Nelson's phrase, "Scatology becomes eschatology" (Skerl 127). This phrase suggests that at the end of life and history we may be superseded by our own chattering assholes, the organs of expulsion and propulsion through which, *Naked Lunch* informs us, we may even now see God in the rearview bulb-flash of omniscient anal orgasm (Burroughs 1969, 131–35).

In this deliberately uproarious vision, which Burroughs develops with undisguised enthusiasm, the upper and lower body fold onto one another like the fused extremities of disparate passages in a cut-up text or film. Recalling the figurines of pregnant senility that Bakhtin celebrates, the paradoxical grotesqueries of Burroughs's mythopoeic end-game have "nothing calm and stable" (Bakhtin 1984b, 25) about them, but posit the carnivalesque concatenation of fecundity, absurdity, profligacy, and decadence as at once a boisterous nightmare and a privileged source of Gnostic energy and metamorphic possibility. The cut-or-folded text, film, and body are a direct line of attack against the Reality Studio and its addictive onslaughts of language, image, and illusion. It is an exploding ticket to the Movie of All Time—profoundly Beat, ineffably Beatified, and coming soon to a Biologic Theater near us all.

NOTES

WORKS CITED

INDEX

NOTES

Introduction: Beats, Visions, and Cinema

1. John Tytell is one commentator who makes this comparison, designating "the social given" as the common enemy of both groups (9).

2. Carr appears as Claude de Maubris, the "falling star Lucifer angel boy demon genius" of a youthful clique, in *Vanity of Duluoz: An Adventurous Education, 1935–46*, one of Kerouac's most important novels. The narrator reports, "Claude kept yelling stuff about a 'New Vision' which he'd gleaned out of Rimbaud, Nietzsche, Yeats, Rilke, Alyosha Karamazov, anything" (Kerouac 1968, 211).

3. Bakhtin's analysis of Rabelais provides useful insights when applied to Beat writing. For instance, just as Rabelais used folk laughter as a source of "ideological weaponry to rescue human consciousness from [a] stultifying conceptual framework," in Gardiner's words, it can be said that the Beats used various forms of spontaneously generated language "to help prevent what [Walter] Benjamin once called the 'paralysis of the imagination.'" Like the language of Rabelais's novel, moreover, that of Beat works often "drew on popular oral sources and reinvested tired clichés and platitudes with new meanings by placing them in unexpected and often disturbing contexts," involving words in "a 'carnival game of negation' which was enlisted to 'serve utopian tendencies.'" Rabelais was certainly an influence on all of the core Beat writers; Ginsberg, for instance, invoked Rabelais's tradition of "social satire" in a petition aimed at exonerating comedian Lenny Bruce from obscenity charges (see Schumacher 410–11).

4. Cf. Terry Eagleton's statement that carnivalesque activity tends to be "a licensed affair in every sense, a permissible rupture of hegemony, a contained popular blow-off" (quoted in Gardiner 231).

5. Kerouac makes a half-serious association between Beethoven and "gloom" in more than one book, including *On the Road*.

6. Charters observes that jazz musician Mezz Mezzrow used "beat" in compound words and phrases in his 1946 book *Really the Blues*, as when he writes, "I was dead beat" and "a beat-up old tuxedo with holes in the pants." It is interesting to note that Kerouac used Mezz as the nickname of Pat Mezz McGillicuddy, the musician character in *Pull My Daisy*.

7. Kerouac, in a 1948 conversation with John Clellon Holmes, is responding to Holmes's suggestion that he succinctly characterize his generation's new attitude (quoted in Charters xix).

8. As glossed by Stephenson, the suggestion is that for Kerouac "the condition of weariness, emptiness, exhaustion, defeat, and surrender is antecedent to and causative of a state of blessedness. In being Beat the ego is diminished and in abeyance" (23).

9. Tytell concisely recounts the evolution of *On the Road* (143). The friend of Kerouac was Ed White, an artist.

10. In a description of Jack Duluoz, his alter ego, Kerouac reports that he "couldn't speak anything but French till [he] was six" (1994, 28).

11. With regard to one more Beat figure and the notion of visual thinking, Lawrence Ferlinghetti was not one of the core Beats but had a longtime association with them; in his prose and poetry, Stephenson finds a complex "Spiritual Optics" that constitutes "a way of being and seeing, a mode of identity and vision" involving a psychic struggle toward "integration of the fragmented, fallen consciousness into a unity" and "reconciliation of subject and object, of ego and nonego, in the communion of creative perception" (140). Note the echoes here of Jacques Lacan's psychoanalytic theory of psychic fragmentation and longing for a lost prelapsarian state.

12. Kerouac's tears flowed "as [the composer] knelt to pray for inspiration."

I. Historical Contexts

1. The atmosphere of the period has been characterized by sociologist Todd Gitlin as "an extreme and wrenching tension between the assumption of affluence and its opposite, a terror of loss, destruction, and failure" (12).

2. These '50s conditions and "the multiple anxieties that still discomforted the prosperous bourgeoisie" (184) are discussed by Pells.

3. Based on a Fannie Hurst novel, Sirk's movie was preceded by a 1934 film version (directed by John M. Stahl) with substantially different narrative details.

4. Goodman wryly adds that indeed, "culturally, the prospect of a great nation playing golf and folk-dancing is dismaying."

5. Goodman is referring to the same group that would be dubbed "the best and the brightest" in later years.

6. Historian Richard H. Pells calls the cold war a "form of cultural combat" that provided a "chance for intellectuals to demonstrate their indispensability" to their country; some of these intellectuals resurrected the notion previously associated with '30s communism that "ideas should be treated as 'weapons' in whatever struggle currently raged" (122, 125, 128).

7. In its technical sense within sociology, "conformity" has been defined as "a change in behavior or belief toward a group as a result of real or imagined group pressure" (Kiesler and Kiesler 2).

8. "I don't associate myself with [the Beat movement] at all, and never have," Burroughs says in the same text, "either with their objectives or their literary style." The tendency to group him, Ginsberg, Kerouac, and Corso is "simply a matter of juxtaposition rather than any actual association of literary styles or overall objectives," he adds.

9. Goodman takes the term "sociolatry" from August Comte.

10. Ehrenreich also notes that "conformity was the most popular topic for major speakers at college commencements" in June 1957 (30).

11. Authors associated or aligned with England's influential Birmingham Center for Contemporary Cultural Studies.

12. The implicitly Foucauldian cast of much of Burroughs's project is suggested by some of the terminology used in biographer Barry Miles's account. He writes that Burroughs "proposed freedom from the dogma and conditioned reflexes of the individual living in authoritarian society" and "looked for the methods of control which perpetuated this unfortunate state of things, for without them such a society cannot exist. He saw them in the church and in the state and . . . he immediately identified the role of sexual suppression and

repression in keeping the population subservient." As an antidote, Burroughs called for what Eric Mottram describes as a "non-subservient model of human nature," doing so in writings that "explored the nature of obedience from every angle, in particular the manipulation of human sexuality" (Miles 1993, 105).

13. Foucault refers here to the period after May 1968, but his remark clearly has wide application.

14. In other contexts, of course, the terms "character" and "personality" may have very different meanings. Consider, for example, their usage in a text on Yoga: "Through the mastery which the yogi attains over his thoughts and his body, he grows into a 'character.' By the subjection of his impulses and propensities to his will, and the fixing of the latter upon the ideal of goodness, he becomes a 'personality' hard to influence by others . . . " (W. James 308). On a level far removed, cf. also the '50s song "Personality" made popular by Lloyd Price, wherein "walk, talk, style" are celebrated.

15. For an application of Susman's analysis to Hitchcock's work and a discussion of *The Wrong Man* as a '50s-related film, see Sterritt 60–62, 65–81.

16. Regarding the Riesman notion of "autonomy," cf. Stallybrass and White on the bourgeois rejection of carnival: "How often we find the post-Romantic writer separating out his or her central character at the moment of carnival or popular festivity, endowing that character with a special sensitivity and isolated self-consciousness over against the crude conviviality of the revellers. There is no more easily recognizable scene of bourgeois pathos than the lonely crowd in which individual identity is achieved *over against* all the others, through the sad realization of not-belonging. That moment, in which the subject is made the outsider to the crowd, an onlooker, compensating for exclusion through the deployment of the discriminating gaze, is at the very root of bourgeois sensibility. Who would not exchange vulgar participation in the jostle of the crowd for the gift of discriminating judgement?" (187). The achievement of "individual identity" by Riesman's "autonomous man" may be considered more illusory than actual, of course.

17. This statement is an interesting precursor of later efforts by Daniel Patrick Moynihan and others to blame elements of "matriarchy" for problems of African-American males.

18. Ehrenreich accurately summarizes the *Playboy* message as "a critique of marriage, a strategy of liberation (reclaiming the indoors as a realm for masculine pleasure) and a utopian vision (defined by its unique commodity ensemble)." She also notes the fundamental conservatism of the publication and its position within the dynamics of '50s-male rebellion (50–51).

19. Linking the "primitivism" of the Beats with that of Jean-Jacques Rousseau as well as such artists as Paul Gauguin, Pablo Picasso, Constantin Brancusi, Paul Klee, and Jackson Pollock, critic Gregory Stephenson finds in this tendency a reaction against the linked secularism, rationalism, and materialism that had been gathering momentum since the time of John Locke and David Hume and had established a nearly unrestricted reign in the nuclear age. The unconventional methods used by the Beats were all aimed at "circumventing or . . . breaking through the rational, logical intelligence, the ego consciousness, to establish contact with the unconscious mind, with the deepest levels of being" (Stephenson 172, 177, 180). Cf. the remark by C. Wright Mills that "[n]either Burke nor Locke is the source of such ideology as the American elite have found truly congenial. Their ideological source is Horatio Alger" (329).

20. The interaction between Ginsberg and Solomon at the Columbia Presbyterian Psychiatric Institute in 1949 is cogently outlined in Bellios (99–100).

21. Marcuse cites Schiller on this point.

22. Maya Deren, James Broughton, Ken Jacobs, Marie Menken, and Sidney Peterson are other members of the "wit's end" clan.

23. Another extension of this "avant-gardist position" is found in Jean-Luc Godard's work. Peter Wollen sums up many of its key characteristics in his table of "deadly sins" and "cardinal virtues" of the cinema, counterposing the classical-film values of narrative transitivity, identification, transparency, single diegesis, closure, pleasure, and fiction against the "revolutionary, materialist" values of narrative intransitivity, estrangement, foregrounding, multiple diegesis, aperture, un-pleasure, and reality (79).

24. Burroughs uses many of the same formulations in his later *Nova Express*, with adjustments to suit that novel's science-fictional tone: "What scared you all into time? Into body? Into shit? I will tell you: *"the word."* Alien Word *"the."* *"The" word* of Alien Enemy imprisons *"thee"* in Time. In Body. In Shit. Prisoner, come out. The great skies are open. I Hassan i Sabbah *rub out the word forever.* If you I cancel all your words forever. And the words of Hassan i Sabbah as also cancel . . . " (12; emphases in original). With regard to Burroughs's identification of "the" as "the time word" and "the shit word," cf. the conclusion of Wallace Stevens's poem "The Man on the Dump," which reads: "Where was it one first heard of the Truth? The the." One commentary glosses this as follows: "'The Truth' is an intangible absolute (like '*the* good'); what it specifies cannot be defined. The *the* itself however represents an urge to seek absolute meaning: to say *the*, not merely *a*" (1484).

25. Note that Brakhage is referring here to needs that he specifically connects with the postwar period.

26. "In the multiverse of the cut-up all time is simultaneous," writes Stephenson of Burroughs's aspiration. "Self and other and *it* melt and merge in the cut-up" (64), he adds later.

27. It was felt that certain Buddhist practices could, in Tytell's description, "result in the annihilation of thought processes so that all would appear as a flow of indistinguishable parts that would carry with it the suppression of accumulated experience" (26). The desired result was a "weightless catharsis beyond madness," which Kerouac and Ginsberg found especially attractive.

28. The phrase "modalities of consciousness" is adapted from Ginsberg, who uses it in his "Kerouac" and attributes it to Humphrey Osmond.

2. Theoretical Frameworks

1. Polsky cites this letter (188), written from prison after Sade had become a writer but before he began writing pornography, as evidence that Sade turned to producing pornography as a means of facilitating masturbation and that, in Albert Camus's words, he "created a fiction in order to give himself the illusion of being."

2. Bakhtin defines the loophole as "the retention for oneself of the possibility for altering the ultimate, final meaning of one's own words" and states that "the loophole left open . . . accompanies the word like a shadow." It is therefore emblematic of unfinalizability, open-endedness, and parodic doubleness, among other important Bakhtinian concepts (see 1984a, 233).

3. Barthes develops this distinction in his *S/Z*.

4. Drawing a connection between Bakhtin and Walter Benjamin, Michael Gardiner notes that Bakhtin "exhorts us to probe the gaps and silences, the fractures and fault-lines that expose the operation of a monologism which seeks to effect an ideological closure in order to 'blast a specific era out of the homogeneous course of history'" (194).

5. Stephenson also characterizes the Duluoz legend as a cyclical construction. Weinreich, who is closer to the mark on this point than Ann Charters and other Beat traditionalists, cites Gertrude Stein's essay on repetition in *Lectures in America* for making clear "the importance of incremental repetition and the ever present 'now' in the truly American utterance" (162). It is interesting to note that Brakhage has cited Stein as a favorite author and an important influence, partly because her work taught him the impossibility of repetition in any literal sense, since meaning is always and necessarily in flux.

6. Literary commentators bear out the carnivalistic leanings of the core Beat group. Although he is not particularly sympathetic to the Beats, literary historian James Atlas (forward to Holmes 1988a, xii–xiii) captures some of their carnivalism in his remarks on John Clellon Holmes's novel *Go*, which tells a tale of Beat adventures and life styles charged with "manic exploration of the unconscious . . . feverish quest for experience . . . glorification of crime." All these preoccupations reflect a rejection of "normal" hierarchical values and therefore connect with what Bakhtin identified as the carnival spirit. So do the free and familiar qualities of what Atlas calls the generation's "self destructive rituals. Disorderly parties in squalid apartments; 'hordes of chattering people' leaping into cabs and racing up and down Manhattan; the incessant quest for 'weed' or 'tea'. . . . " Stated in a more positive manner, a similar sense of carnivalesque ambivalence and open-endedness underlies the assertion by Gene Feldman and Max Gartenberg that unlike the square, "whose every move must be within clearly marked limits," the Beat thinker "accepts chaos as being the real world—shifting, changing, perpetually slipping out of his grasp and his attempts to engage it" (15). More recently Blaine S. Allan, also recognizing in Beat culture the carnivalesque quality of life turned inside out, has stated (without reference to Bakhtinian theory) that the "beats inverted the values most prized by dominant culture in the United States" (1984, 44).

7. *Rabelais and His World* is Bakhtin's most extended treatment of the carnival spirit.

8. Peter Stallybrass and Allon White write cogently of an "uncritical populism" whereby carnival "often violently abuses and demonizes weaker, not stronger, social groups—women, ethnic and religious minorities, those who 'don't belong'—in a process of displaced abjection" (19). The harshness of *The Wild Boys* is articulately captured by Tytell when he describes its title characters as a ritualized group who make "sacraments" of sex and hashish, who "attack with fanatical devotion," and who fashion drug pouches from human testicles as they propel their eponymous novel "between scenes of incredible violence and homoeroticism without love, existing almost for the sake of sensation itself" (137).

9. What would have been experienced by these youths if they had traversed a "normal" period of adolescence is, in sociologist Bernice Martin's description, "an interlude of socially sanctioned immediacy and of relative freedom from the all-defining roles and structures of dependent childhood behind and full social maturity ahead. In all classes [of Western society] the adolescent is expected to rebel a little, especially the boy, and to be a bit wild and irresponsible before settling down" (139).

10. Burroughs's comment was made during a promotional junket with Cronenberg to

publicize the latter's film of *Naked Lunch*, and Krutnik quotes it as a revealing sign of Lewis's reputation. "Burroughs deems it appropriate that the French Order of Arts and Letters should include a wife-murdering ex-addict novelist and a maker of visceral horrorfests," he uncharitably writes, "but Lewis—comedian, film-maker, and Telethon-host—cannot be tolerated within such exalted company. Rarely has a public media figure been so deeply loved, and so intensively and so easily vilified" (12).

11. The unabashed pro-urban and anti-rural bias in Sarris's formulations is also worth noting.

12. Bakhtin's biographers report that while staying at the Soviet Writers Union during a vacation in the mid-'60s, when he was over seventy years old, he "loved to go to the movies shown there, which included foreign films not shown to the general public, even though it meant climbing the stairs to the cinema hall on his one leg" (Clark and Holquist 336).

13. Guimond adds, "There might have been some outsiders or other isolated people in the picture magazines—'troubled' children who needed foster homes, for example—but these magazines always emphasized how this isolation, like other social problems, could be solved by the proper functioning of middle-class institutions" (312). Cf. the postwar social-science view that, as Goodman paraphrased it, modern Americans have "apparently reached the summit of institutional progress, and it only remains for the sociologists and applied-anthropologists to . . . iron out the kinks" (1960, 10).

14. Guimond cites William Stott on the change in "I've seen America" discourse from a vehicle for progressive ideas to a set of conservative clichés. On the solving of social problems, note yet again the recurrence of the idea that finding the right measures in the modern American milieu is surely only a matter of hard work, patience, and good will.

15. Burroughs also targeted *Time* and *Life*, or rather the controlling forces behind them, as particular enemies of free thought. An early passage in *Nova Express* reads, "Who monopolized Immortality? Who monopolized Cosmic Consciousness? Who monopolized Love Sex and Dream? Who monopolized Life Time and Fortune? Who took from you what is yours? Now they will give it all back? Did they ever give anything away for nothing? Did they ever give any more than they had to give? Did they not always take back what they gave when possible and it always was? *Listen*: Their Garden of Delights is a terminal sewer . . ." (13). Note the punning use Burroughs makes of the magazines' names. Also relevant is the *Time* cover prominently displayed on Jack Smith's wildly costumed torso in a scene of Ken Jacobs's 1957 film *Star Spangled to Death*.

16. "The path to salvation, social engineers explain, lies in a trained elite that will benevolently manipulate us into group harmony," Whyte writes. "And who's to be the elite? Social engineers modestly clear their throats" (1952, 114).

17. Kerouac's concern about the stultifying power of mass media recalls the Frankfort School's analysis, and so does work by other Beat-related authors. Stephenson juxtaposes Kerouac's antisuburban statements with Ginsberg's lament that "among the abundance and the affluence . . . among the automobiles, the televisions, the household appliances, the hi-fi-sets, the fallout shelters, the SAC bombers, and the nuclear missiles, we had misplaced or displaced 'the lost America of love.'" He also adds Lawrence Ferlinghetti's lines describing "freeways fifty lanes wide / on a concrete continent / spaced with bland billboards / illustrating imbecile illusions of happiness" (175–76). What lends a Foucauldian cast to such observations is their recognition that power has its effects not just in Master Switch control centers but in the daily, voluntary lives of those enmeshed in the social system. Work by other

writers as diverse as Gregory Corso and Aldous Huxley also comes readily to mind in this context.

18. See for instance *The Soft Machine*, a key Burroughs novel. And regarding this thought, cf. the question in Bakhtin's favorite author, Dostoevsky, as to whether "if God doesn't exist, everything is permitted."

19. Citing sociologist Edwin Sutherland's study of white-collar crime, Polsky states that the "social processes involved in deciding which pornography shall be permitted, and even some (though by no means all) of the selective criteria used, are roughly analogous to the way that . . . our society permits certain types of criminals, notably businessmen who commit crimes in their corporate capacities, to escape penological consequences and even public stigma. The . . . classier the pornography the more likely it is to be permitted" (196–7).

3. Social Criticism

1. The volume contains eighty-three photographs plus a triptych on the final page that includes "outtakes" related to the last full-page image. Its initial French edition, with text edited by Alain Bosquet, was published by Robert Delpire Editeur in Paris; its first American edition was from Grove Press in New York.

2. Jack Duluoz, the character representing Kerouac, gives this instruction as a reminder to Raphael Urso, the character representing Gregory Corso, in the 1965 novel *Desolation Angels* (128).

3. It appears in Frank's 1989 collection *The Lines of My Hand*, in a section labeled "United States 1955–1956." An earlier version was printed privately in the early '70s.

4. Her singing of the lyrics eventually changes to wordless vocalese, anticipating (and sounding very much like) the crooning of the Stella Stevens character in John Cassavetes' jazz movie *Too Late Blues*, released in 1961. It is interesting to contrast the smooth, sexy allure of this characteristically '50s-style sound with the aggressive parody of high-pitched female vocalizing constructed by Frank Tashlin and Jayne Mansfield in *The Girl Can't Help It* (1956).

5. The poem was published in the Beat-oriented magazine *Neurotica* in 1950 as "Fie My Fum." Blaine Allan attributes the poem to Kerouac, Ginsberg, and Cassady. Nicosia attributes it to Kerouac and Ginsberg alone (Nicosia 583), as do the credits for Amram's later recording of the song. The published version of the lyrics, in Grove Press's book based on the film, also attributes the incomplete version of the poem sung by Ellis to Kerouac and Ginsberg, and does not add Cassady's name to these credits when it presents the complete version on the succeeding pages. It also notes that the movie version was "sung under the protest of the authors, who insist that the line 'Hop my heart song' should be 'Hop my heart on' as it appears in the original, integral version" (Kerouac 1961b, 9). (On this and other matters below see also Allan 1988, 185–205.)

6. Orlovsky is listed as Peter Orlofsky in the credits. The cast also includes actor Richard Bellamy (listed as Mooney Peebles) as the Bishop; painter Larry Rivers as Milo, the Neal Cassady surrogate; painter Alice Neel (listed as Alice Neal) as the Bishop's mother; and Delphine Seyrig (listed as Beltiane) as Milo's wife Carolyn. Nicosia, McNally, and Allan all indicate that Ginsberg and Orlovsky are meant to be playing themselves in the film while Corso is playing Kerouac; however, Kerouac's narration specifically identifies Corso as Gregory Corso within the diegesis. It is possible that Kerouac decided to distance himself from

Corso's portrayal because Corso's appearance did not please (or flatter) him. "Spotting the awkwardness of Gregory's attempts to act like him," Nicosia writes, referring to Kerouac's on-set observation of some of the shooting, "Jack told him: 'Be yourself'" (584).

7. Allan's account is overeager to find that planning and professionalism outweigh cinematic spontaneity, but it remains the richest source of factual information on the *Pull My Daisy* production history.

8. McNally indicates that Leslie had long wanted to make films but gave this ambition up as a teenager in order to concentrate on painting; his return to film was motivated by disillusionment with "emotionless" surrealist painting and an ambition "to make non-Hollywood but popular narrative movies" (262).

9. Nicosia mysteriously reports that one of the repeat performances "was executed mostly in a Chinese accent" (584).

10. It is a double irony that Frank had journeyed to Florida with Kerouac two years earlier to work on an illustrated essay for *Life*, which then "never ran the bleak pictures that Frank brought back."

11. The first described was taken by Joern Gerdts, the second by Loomis Dean, and the third by J. Philip Shambaugh for the *Daily Princetonian*.

12. Ehrenreich suggests the consolidation of such a genre (62).

13. Interest was enhanced by the still-growing American infatuation with television and everything that pertains to it, and also by the eagerness of print journalists to capitalize on the discovery of fraud and chicanery in the newly arrived medium that was subjecting traditional journalism to stiff and often damaging competition.

14. This holds even though one insert shot shows her aiming an admiring and perhaps sexually charged gaze at one of her husband's friends, suggesting a subplot that is not followed up elsewhere in the film.

15. Pells discusses these points (212). Goodman's analysis in *Growing Up Absurd* is the basis for his observations.

16. Charters reports that the Beats lived over the years "in various rooms and apartments scattered throughout New York, first around Columbia University and Times Square, then on the Lower East Side, Brooklyn, Harlem, the Bronx, and Lexington Avenue. Greenwich Village was rarely in the picture. Its heyday as a center for radical literary and political activity had passed . . . in the early 1940s. . . . [The early Beats] didn't identify with turn-of-the-century Greenwich Village anarchists like Alexander Berkman or World War I–era Greenwich Village literary innovators like Alfred Kreymborg." Rather, they relied on their passion for new kinds of shared experience as the basis for their own "family of friends," in Alfred Kazin's term, and maintained their closeness despite a geographical restlessness that culminated in their dispersal as a group in the early '50s (2–3).

17. It should be added that the underground period was not a time of complete absence from the public eye. While there were few references to the Beat Generation in widely visible pop-culture outlets during much of the early '50s, exceptions did arise, such as the promotion of the late John Horne Burns's novel *A Cry of Children* in 1953 as "A merciless novel of America's 'beat generation,'" treating its readers to "young love in the bohemian fringe-world," as the front cover of the Bantam Books paperback put it. A quote from [John] Clellon Holmes, identified as the author of *Go*, appears on the first page of this volume, underneath a plot synopsis and a Beat-conscious advertising blurb: "From the bop records at all-night parties and the juke-boxes in Bohemian bars comes this violent cry of today's young

Americans—'*The Beat Generation.*'" Burns's earlier books had been *The Gallery*, a mildly successful war novel in the late '40s, and the unsuccessful *Lucifer With a Book*, also about young people; he was rarely, if ever, linked to the Beats before his death in 1952. What suggested the connection to his posthumous publisher may have been Holmes's statement (in the *Glamour* magazine quote used to promote the paperback) that "behind the excess of drink, promiscuity and speed exhibited by many young people today there lies . . . the fumbling, earnest search for a moment of warmth or meaning or joy which might redeem the blackness of reality." Burns's "brilliant and different novel" centers on a male character "who searched through love for his 'moment of warmth' and the comfort of faith, but awoke to the realities of a private hell. . . . "

18. Ginsberg had long been fond of "Jubilate Agno" ("Rejoice in the Lamb") by Christopher Smart, an eighteenth-century English poet who "devised an alternative means— spurred by madness—of extending the lyric moment into a long poem. Smart's was a kind of cumulative method, composing one line a day to create a long poem whose narrative is characterized by its very disconnectedness." Kerouac was also influenced by Smart, notably in the "230th Chorus" of *Mexico City Blues* (Jones 163).

19. The other necessary conditions are "the right physical combination, the right mental formation, the right courage, the right sense of prophecy, and the right information," along with the correct intentions and ambition.

20. From "Notes for *Howl and Other Poems*," liner notes for a Fantasy record album.

21. Fellaheen as conceived by Kerouac were to be found just about anywhere; the Mexican character Tristessa is described at one point as resembling "a junkey on a corner in Harlem or anyplace, Cairo, Bang Bombayo and the whole Fellah Ollah Lot from Tip of Bermudy to wings of albatross ledge befeathering the Arctic Coastline, only the poison they serve out of Eskimo Gloogloo seals and eagles of Greenland, ain't as bad as that German Civilization morphine she (an Indian) is forced to subdue and die to, in her native earth" (Kerouac 1992, 28).

22. The phrase "said and imagined . . . " is quoted by Bakhtin from Rabelais.

23. The phrase is from committee chair J. Parnell Thomas, Republican of New Jersey. Regarding this charge, Cook cites the later observation by screenwriter John Howard Lawson that the American film industry was actually one of the nation's most conservative elements at that time, but asserts that the "predominantly liberal" problem, semidocumentary, and *noir* pictures gave a different impression, especially when examined in conjunction with wartime movies of a pro-Russian bent and with the fact (proven or alleged, depending on each individual case) that some well-known Hollywood workers had contributed to or been affiliated with the Communist party or causes allied with it during the prewar years (Cook 472).

24. Stephenson discusses *Desolation Angels* in terms of acedia, "an affliction of the spirit—a spiritual dryness that manifests itself as melancholia, apathy, listlessness, and a sense of disillusionment and disgust with life," noting that the novel's protagonist (a Kerouac surrogate) is "overtaken and overthrown" by this malady (40). Similar things could be said of the Robert Stack character and his condition in *Written on the Wind*.

25. This phrase, in the "113th Chorus" of *Mexico City Blues*, a book-length poetic work, is preceded by the words, "You start with the Teaching / Inscrutable of the Diamond / And end with it . . . " (113). Stephenson quotes it at the beginning of an essay that refers to Kerouac's multinovel "Duluoz legend" as a "circular journey" (17).

26. Peary goes on to claim that while this movie "makes one aware of the economic

shame of the cities," filmmaker Polonsky nevertheless "shies away from making a real plea for social change or suggesting how group (class) action could change the capitalist power structure," concentrating instead "on the individual" and advancing "the common Hollywood theme 'Don't sell out'" (158). Similar charges were made against the Beats, of course, in their role as sociopolitical commentators. Another critic asserts that both Polonsky and Garfield were "blacklisted as much for the tone of their films as their politics" (Rob Edelman in Lyon 1986, 422).

27. Lowry goes on to state that later Aldrich films, such as the 1956 war movie *Attack!* and the 1956 "women's melodrama" *Autumn Leaves*, embody genre reinterpretations so extreme as to betray "a cynicism so bitter that it could only arise from a liberal sensibility utterly disillusioned by an age in which morality has become a cruel joke. In fact, the shattering of illusions is central to Aldrich's work, and it is a powerfully self-destructive process, given the sweetness of the illusions and the anger of his iconoclasm" (Lyon 1986, 9).

28. Aldrich identifies the film's "basic significance in *our* political framework" (italics in original) as a statement that "the ends did not justify the means" (Higham and Greenberg 28), intended as a rejoinder to the anticómmunist investigations of Senator Joseph McCarthy.

29. Odets was another screenwriter (and playwright) with recognized left-wing connections and related career difficulties.

30. Baxter quotes Houston's comment from her "Glimpses of the Moon," in *Sight and Sound* (Spring 1953).

4. Beats, Films, and Liminality

1. The threshold dialogue flourished as a genre from Hellenistic and Roman times through the Renaissance and the Reformation.

2. Winnicott acknowledges that a transitional object is symbolic of some part-object, such as the breast, but he holds that its importance lies more in its actuality than in its symbolic value. The concept of the transitional object therefore differs from Melanie Klein's notion of the internal object, since the internal object equals a mental concept while the transitional object equals a possession—yet without actually being an external object to the baby's perception (6, 9).

3. Turner cites Roger Abrahams on this point. Note also the important distinction between liminal and liminoid phenomena in Turner's work. As summarized by Robert L. Moore, liminal phenomena "are more characteristic of transitions in tribal societies. They tend to be collective and to be related to biological, calendrical, and other sociostructural rhythms as well as to social crises." Liminoid phenomena, "more characteristic of complex modern societies, are usually individual products, although they may have a widespread effect on the society. Not cyclical in nature, they develop independently of the central political and economic processes of the culture" and are more "fragmentary, plural, and experimental in character than liminal states" (Schwartz-Salant and Stein 22).

4. James A. Hall, a Jungian psychoanalyst, also sounds a Bakhtinian note (as well as a Jungian one) in his essay "The Watcher at the Gates of Dawn: The Transformation of Self in Liminality and by the Transcendent Function" when he notes the prevalence of folklore figures steeped in liminality. Among these figures are holy beggars, third sons, little tailors, simpletons, and the Lone Ranger-like hero described by Turner as the "homeless and

mysterious 'stranger' without wealth or name who restores ethical and legal equilibrium" (Schwartz-Salant and Stein 40).

5. Stephenson goes on to cite Mircea Eliade on the importance of initiation to the sustenance of tribal society, the ratification of inherited culture, and the renewal of spiritual traditions.

6. See Miles (1989) for the major elements appropriated by Ginsberg into his new style.

7. Schumacher notes that for Ginsberg the elements of pitch and tone, largely suggested by vowel sounds, "governed the physiology when the poem was read aloud. . . . The length of a line not only dictated the physical act of drawing a breath but it also suggested the union of the physical and emotional states during the actual composition of the poem itself" (209).

8. Burroughs has cited Von Neumann's work as an example of the cut-up's utility in nonliterary fields. In the latter's *Theory of Games and Economic Behavior*, he "introduces the cut-up method of random action into game and military strategy: assume that the worst has happened and act accordingly. If your strategy is at some point determined . . . by random factor [*sic*] your opponent will gain no advantage from knowing your strategy since he cannot predict the move." The method also has promise for processing scientific data, Burroughs adds, and can "add new dimension to films" (1982, 36). The foregoing account of the origin of the cut-up method draws on Morgan (321).

9. The specific influence of Konitz is identified by Tom Clark (102).

10. "Walking on Russian Hill [in San Francisco] one night, [Kerouac] discovered a movie crew filming Joan Crawford in *Sudden Fear*. After rushing home for his notebook, he spent hours sketching the crowd, the cops, the neighbors, the technicians, and the tired actress repeating her performance a dozen times under klieg lights glaring through the fog. Jack was so excited he stayed up all night typing the piece. . . . Later he would universalize the character of Joan Crawford with the name 'Joan Rawshanks'" (Nicosia 364).

11. An influential strain of contemporary film theory conceptualizes this practice in terms of classical film's ability to provide the fractured, inherently chaotic psyche (forever split among turbulent conscious and unconscious forces) with a comforting illusion of unity by positioning the spectator as a privileged, autonomous subject for whose transcendent gaze the spectacle (along with its embedded interpellations) unfolds as a "natural" event free of ideological content; see the broad range of theory drawing on Lacan, philosopher Louis Althusser, and their epistemological descendants. Although this explanation seems reductive and deterministic in some respects, it remains persuasive in instances where conditioned and cooperative spectators may be assumed.

12. This essay in included in Burroughs 1993, 125–27. Miles attempts to raise a partial defense of Burroughs in this area, contending that Burroughs disliked only "the woman still playing the traditional role, demanding security and protection, looking to her man for money, flattery and love, restricting his freedom, tying him down to house and family." As feminist ideas gained ground in the '70s, this argument continues, Burroughs saw that "liberated women" did not threaten him and noted approvingly that members of the "women's movement" are "opposed to the matriarchal society" and "don't want to be treated as women." Sexual difference, Burroughs had concluded by 1977, is "certainly more sociological than biological" (1993, 138). While it is heartening to observe Burroughs's evolution, it

remains disturbing to encounter his earlier statements, which remain in wide circulation—for example, "Of course women have poison juices I always say," as he comments in a 1954 letter to Kerouac written from Tangiers (Harris 213).

13. That is to say, Bud Powell, Thelonious Monk, or even John Lewis would have been more credible exemplars of Beat-style piano playing. Then again, taste in such an area can be mercurial and mysterious; in *On the Road* a veritable epiphany is constructed out of an appearance by George Shearing, a fine pianist but one who is generally regarded as far more square than most in the Beat pantheon. (Years later, Ginsberg was still making an apologia for Kerouac's sometimes eccentric tastes, admitting that "possibly Kerouac in his enthusiasm overpraised" Shearing and others but contending that he nonetheless provided a perfect "time capsule" reflecting the period of which he was writing (1983, 66–68).

14. The sound-track album for *Beat Girl* was the first sound-track record issued in England, and was reissued in a later era by Elvis Costello's record company (see *The Beat Generation* 46–51).

15. This association is justified by Algren's own tastes. He evidently thrilled Kerouac by telegraphing his praise for *On the Road* soon after Viking first published it (Nicosia 559.)

16. The saga of the *On the Road* movie rights is detailed in Nicosia 559–82.

17. Of the $110,000 offer from Warner Bros. for rights to the novel and Kerouac's appearance in the movie, Kerouac wrote Cassady that his "agent turned it down because it wasn't enough money or something—Everybody asking me 'WHO will play Dean Moriarty?' and I say 'He will himself if he wants to,' so boy maybe truly you can become movie star with luck (tho my girl Joyce says not to wish that fate on you)" (quoted in C. Cassady 290).

18. Kerouac found this act "utterly repugnant," according to McNally (278).

19. Kerouac made this complaint in a letter to the Beat-sympathetic *New York Post* reporter Alfred G. Aronowitz in January 1959. Interestingly, he did not seem bothered by moments of similar but even more childish "violence" that occur earlier in *Pull My Daisy*; these are not depicted in closeup, so perhaps it was not merely the content but rather the emphatic mise-en-scène of the moment that provoked Kerouac's anger. It is also ironic that, since Kerouac provides all the "dialogue" in *Pull My Daisy*, it is his own voice that provides the "Pow" in question (quoted in McNally 263; see also Allan 1988, 199).

20. The make of the starring automobile was no coincidence, since *Route 66* had Chevrolet as a sponsor. Chevy was a big spender on television advertising in this period, with budgets of some $90 million per year; other programs carrying its message included *My Three Sons* on ABC and *Bonanza* on NBC (Halberstam 631).

21. Noting some of the clearly cinematic qualities of the "Joan Rawshanks in the Fog" episode—the protagonist's eye "seems to function as a camera eye" at many points—critic Jaap van der Bent cites Tim Hunt's observation that Kerouac organizes the action "through narrative techniques such as crosscuts and dolly shots . . . alternately sweeps different areas of the scene and moves in for close-ups . . . flashes back and projects ahead." Van der Bent also notes that for Kerouac, "modern Hollywood stands for a corruption of the American dream of freedom and harmony" (151).

22. Weinreich observes that Kerouac's persona "retreats further and further away from the distractions of this world to the inwardness of writing" (34).

23. The only one of the core Beats to sport a middle initial in his authorial signature, William S. Burroughs, may have adopted this formulation in ironic homage to his

ultrarespectable lineage as a member (and official black sheep) of the wealthy Burroughs Adding Machine Company clan. He was named after his paternal grandfather, William Seward Burroughs; a biographer reports that the elder Burroughs's middle name was inspired by "Lincoln's far-sighted secretary of state, who bought Alaska from the Russians," and "was an expression of hope that the boy would make something of himself" (Morgan 14). The younger Burroughs must have found all of this hilarious.

24. When jazz is played at Waldo's, it is generally performed by an all-white combo. It is interesting to note how many films and television shows have unashamedly depicted the New York jazz scene as mainly or wholly white; another egregious example is *The Gene Krupa Story*, a Hollywood feature directed by Don Weis in 1959.

25. "The score for *The Man With the Golden Arm* is not a jazz score. It is a score in which jazz elements were incorporated toward the end of creating an atmosphere, I should say a highly specialized atmosphere, specific to this particular film," wrote Bernstein in *Film Music Notes* in 1956. "Now there are a rash of unpleasant films using jazz more or less skillfully," he added, lamenting the imitators who insisted his score *was* jazz despite its lack of improvisation and other markers of the real thing. "In the future, therefore, it will be difficult, if not impossible, to create a highly specialized atmosphere merely by using jazz elements" (quoted in Prendergast 109, 119).

26. *Gunn* became a theatrical movie in 1967, directed by Edwards from a screenplay he wrote with William Peter Blatty. Stevens was again the star, but popular supporting players Herschel Bernardi and Lola Albright did not appear.

27. His affinity for the urban scene is clear even earlier, in his acting for such Hollywood productions as *Crime in the Streets* (1956, directed by Don Siegel) and *Edge of the City* (1957, directed by Martin Ritt).

28. Parker Tyler has a different assessment, expressing his "genuine surprise that . . . *Too Late Blues* . . . sustains nearly all the original and interesting qualities of *Shadows*, even if we see them, as it were, in the disguise of certain commercial formulas" (Sitney 1970, 115–16).

29. This form of entertainment was not uncommon in this period, when such offbeat personalities as Henry Morgan and Long John Nebel held forth on everything from Asian culture to flying saucers on free-form radio shows. To give an idea of the flavor of Shepherd's program, he would often accompany recorded music with his own whistling or kazoo playing. He also wrote for *Mad* magazine ("The Night People vs. Creeping Meatballism" humorously contrasted hipsters and squares), performed as a stand-up comedian in nightclubs, and published books; a portion of his *In God We Trust (All Others Pay Cash)* became the basis for his narration of Bob Clark's 1983 film comedy, *A Christmas Story*. Shepherd's work directly anticipates that of such different performers as Spalding Gray, Mike Feder, and Garrison Keillor.

30. Carney discusses the two different versions of the film, noting that the end-credits "improvisation" statement in the second, mostly scripted, version is regrettably inaccurate but reflects Cassavetes' gratitude to his performers for their crucial role in the development of the work (26). The final budget of *Shadows*, for which about thirty hours of film were exposed, is reported by J. Hoberman and Sheldon Renan as about $15,000 (for Hoberman see D. James 1992, 105; for Renan see Renan 100).

31. For more detail, see Carney (50–65). As he puts the last-mentioned point, "In the depths, consciousness is not static, simple, monotonic, or reducible to basic intentions and

motives. On the surfaces, expressions are slippery, oblique, indirect, guarded, posed, and stylized."

32. Although this quality has detracted from the mass-audience popularity (and hence the accessibility for viewing) of Cassavetes' work, it has been recognized by some critics as taking narrative convention in fresh and provocative directions. Carney turns to other arts (in Beat-related forms) when trying to evoke the nature of Cassavetes' approach. In musical terms, jazz aesthetics are more relevant than the symphonic tradition since "[r]ather than attempting to plumb depths, Cassavetes' viewers must learn to skate on shifting surfaces." Simultaneously, fidelity to the performative impulse makes his films "the Jackson Pollocks of cinema" (52, 65). Other critics have taken other paths to an understanding of Cassavetes' work in terms of autotelic idiosyncrasy rather than communicative rationality. Jonathan Rosenbaum aptly calls him a filmmaker of doubt, "for whom a shot is often a question rather than an answer, a hypothesis rather than a fact" (281). George Kouvaros and Janice Zwierzynski develop this insight by noting that Cassavetes' works "question the very possibility of both moral judgment and secure knowledge" (27–28).

33. The award citation is dated January 26, 1959. *Pull My Daisy* received the second such award on April 26, 1960.

34. Kerouac wrote to a friend who had been introjected into his prose, "You see, if I were a big Russian novelist writing fiction it would be so easy. I hope you appreciate the fact I feel, well, shamed? awful? shitty? for writing about everybody as they are. I always make an effort to clean up the mess by changing names, times, places, circumstances. But in years from now no one will see a 'mess' there, just people, just Karma, the gaging [*sic*] Karma of all of us" (letter to Carolyn Cassady, quoted in Knight and Knight 50).

35. James's description of Hugh as "skilled" has little on-screen support.

36. Carney appears to recognize this link with Lacan when he notes the importance to Cassavetes of the idea that from the earliest beginnings of experience, "cultural and artistic arrangements of knowledge are in place waiting to ensnare us. The world is not a blank slate on which we write our dreams: It is power saturated and convention imbued." To this implicitly Foucauldian statement Carney might have added "scientific" arrangements of knowledge; and he might have stressed the importance of linguistic patterns in the forms that have been codified by Ferdinand de Saussure, postulated as oedipal Law by Lacan, and astutely recontextualized by the "translinguistics" of Bakhtin and associates. Also to the point is Carney's quotation from Henry James's novel *The Portrait of a Lady*: "Nothing that belongs to me is any measure of me; on the contrary, it's a limit, a barrier, and a perfectly arbitrary one. Certainly, the clothes which, as you say, I choose to wear, don't express me; and heaven forbid they should!" This statement is fully compatible with Cassavetes' aesthetic and philosophical ethos (Carney 71, 27).

37. Cassavetes has occasionally allowed a character to express his (Cassavetes') own distaste for conventional film-narrative construction, for example, the Gena Rowlands figure in *Minnie and Moskowitz*.

5. Heading Underground

1. The Antonin Artaud letter known as "Coleridge the Traitor" was written to Henri Parisot, November 17, 1946 (Sontag 1988, 476).

2. The basics of this event are given in "The First Statement of the New American

Cinema Group," printed in *Film Culture* (22–23; Summer 1961) and reprinted in Sitney (1970, 79–83).

3. Active members of the Film Artists Society included Shirley Clarke, Francis Lee, Ian Hugo, Willard Maas, Francis Thompson, and Lewis Jacobs. It was succeeded by the Independent Film Makers Association, with such new members as Brakhage, Rudy Burkhardt, and Hilary Harris.

4. Cf. the observation by David Curtis that "[w]hen the 'complete alternative' presented itself as a well-established fact (in the form of the New York Film-makers Co-operative [*sic*] and the so-called college circuit of exhibition outlets) in the mid-sixties, the position of feature film-makers on Jonas Mekas' list [of "significant new film-makers" in *Film Culture* 20, 1960] became clearer. Shirley Clarke and Jonas Mekas moved towards the Co-op; . . . [Joseph] Strick and Cassavetes moved back towards the commercial cinema, which in turn was already moving towards them" (135).

5. Mekas has been aptly described by Paul Arthur as "translating constant pressures of estrangement into a manifold form of praxis" (D. James 1992, 46).

6. Arthur states outright that "much of what Mekas admired and attempted to consolidate was a direct inheritance of the Beat ethos" (D. James 1992, 43). More specifically, Maureen Turim links the New American Cinema's romantic emphasis on "the person behind the camera (and behind the editing machine)" with Beat poetry and abstract expressionism, which likewise stress "the artist as unique individual" (D. James 1992, 198).

7. The year 1959, when public interest (negative and positive) in Beat activity reached a pinnacle, marks the point at which "underground" became an adjective of choice in the present context. Renan notes that Lewis Jacobs wrote of "film which for most of its life has led an underground existence" in his article "Morning for the Experimental Film," in *Film Culture* 19, Spring 1959, and that Stan VanDerBeek claimed to have coined the "underground" usage around the same time to describe films like his own. Renan associates the term "avant-garde" with films linked to modernist art movements in the '20s, and the term "experimental" with Soviet montage films of the '20s and works by such Americans as Maya Deren, Kenneth Anger, and Sidney Peterson in the '40s; he also notes that the term "independent" existed alongside "underground" starting in the late '50s, and points out that the latter term was first used by critic Manny Farber to describe "low-budget masculine adventure films" produced in the '30s and '40s. Also coexistent with "underground" was the categorical use of "New American Cinema," which includes "underground" film but is not limited to it (Renan 22–23).

8. Richard Sylbert was production designer for the film, and Albert Brenner (later to become an important Hollywood production designer) served as art director. Clarke, who is credited as both director and editor, also produced the movie with Lewis Allen. In addition to pianist Freddie Redd, the jazz combo consists of saxophonist Jackie McLean, drummer Larry Ritchie, and bassist Michael Mattos.

9. For an analysis, see Lauren Rabinovitz (116–22).

10. Clarke traveled to the Cannes Film Festival for the film's 1961 premiere with the Beat trio of Ginsberg, Corso, and Orlovsky—all veterans of *Pull My Daisy*—in tow.

11. This contention comes from Elayne Zalis, "Cross-examining the Lawmakers: *The Connection* (Play and Film) as Seen through Patriarchal Eyes" (University of Iowa, 1986), 9–11.

12. Brakhage cites James's *Allegories of Cinema* as an example of the "case" he is discussing. Note the interesting implication, in Brakhage's allusion to Martin Luther, that Protestantism is to Roman Catholicism as the avant-garde is to Hollywood.

13. The departing Jarrell and Corso figures are on their way to visit Carl Sandburg, of all people. Duluoz insists that he doesn't mind being left out because he knows Sandburg already, and in fact, Sandburg once hugged him.

14. "Drugs—especially alcohol—intensified the chaos of loose living and created a kind of artificial spontaneity by partially removing the controls of will and conscience," Jones adds. He also suggests that psychoanalytic theory (Burroughs practiced lay analysis on Kerouac) and the Surrealist interest in dreams influenced Kerouac's preoccupation with spontaneity. Existentialist philosophy is relevant, as well, since its demand for "the deepest and most honest relations with other human beings at every moment" necessitates "supple and resilient reflexes." Jones also quotes Nicosia's report that Kerouac was aware of "writing by free association" in the work of Proust and many Romantic poets including Wordsworth and Coleridge, and knew that roots of this practice could be traced to ancient Greek and Roman lyrical poets. Still other inducements to spontaneity were the beauties of jazz improvisation and the Buddhist valorization of intuition over logic (147–50).

15. Brakhage shares an interest in dreams with Kerouac and the Surrealists; cf. his call to "[a]llow so-called hallucination to enter the realm of perception . . . accept dream visions, day-dreams or night-dreams, as you would so-called real scenes," quoted in Part Two above.

16. The core Duluoz Legend novels are *The Town and the City, On the Road, Visions of Cody,* and *Desolation Angels.*

17. Jones is endorsing Nicosia's biographical argument.

18. Bernice Martin expresses a similar view from a sociological perspective when she writes that in literature and (perhaps somewhat less) in other arts, "the avant-garde violation of accepted form relies very heavily for its success on *not* destroying totally the reader's memory of the code and structure which are being bent, twisted or denied. Literature has always depended on the layered accumulation of meaning in words, images and linguistic forms: if these are all simply erased, neither Joycean private meaning nor Dadaesque and Beat shock value can be achieved since the shock (or expansion of consciousness) depends on the reader's *awareness* that something he has erstwhile taken for granted has been presented to him in a new guise. . . . All these [avant-garde] techniques serve to blur boundaries and to undermine clarity and sequence, but they need readers who know what the rules are (or were) before the effects of the violation can be appreciated. Thus the old rejected form always remains as a necessary sub-text lying implicit beneath the surface text: anti-structure is parasitic on the covert retention of structure if it is to avoid sheer incomprehensibility" (98). Also relevant is Luis Buñuel's claim that anything that does not come out of tradition is plagiarism.

19. Cf. his statement, "In the act of editing film I am enough detached from motion to be directly involved with the move meant" (Brakhage 1963, n.p.).

20. *The Text of Light* is an "abstract" film made from closeups of a glass ashtray.

21. Cf. Brakhage's description of his *The Domain of the Moment* (1977), a four-film cycle "in contemplation upon those events which are so centered upon one moment that chronology seems almost obliterated or at least unimportant in remembrance [*sic*]" (Film-Makers' Cooperative Catalogue No. 7, 54).

22. "Respond Dance" is included in Brakhage 1963, n.p.

23. There are certain very noteworthy exceptions, including the extraordinary *Song 23: 23rd Psalm Branch* (1966/78) and *Murder Psalm* (1981).

24. Note that Brakhage also considers music to be a basic reference point in his film-making. Although he has rather different attitudes toward associative links between montage and music and toward the actual use of music on sound tracks, he continually employs music metaphors in describing and explicating his films; and several works from his earliest and latest phases have musical sound tracks. Still, most of his films are silent, indicating (as one of several motivations for this crucial aesthetic decision) a wish to explore and celebrate visual rhythm for its own sake without setting up counterpoints and/or competitions with musical rhythm.

25. This statement appeared in the program notes for a fund-raising screening of *The Queen of Sheba Meets the Atom Man*, January 28, 1963. It was reprinted in R. Rice (121).

26. Carmines gave this sermon at the Judson Memorial Church in New York on August 12, 1962; it was reprinted in R. Rice (124–25). Carmines was a prominent supporter of avant-garde expression in the arts; among his own accomplishments is the theater piece *In Circles*, an ambitious musical setting of words by Gertrude Stein, who is cited as a key influence by many experimentalists including Kerouac, Ginsberg, and Brakhage. Carmines considered *The Flower Thief* to be "a parable of the entire 'beat' movement, and its meaning . . . the meaning of the beat in our time." Rice considered Carmines's sermon "his most favorite review" (see Mekas's introduction in R. Rice [87]).

27. J. Hoberman suggests that the title might refer to Jean-Luc Godard's *Breathless* (1959) and to the hope that this and similar works might spark an American version of the French *Nouvelle Vague* (D. James 1992, 117).

28. Markopoulos gave this lecture at Idaho State University in 1964.

29. The villain's three major names—Mr. Bradly Mr. Martin, Mr. and Mrs. D, the Ugly Spirit—appear together on p. 55 of *The Ticket That Exploded*, among other places.

30. Cf. the suggestion by Rick Altman that in classical cinema "the sound track is a ventriloquist who, by moving his dummy (the image) in time with the words he secretly speaks, creates the illusion that the words are produced by the dummy/image whereas in fact the dummy/image is actually created in order to disguise the source of the sound. Far from being subservient to the image, the sound track uses the illusion of subservience to serve its own ends" and to permit filmmakers "to speak their sub-conscious mind—their belly—without fear of discovery" (67, 79).

31. Burroughs also describes the human body as "an image on screen talking" (1987b, 178).

32. Jacques Lacarrière calls the world's earthly rulers "pseudanthropes" (10), shadows or semblances of humanity who possess only the shadow of true consciousness.

WORKS CITED

Albert, Judith Clavir, and Stewart Edward Albert. 1984. *The Sixties Papers: Documents of a Rebellious Decade*. New York: Praeger.

Allan, Blaine. 1984. *The New American Cinema and the Beat Generation: 1956–1960*. Diss. Northwestern University.

———. 1988. "The Making (and Unmaking) of *Pull My Daisy*." *Film History* 2:185–205.

Allen, Donald M., and Warren Tallman, eds. 1973. *Poetics of the New American Poetry*. New York: Grove Press.

Altman, Rick. 1980. "Moving Lips: Cinema as Ventriloquism." *Yale French Studies* 66: 67–69.

Ansen, Alan. 1959. "Anyone Who Can Pick Up a Frying Pan Owns Death." *Big Table* 2 (Summer): 32–41. In Skerl and Lydenberg, 25–29.

Arato, Andrew, and Eike Gebhardt, eds. 1990. *The Essential Frankfort School Reader*. New York: Continuum.

Bakhtin, M. M. 1981. *The Dialogic Imagination: Four Essays*. Trans. Caryl Emerson and Michael Holquist. Austin: University of Texas Press.

———. 1984a. *Problems of Dostoevsky's Poetics*. Trans. Caryl Emerson. Minneapolis: University of Minnesota Press.

———. 1984b. *Rabelais and His World*. Trans. Hélène Iswolsky. Bloomington: Indiana University Press.

———. 1986. *Speech Genres and Other Late Essays*. Trans. Vern W. McGee. Austin: University of Texas Press.

Bakhtin, M. M., and P. N. Medvedev. 1985. *The Formal Method in Literary Scholarship: A Critical Introduction to Sociological Poetics*. Trans. Albert J. Wehrle. Cambridge: Harvard University Press.

Barthes, Roland. 1974. *S/Z*. New York: Hill and Wang.

Battcock, Gregory, ed. 1967. *The New American Cinema: A Critical Anthology*. New York: E. P. Dutton.

Baxter, John. 1970. *Science Fiction in the Cinema*. New York: A. S. Barnes.

Bazin, André. 1967. *What Is Cinema?* Trans. Hugh Gray. Berkeley: University of California Press.

The Beat Generation. 1992. Album booklet. Rhino Records R2 70281.

Bellios II, John G. 1977. *The Open Road: A Study in the Origins of the Beat Generation, 1944–1955*. Diss. University of North Carolina.

Bohn, Thomas W., and Richard L. Stromgren. 1987. *Light and Shadows: A History of Motion Pictures.* Mountain View: Mayfield Publishing.

Bordwell, David, Janet Staiger, and Kristin Thompson. 1985. *The Classical Hollywood Cinema: Film Style & Mode of Production to 1960.* New York: Columbia University Press.

Brakhage, Stan. 1963. *Metaphors on Vision.* New York: Film Culture.

———. 1989. *Film at Wit's End: Eight Avant-Garde Filmmakers.* Kingston: McPherson & Co.

Bukatman, Scott. 1993. *Terminal Identity: The Virtual Subject in Postmodern Science Fiction.* Durham: Duke University Press.

Burroughs, William S. 1969. *Naked Lunch.* New York: Grove Press.

———. 1970. *Electronic Revolution.* Bonn: Expanded Media Editions.

———. 1980. *The Soft Machine, Nova Express, The Wild Boys.* New York: Grove Press.

———. 1982. "The Cut-Up Method of Brion Gysin." *Re/Search* 4/5, 35–36.

———. 1987a. *Queer.* New York: Penguin Books.

———. 1987b. *The Ticket That Exploded.* New York: Grove Press.

———. 1993. *The Adding Machine: Selected Essays.* New York: Arcade Publishing.

Burroughs, William S., and Allen Ginsberg. 1963. *The Yage Letters.* San Francisco: City Lights Books.

Carney, Ray. 1994. *The Films of John Cassavetes: Pragmatism, Modernism, and the Movies.* New York: Cambridge University Press.

Carroll, Noël. 1989. *The Philosophy of Horror, or, Paradoxes of the Heart.* New York: Routledge.

Cassady, Carolyn. 1990. *Off the Road: My Years with Cassady, Kerouac, and Ginsberg.* New York: Penguin Books.

Cassady, Neal. 1993. *Grace Beats Karma: Letters From Prison 1958–60.* New York: Blast Books.

Charters, Ann. 1992. *The Portable Beat Reader.* New York: Viking.

Clark, Katerina, and Michael Holquist. 1984. *Mikhail Bakhtin.* Cambridge: Harvard University Press.

Clark, Tom. 1990. *Jack Kerouac: A Biography.* New York: Paragon House.

Collier, James. 1964. *The Hypocritical American: An Essay on Sex Attitudes in America.* Indianapolis: Bobbs-Merrill.

Cook, Bruce. 1971. *The Beat Generation.* New York: Charles Scribner's Sons.

Cook, David A. 1990. *A History of Narrative Film.* New York: W. W. Norton.

Cotkin, George. 1985. "The Photographer in the Beat-Hipster Idiom: Robert Frank's *The Americans.*" *American Studies* 26.1: 19–33.

Coursodon, Jean-Pierre, with Pierre Sauvage. 1983. *American Directors.* New York: McGraw-Hill.

Curtis, David. *Experimental Cinema.* 1971. New York: Universe Books.

Donaldson, Scott, ed. 1979. *On the Road: Text and Criticism*. New York: Viking.

Dyer, Richard. 1986. *Heavenly Bodies: Film Stars and Society*. New York: St. Martin's Press.

Ehrenreich, Barbara. 1983. *The Hearts of Men: American Dreams and the Flight from Commitment*. New York: Anchor Books.

Fassbinder, Rainer Werner. 1975. "Fassbinder on Sirk." Trans. Thomas Elsaesser. *Film Comment* 11 (November): 23.

Feldman, Gene, and Max Gartenberg, eds. 1959. *The Beat Generation and the Angry Young Men*. New York: Dell.

Film-Makers' Cooperative Catalogue No. 7. 1989. New York: Film-Makers' Cooperative.

"The First Statement of the New American Cinema Group." 1961. *Film Culture* (Summer): 22–23.

Foster, Edward Halsey. 1992. *Understanding the Beats*. Columbia: University of South Carolina Press.

Foucault, Michel. 1972. "Intellectuals and Power." In *Language, Counter-Memory, Practice: Selected Essays and Interviews*. Ed. Donald F. Bouchard. Ithaca: Cornell University Press, 205–17.

——. 1980. *Power/Knowledge: Selected Interviews and Other Writings, 1972–1977*. Trans. Colin Gordon, Leo Marshall, John Mepham, and Kate Soper. New York: Pantheon Books.

——. 1984. *The Foucault Reader*. Ed. Paul Rabinow. New York: Pantheon Books.

Frank, Robert. 1959. *The Americans*. Millerton: Aperture.

——. 1989. *The Lines of My Hand*. New York: Pantheon Books.

French, Warren. 1986. *Jack Kerouac*. Boston: Twayne.

Gardiner, Michael. 1992. *The Dialogics of Critique: M. M. Bakhtin and the Theory of Ideology*. London: Routledge.

Geismar, Maxwell. 1958. *American Moderns: From Rebellion to Conformity*. New York: Hill and Wang.

Ginsberg, Allen. 1959. "Notes for *Howl and Other Poems*." Notes for record album Fantasy 7006. Reprinted in Allen and Tallman.

——. 1963. *Reality Sandwiches: 1953–60*. San Francisco: City Lights Books.

——. 1983. *Composed on the Tongue: Literary Conversations, 1967–1977*. San Francisco: Grey Fox Press.

——. 1984. *Collected Poems 1947–1980*. New York: Harper & Row.

Gitlin, Todd. 1987. *The Sixties: Years of Hope, Days of Rage*. Toronto: Bantam Books.

Goodman, Paul. 1960. *Growing Up Absurd: Problems of Youth in the Organized Society*. New York: Vintage Books.

——. 1962. *Drawing the Line*. New York: Random House.

———. 1968. *People or Personnel: Decentralizing and the Mixed Systems*, published with *Like a Conquered Province: The Moral Ambiguity of America*. New York: Vintage Books.

Gramsci, Antonio. 1988. *An Antonio Gramsci Reader: Selected Writings, 1916–1935*. Ed. David Forgacs. New York: Schocken Books.

Guimond, James. 1991. *American Photography and the American Dream*. Chapel Hill: University of North Carolina Press.

Halberstam, David. 1993. *The Fifties*. New York: Villard Books.

Halliday, Jon. 1972. *Sirk on Sirk: Interviews with Jon Halliday*. New York: Viking.

Harris, Oliver, ed. 1993. *The Letters of William S. Burroughs 1945–1959*. New York: Viking.

Haskell, Molly. 1974. *From Reverence to Rape: The Treatment of Women in the Movies*. New York: Holt, Rinehart and Winston.

Hassan, Ihab. 1961. *Radical Innocence: Studies in the Contemporary American Novel*. Princeton: Princeton University Press.

Higgins, Garym, Rodrigo Garcia Lopes, and Thomas Connick. 1992. "Grisled Roots: An Interview With Stan Brakhage." *Millennium Film Journal* 26 (Fall): 56–66.

Higham, Charles, and Joel Greenberg. 1969. *The Celluloid Muse: Hollywood Directors Speak*. Chicago: Henry Regnery Company.

Hoberman, J. 1992. "The Forest and *The Trees*." In James 1992, 100–120.

Hofstadter, Douglas R. 1986. *Metamagical Themas: Questing for the Essence of Mind and Pattern*. New York: Bantam Books.

Holmes, John Clellon. 1952. "This Is the Beat Generation." *New York Times Magazine*, November 16.

———. 1988a. *Go*. New York: Thunder's Mouth Press.

———. 1988b. *Passionate Opinions: The Cultural Essays*. Fayetteville: University of Arkansas Press.

Horkheimer, Max, and Theodor W. Adorno. 1991. *Dialectic of Enlightenment*. Trans. John Cumming. New York: Continuum.

Howard, Gerald, ed. 1991. *The Sixties: Art, Politics and Media of our Most Explosive Decade*. New York: Paragon House.

Howe, Irving. 1955. "America, the Country and the Myth." *Dissent* II (Summer): 242–44.

Hughes, Douglas A., ed. 1970. *Perspectives on Pornography*. New York: St. Martin's Press.

Hunt, Tim. 1981. *Kerouac's Crooked Road: Development of a Fiction*. Hamden: Archon Books.

Inglis, Ruth A. 1947. "Need for Voluntary Self-Regulation." In *The Annals of the American Academy of Political and Social Science*. Ed. Gordon S. Watkins, Ph.D. *The Motion Picture Industry*. Philadelphia: The American Academy of Political and Social Science, 153–59.

Jacobs, Lewis. 1959. "Morning for the Experimental Film." *Film Culture* 19 (Spring).

James, David E. 1988. *Allegories of Cinema: American Film in the Sixties*. Princeton: Princeton University Press.

——, ed. 1992. *To Free the Cinema: Jonas Mekas & the New York Underground*. Princeton: Princeton University Press.

James, William. 1958. *The Varieties of Religious Experience: A Study in Human Nature*. New York: Mentor.

Jones, James T. 1992. *A Map of Mexico City Blues: Jack Kerouac as Poet*. Carbondale: Southern Illinois University Press.

Kerouac, Jack. 1950. *The Town and the City*. New York: Harcourt, Brace.

——. 1958. "The Philosophy of the Beat Generation," *Esquire*, March.

——. 1959a. "Belief & Technique for Modern Prose." *Evergreen Review* 2.8 (Spring): 57.

——. 1959b. "The Origins of the Beat Generation." *Playboy*, June.

——. 1961a. *Book of Dreams*. San Francisco: City Lights Books.

——. 1961b. *Pull My Daisy*. New York: Grove Press.

——. 1970. *Scattered Poems*. San Francisco: City Lights Books.

——. 1976. *The Dharma Bums*. New York: Penguin Books.

——. 1980. *Desolation Angels*. New York: Perigee Books.

——. 1981. *Big Sur*. New York: Penguin Books.

——. 1987. *Doctor Sax: Faust Part Three*. New York: Grove Weidenfeld.

——. 1988. *Satori in Paris and Pic: Two Novels*. New York: Grove Weidenfeld.

——. 1989. *The Subterraneans*. New York: Grove Weidenfeld.

——. 1990. *Mexico City Blues*. New York: Grove Weidenfeld.

——. 1991. *On the Road*. New York: Penguin Books.

——. 1992. *Tristessa*. New York: Penguin Books.

——. 1993. *Visions of Cody*. New York: Penguin Books.

——. 1994. *Vanity of Duluoz: An Adventurous Education, 1935–46*. New York: Penguin Books.

Kiesler, Charles A., and Sara B. Kiesler. 1969. *Conformity*. Reading: Addison-Wesley.

Klein, Marcus, ed. 1969. *The American Novel Since World War II*. Greenwich: Fawcett Publications.

Knight, Arthur, and Kit Knight, eds. 1986. *The Beat Vision: A Primary Sourcebook*. New York: Paragon House.

Kouvaros, George, and Janice Zwierzynski. 1992. "Blow to the Heart: Cassavetes' *Love Streams*." *Post Script* 11.2 (Winter): 27–36.

Kovel, Joel. 1988. *The Radical Spirit: Essays on Psychoanalysis and Society*. London: Free Association Books.

Krutnik, Frank. 1994. "Jerry Lewis: The Deformation of the Comic." *Film Quarterly* 48.1 (Fall): 12–26.

Lacarrière, Jacques. 1989. *The Gnostics.* Trans. Nina Rootes. San Francisco: City Lights Books.

Lindner, Robert. 1961. *Must You Conform?* New York: Grove Press.

Livingston, Jane. 1992. *The New York School Photographs 1936–1963.* New York: Stewart, Tabori & Chang.

Lucanio, Patrick. 1987. *Them or Us: Archetypal Interpretations of Fifties Alien Invasion Films.* Bloomington: Indiana University Press.

Lyon, Christopher, ed. 1985. *The International Dictionary of Films and Filmmakers: Films.* New York: The Putnam Publishing Group.

———, ed. 1986. *Directors/Filmmakers: The International Dictionary of Films and Filmmakers: Volume II.* New York: The Putnam Publishing Group.

MacDonald, Scott. 1987. *A Critical Cinema: Interviews with Independent Filmmakers.* Berkeley: University of California Press.

Mailer, Norman. 1957. "The White Negro." In *The Portable Beat Reader.* Ed. Ann Charters. New York: Viking, 586–609.

Marcuse, Herbert. 1955. *Eros and Civilization: A Philosophical Inquiry into Freud.* Boston: Beacon Press.

Martin, Bernice. 1981. *A Sociology of Contemporary Cultural Change.* New York: St. Martin's Press.

Mast, Gerald. 1986. *A Short History of the Movies.* New York: Macmillan Publishing.

May, Elaine Tyler. 1989. "Explosive Issues: Sex, Women, and the Bomb." In *Recasting America: Culture and Politics in the Age of Cold War.* Ed. Lary May. Chicago: The University of Chicago Press, 155–66.

McNally, Dennis 1990. *Desolate Angel: Jack Kerouac, the Beat Generation, and America.* New York: Delta.

Mead, Taylor. 1963. "The Movies Are a Revolution." *Film Culture* 29 (Summer). In Battcock 1967, 47–48.

Mekas, Jonas. 1955. "The Experimental Film in America." *Film Culture* 3, May–June. Reprinted in *Film Culture Reader.* Ed. P. Adams Sitney. New York: Praeger Publishers, 21–26.

———. 1959–70. *Diaries.* New York: Anthology Film Archives.

———. 1962. "Notes on the New American Cinema." *Film Culture* 24 (Spring).

Michelson, Annette. 1971. "Toward Snow." *Artforum,* June. In Sitney 1987, 172–183.

———. 1973. "Camera Lucida/Camera Obscura." *Artforum* 11.5, January, 37.

———. 1991. "'Where Is Your Rupture?': Mass Culture and the Gesamtkunstwerk." *October* 56 (Spring): 42–63.

Miles, Barry. 1989. *Ginsberg: A Biography.* New York: Simon and Schuster.

———. 1993. *William Burroughs: El Hombre Invisible: A Portrait.* New York: Hyperion.

Mills, C. Wright. 1956. *The Power Elite.* London: Oxford University Press.

Moore, Robert L. 1991. "Ritual, Sacred Space, and Healing: The Psychoanalyst as Ritual Elder." In Schwartz-Salant and Stein, 22–24.

Morgan, Ted. 1990. *Literary Outlaw: The Life and Times of William S. Burroughs.* New York: Avon Books.

Naremore, James. 1988. *Acting in the Cinema.* Berkeley: University of California Press.

Nicosia, Gerald. 1986. *Memory Babe: A Critical Biography of Jack Kerouac.* London: Penguin Books.

Odier, Daniel. 1989. *The Job: Interviews with William S. Burroughs.* New York: Penguin Books.

O'Neil, Paul. 1959. "The Only Rebellion Around." *Life* 47, November 30.

Peary, Danny. 1986. *Guide for the Film Fanatic.* New York: Simon & Schuster.

Pells, Richard H. 1989. *The Liberal Mind in a Conservative Age: American Intellectuals in the 1940s and 1950s.* Middletown: Wesleyan University Press.

Podhoretz, Norman. 1958. "The Know-Nothing Bohemians." In Donaldson, 342–56.

Poggioli, Renato. 1968. *The Theory of the Avant-Garde.* Trans. Gerald Fitzgerald. Cambridge, Mass.: The Belknap Press.

Polsky, Ned. 1969. *Hustlers, Beats, and Others.* New York: Doubleday.

Prendergast, Roy M. 1991. *Film Music: A Neglected Art: A Critical Study of Music in Films.* New York: W. W. Norton.

Price, Byron. 1947. "Freedom of Press, Radio, and Screen." In *The Annals of the American Academy of Political and Social Science.* Ed. Gordon S. Watkins. *The Motion Picture Industry.* Philadelphia: The American Academy of Political and Social Science, 137–39.

Rabinovitz, Lauren. 1991. *Points of Resistance: Women, Power & Politics in the New York Avant-Garde Cinema, 1943–71.* Urbana: University of Illinois Press.

Renan, Sheldon. 1967. *An Introduction to the American Underground Film.* New York: E. P. Dutton.

Rice, Elmer. 1952. "The Industrialization of the Writer." *Saturday Review* 35, April 12.

Rice, Ron. 1965. "Diaries, Notebooks, Documents." *Film Culture* 39 (Winter): 87–125.

Richie, Donald. 1961. "Letter from Cannes." *Nation* 192, June 17.

Riesman, David, with Nathan Glazer and Reuel Denney. 1961. *The Lonely Crowd: A Study of the Changing American Character.* New Haven: Yale University Press.

Rosenbaum, Jonathan. 1988. "Raging Messiah." *Sight and Sound* 57.4 (Autumn): 281.

Ross, Andrew. 1989. *No Respect: Intellectuals & Popular Culture.* New York: Routledge.

Roud, Richard, ed. 1980. *Cinema: A Critical Dictionary: The Major Film-Makers.* London: Secker & Warburg.

Rudolph, Kurt. 1987. *Gnosis: The Nature and History of Gnosticism.* Trans. Robert McLachlan Wilson. San Francisco: HarperSanFrancisco.

Sarris, Andrew. 1968. *The American Cinema: Directors and Directions 1929–1968.* New York: E. P. Dutton.

———. 1978. *Politics and Cinema.* New York: Columbia University Press.

Satin, Joseph, ed. 1960. *The 1950's: America's "Placid" Decade.* Boston: Houghton Mifflin.

Schechner, Richard. 1985. *Between Theater & Anthropology.* Philadelphia: University of Pennsylvania Press.

Schrader, Paul. 1972. "Notes on Film Noir." *Film Comment* 8.1 (Spring). In *Film Genre Reader.* Ed. Barry Keith Grant. Austin: University of Texas Press, 1986, 213–26.

Schumacher, Michael. 1992. *Dharma Lion: A Critical Biography of Allen Ginsberg.* New York: St. Martin's Press.

Schwartz-Salant, Nathan, and Murray Stein, eds. 1991. *Liminality and Transitional Phenomena.* Wilmette: Chiron Publications.

Sitney, P. Adams, ed. 1970. *Film Culture Reader.* New York: Praeger.

———. 1979. *Visionary Film: The American Avant-Garde 1943–1978.* Oxford: Oxford University Press.

———, ed. 1987. *The Avant-Garde Film: A Reader of Theory and Criticism.* New York: Anthology Film Archives.

Skerl, Jennie, and Robin Lydenberg, eds. 1991. *William S. Burroughs at the Front: Critical Reception, 1959–1989.* Carbondale: Southern Illinois University Press.

Sklar, Robert. 1975. *Movie-Made America: A Social History of American Movies.* New York: Random House.

Sontag, Susan. 1988. *Antonin Artaud: Selected Writings.* Trans. Helen Weaver. Berkeley: University of California Press.

———. 1990. *On Photography.* New York: Anchor Books.

Spigland, Ethan. 1990. "A Conversation with Raúl Ruiz." *Persistence of Vision* 8: 72–84.

Staccato. Record album composed and conducted by Elmer Bernstein. Capitol T-1287.

Stallybrass, Peter, and Allon White. 1986. *The Politics and Poetics of Transgression.* Ithaca: Cornell University Press.

Stam, Robert. 1989. *Subversive Pleasures: Bakhtin, Cultural Criticism, and Film.* Baltimore: The Johns Hopkins University Press.

Stephenson, Gregory. 1990. *The Daybreak Boys: Essays on the Literature of the Beat Generation.* Carbondale: Southern Illinois University Press.

Sterritt, David. 1982. Personal interview with Bruce Conner.

———. 1993. *The Films of Alfred Hitchcock*. Cambridge: Cambridge University Press.

Stevens, Wallace. 1979. "The Man on the Dump." In *The Norton Anthology of World Masterpieces*. Ed. Maynard, Mack, et al. New York: W. W. Norton.

Susman, Warren I. 1985. *Culture as History: The Transformation of American Society in the Twentieth Century*. New York: Pantheon Books.

Turner, Victor. 1986. *The Anthropology of Performance*. New York: PAJ Publications.

Tyler, Parker. 1962. "For *Shadows*, Against *Pull My Daisy*." *Film Culture* 24 (Spring).

Tytell, John. 1976. *Naked Angels: The Lives & Literature of the Beat Generation*. New York: McGraw-Hill.

van der Bent, Jaap. 1988. "How Low Can You Go: The Beat Generation and American Popular Culture." *European Contributions to American Studies* (Netherlands) 13: 145–56.

Volosinov, V. N. 1986. *Marxism and the Philosophy of Language*. Trans. Ladislav Matejka and I. R. Titunik. Cambridge: Harvard University Press.

Weinreich, Regina. 1990. *The Spontaneous Poetics of Jack Kerouac: A Study of the Fiction*. New York: Paragon House.

Whyte, William H., Jr. 1952. "Groupthink," *Fortune* 45, March.

———. 1953. "The Transients." *Fortune*, May-August.

William Klein. 1991. Catalogue. Tokyo: Pacific Press Service.

Winnicott, D. W. 1971. *Playing and Reality*. New York: Basic Books.

Wollen, Peter. 1982. *Readings and Writings: Semiotic Counter-Strategies*. London: Verso.

INDEX

DAVID STERRITT is an associate professor of film at the C. W. Post Campus of Long Island University and film critic of *The Christian Science Monitor*. He is also on the film studies faculty at Columbia University and served for several years on the New York Film Festival selection committee. He is the author of *The Films of Alfred Hitchcock*, and his collected film criticism is housed by invitation in the Harvard Film Archive at Harvard University.